Poverty and Wealth in America

Poverty and Wealth in America

Edited with an Introduction by

Harold L. Sheppard

❦ a New York Times Book

Quadrangle Books

CHICAGO

Library of Congress Catalog Card Number: 76-78325

The publishers are grateful to the contributors herein for permission to reprint their articles.

Contents

Introduction   *3*

1. Other Americas: Past and Present

Building Up a Country to Reduce Its Poverty   *19*
  by Dexter S. Kimball

The Inaugural Address, 1937   *26*
  by Franklin D. Roosevelt

The Unknown and Unseen   *32*
  by A. H. Raskin

2. The Anatomy of Income and the Nature of Poverty

More Data Sought on the Poorest Third   *38*
  by John H. Crider

The Battle of the Family Budget   *41*
  by Richard L. Neuberger

The High Cost of Low Incomes   *48*
  by Sumner H. Slichter

Is the Income Gap Closed? "No!"   *56*
  by Herman P. Miller

Our 398 Millionaires—A New Breed   *64*
  by Alvin Shuster

New Definition of Our "Poor"   *69*
  by Herman P. Miller

Poverty Is a Tougher Problem Than Ever   *76*
  by Robert Bendiner

3. Wealth: Its Potential Use and Misuse

Our Fear of Abundance   *91*
  by Walter P. Reuther

"This Is a World I Never Fought For"   *99*
  by Richard L. Neuberger

Next Step—A 600-Billion-Dollar Economy?   *105*
  by Leon H. Keyserling

4. More Than Dollars: Housing, Health, and Justice

A Home Is a Strain to 7 of 10 Families   *118*
  by Charles Grutzner

"You Shove Out the Poor to Make Houses for the Rich"   *121*
  by William Lee Miller and L. Thomas Appleby

Battle of Hunger   *129*
  by Dr. Ancel Keys

The State of the Union's Health   *133*
  by Howard A. Rusk

Equal Justice for the Poor, Too   *138*
  by Arthur J. Goldberg

5. Poverty Groups, Poverty Areas

The Pressing Problem of Old-Age Security   *150*
   by Sumner H. Slichter

New York Plans Aid for Puerto Ricans   *161*

A Plea for a Square Deal for the Indians   *163*
   by Oliver La Farge

The Negro Since 1900: A Progress Report   *170*
   by W. E. B. DuBois

The Negro—Progress and Challenge   *180*
   by Chester Bowles

The Negro's Middle-Class Dream   *189*
   by C. Eric Lincoln

Hard-Core Unemployment a Rising National Problem   *200*
   by A. H. Raskin

White House Seeks Cure for Unemployment Blight   *210*
   by A. H. Raskin

6. Solutions, Strategies, and Tactics

Relief Through Work   *222*
   by Harry L. Hopkins

For a Guaranteed Income   *227*
   by Michael D. Reagan

The Grand Design of the Poverty Program   *235*
   by Nathan Glazer

Making Trouble Is Alinsky's Business   *247*
   by Patrick Anderson

Review of *Maximum Feasible Misunderstanding*   *263*
   by Adam Walinsky

Suggested Reading   *272*

Index   *274*

Poverty and Wealth in America

Introduction

FOR MANY YEARS before the formally declared "War Against Poverty" in the mid-1960's, America was fighting poverty in a variety of ways and using various terminologies to describe the problem. At times these efforts were defined in terms of raising minimum and hourly wages; of making more equal the distribution of national income; of combatting unemployment through such devices as tax and monetary policies, or area economic development programs; or of creating and then improving a system of Social Security, as well as educating newcomers to the American urban-industrial environment and increasing personal and national wealth through other private and public actions.

In these efforts the term "poverty" was not always a key to motivation. Until late 1963, in fact, what we now call the antipoverty program was better known by its individual components —programs aimed at solving the problems of high school dropouts and juvenile delinquents; ideas such as a domestic Peace Corps; or measures designed to correct the status of the aged and of Negroes, to name some of them. For many years it was easier to gain support and approval of reform if specific targets were designated for attack, rather than if some all-embracing term such as poverty were made the central focus.

Some observers have argued that the swift concentration of blacks in American cities created a form of social dynamite that needed de-fusing with a new policy. But a new program could be sold to white America only if it were couched in words that encompassed, passionately and with color-blindness, all the marginal groups in the society. A "War on Poverty" might just do the trick, especially as whites do make up two-thirds of all the poor in the nation.

Decline in Poverty

America's poverty population has been declining over the decades, both in total numbers and proportionately, despite the impression created by the semantics of a new focus on unsolved problems. From the Great Depression to the present day, the country has moved—with varying speed and occasional regressions—to reduce its total incidence of poor living conditions.

For example, the Council of Economic Advisers reports (in *The Economic Report of the President* for 1969) that over the twenty-year span beginning in 1947 the number and proportion of families who received less than $3,000 income—in 1967 prices —declined substantially. In 1947 there were 10.2 million families living on such low incomes, but by 1967 there were only 6.2 million. These two figures respectively represented slightly more than 27 per cent of all American families in 1947, and less than 13 per cent in 1967.

During the same period the median family income rose, in 1967 prices, from approximately $4,500 to nearly $8,000. This amounts to more than a 75 per cent increase in the twenty-year period. And despite the current social "definition of the situation" that would have us believe that things are getting worse for America's nonwhites, the median family income of nonwhites grew at a greater rate than that of whites—by more than 110 per cent from 1947 to 1967 (from $2,418 to $5,141).

Economic Policies and Political Parties

Perhaps more interesting than the raw statistics are the political aspects of changes in income distribution. One simple way of raising this issue (but not necessarily resolving it) is to consider the different rates of increase in family incomes according to which political party controlled the White House. We can use the same yardstick to compare white and nonwhite rates of progress. The following table presents the average annual rate of growth in median family income for whites and nonwhites in three different time periods: 1947–1953, the Truman years for which data from the Council of Economic Advisers are available; 1953–1961, the Eisenhower era; and 1961–1967, the most recent Kennedy-Johnson years reported by the Council:

Average Annual Rates of Growth in Median Family Income for Whites and Nonwhites in Three Selected Periods, 1947 Through 1967 (in per cent)

	All	Whites	Nonwhites
1947–53	2.88	2.82	4.65
1953–61	2.60	2.81	1.90
1961–67	4.04	3.73	7.38
1964–67	4.23	4.00	8.10

The data in this table lead to four major generalizations about the growth of family income during the two decades involved:

(1) Median family incomes have grown at a faster annual rate under the two Democratic administrations than under the one Republican administration.

(2) This is especially true in the case of nonwhite families.

(3) For these minority-group families, the rate of progress in family income has been *greater* than for white families under the Democrats, but *lower* than for whites when the Republicans were in the White House.

(4) The greatest rate of growth has taken place during the three last years covered in the analysis, 1964–1967. This is true for whites as well as nonwhites, but nonwhites have done twice as well as white families in terms of growth rates.

There are, of course, many reasons for these differences, but a major explanation is the different economic policies of the two political parties during these years. It may be too early to judge the impact of the current Republican administration, but indications are that its efforts to combat a strong inflationary trend may result in the same kinds of changes revealed in the table above.

These anti-inflation efforts would be felt first by the low-income men and women who have only recently begun to climb from the bottom of the ladder of economic security and income growth. Their situation would be worsened at the very time when more advantaged Americans (including employers and trade union members and leaders) are being implored to hire the "hard-core unemployed and underemployed." We would then be in for a dangerous reaction from an army of "two-time losers." If my reading of American economic history is correct, we have never succeeded in combatting inflation without increasing unemployment. Even more ominous could be the reaction from the "new middle class" of workers who now enjoy unprecedented levels of family income—especially those skilled and semi-skilled workers with two or more wage-earners in their homes. They, too, would suffer relative losses in total income if an anti-inflation push moved too far out of control.

In addition to the Democrats' more active economic growth policies (as shown in such fiscal-monetary decisions as the 1964 tax cut, and in such structural programs as manpower and area development efforts), we cannot overlook the effect on incomes of both the Korean and Vietnam wars. International as well as domestic factors affect wealth and poverty in the United States.

Now, it would also be tempting to attribute the higher rates of family income growth since 1964 directly to the formal "War Against Poverty," and especially to the programs associated with the passage of the Economic Opportunity Act of 1964. But such a judgment may be premature. After all, its programs did not really get underway until late in 1965. Much of its funds and energies were devoted to children (Head Start) and to adolescents (Neighborhood Youth Corps and Job Corps), whose improvement could hardly be expected to affect a change in family incomes. Equally important, the collection of data for the purpose of evaluating Economic Opportunity programs was not among the most important projects of Poverty Warriors, especially at the local community level.

From Poverty to Wider Income Gaps and Crises of Affluence

The progress in raising median family incomes—and in reducing the incidence of poverty—does not necessarily mean, however, that we have also achieved a more even distribution of the nation's wealth. Economic opportunity is not the same as economic equality, as the following analysis reveals.

Any discussion of trends in income should not be confined simply to analysis of *median* incomes. A more complete assessment would include a focus on the *range* of income distribution. For example, in 1959, the bottom one-fourth of American families received incomes of $4,000 or less (in 1967 prices), while the top tenth received a minimum of $13,500—a range of $9,500. Eight years later, in 1967, the corresponding figures were approximately $4,900 and $16,300—a range of $11,400. The range expanded.

In other words, while average family income was increasing during this period (and the rate of poverty was declining), we should not blind ourselves to the fact that the "income gap" in the United States was widening. Many Americans adhere to the national myth that in our equalitarian society incomes become more and more evenly distributed. "Economic opportunity" tends to become confused with more equitable income distribution. For the less sophisticated, it is confusing to be told that we are simultaneously (a) lowering the proportion of families living in poverty *and* (b) increasing the dollar gap between the bottom and the top families in an "equalitarian" society.

This paradox is even more glaring in the urban scene. While the maximum income for the bottom quartile of families in urban areas of one million or more rose from $5,200 in 1959 to $6,000 in 1967 (an increase of 15 per cent), the minimum income for the top ten per cent climbed from $15,000 to $18,750 (an increase of 25 per cent). In 1959 the income gap was only $9,800, but by 1967 it had widened to $12,750. This "Big Metro" income gap is greater than for the country as a whole ($11,400 as previously cited). The gap in Big Metro increased by 30 per cent, but only 20 per cent for the total country.

The significance of these and similar facts and figures lies in the social-psychological sphere, and not in simple economics. In the urban context especially, the contrasts between the "rich" and the "poor" are much more visible. Indeed, they become more pronounced. Relative deprivation and *ressentiment* are magnified and crystallized in large urban mass society, because of its con-

Distribution of Family Income,
1959 and 1967
(in 1967 prices)

		1959	1967	% Change
I.	*Total U.S. Families*			
	A. Bottom fourth *(maximum)*	$ 4,000	$ 4,900	+23
	B. *Median*	$ 6,398	$ 7,973	+25
	C. Top tenth *(minimum)*	$13,500	$16,300	+21
	"Income Gap" between			
	C and A	*$ 9,500*	*$11,400*	*+20*
II.	*Families in Standard Metropolitan Areas of 1 million or more (1960 population)*			
	A. Bottom fourth *(maximum)*	$ 5,200	$ 6,000	+15
	B. *Median*	$ 7,747	$ 9,122	+18
	C. Top tenth *(minimum)*	$15,000	$18,750	+25
	"Income Gap" between			
	C and A	*$ 9,800*	*$12,750*	*+30*

Source: Unpublished preliminary tables, Bureau of Census.

trasts. The men and women in the bottom fourth of the income distribution concentrate less on their own progress over time; they are less concerned with how much better off they are than their cousins in the smaller cities and rural areas. They are instead more preoccupied with what their *neighbors* have—and how much more those neighbors have reaped the fruits of the urban-technological cornucopia than they have. They have little patience with, and less understanding of, the argument that their own rise in income is partly made possible by the incentives of the wealthy to make even more.

The growing income heterogeneity of the large, sprawling, and burgeoning urban society (a heterogeneity too frequently obscured by the *averages* typically reported in the popular press) indicates the basis of the discontent that baffles the casual chronicler of "affluent America." We are now entering an era of crises stemming from this affluence. And many of these crises are fed by the emergence of "relative deprivation" among urban families and individuals who, "objectively" speaking, are experiencing un-precedented growth in incomes, goods, and services. More than a hundred years ago, Marx observed that ". . . although the enjoy-ments of the workers have risen, the social satisfaction they have has fallen *in comparison* with the increased enjoyments of the capitalists. . . . Our desires and pleasures spring from society; we measure them, therefore, by society and not by the objects which serve their satisfaction."

Or, as a conservative might express it, "things have to get better before they get worse." It is possible for more and more of the poor in urban America to have color television and late-model cars—and feel even more deprived than ever. It is possible, fur-thermore, for this new and confusing phenomenon to occur in a Big Metro urban setting populated entirely by whites. The crisis is not a symptom of a "racist" society. The presence of blacks and Puerto Ricans has served only to aggravate the social dynamite of the income and wealth dynamics of American society. Their presence does not fully explain the new crises of affluence. The dollar gap between the bottom one-fourth and the top one-tenth has occurred among white as well as among Negro families in Big Metro. In fact, *within* the Negro population of our largest urban areas, the income gap between the lowest and highest families widened at a greater rate than within the white population.

Beyond Income

As indicated at the outset, America's fight against poverty and the improvement of the incomes of its citizens did not begin as late as 1964. After pondering over the present selection of *New York Times* articles, the reader may note many failures and unmet challenges as well as successes. But the overwhelming truth is that American society in the last four decades has been successful in moving vast, although selective, portions of its members out of low-income, subsistence lives. The current preoccupation with wealth and poverty is unique in that it espouses the taking of *all* segments of the population out of poverty—and placing them well above the current subsistence-income levels used by official reports as a monetary definition of "poverty." Furthermore, and in spite of such statements as "The poor are poor because they do not have enough money," the preoccupation now is with more than income problems per se. Style of life, participation in the decision-making processes that affect the poor, and "community control" have also become matters of central concern.

The search for a way out of poverty has become fused with a movement devoted to an expanded participatory democracy. Many of the new bureaucrats of the anti-poverty struggle are devoted advocates of the philosophy that a feeling of individual and collective self-confidence among the poor is an indispensable condition for the escape from poverty. "Maximum feasible participation" of the poor (for example, in neighborhood activities and in agency boards associated with these activities) is considered at least an indirect means of creating new feelings of personal and group efficacy in facing individual and community problems related to being poor. Poverty thus becomes synonymous with political impotence and personal inefficacy. Of course, whether this emphasis on participation has any effect on rates of poverty will not be measurable in any short-term period. The quest for self-confidence is a highly subtle and delicate process. At times, in the view of Kenneth Clark and others, it has often meant that the poor have been stimulated into wasting their valuable energies in such things as internal power and personality struggles.

For many more fortunate, higher-income Americans, a feeling of personal efficacy is taken for granted, not even recognized as a vital prerequisite for their own success and well-being. They frequently cannot tolerate the growing pains involved in the poverty warriors' attempts, however clumsy, to create the same condition among the poor.

From Affluent Indifference to Groping Concern

Before the focus on such issues, it could be said with some factual justification that the post-depression poor were "invisible" to most other Americans, many of whom were just beginning to enjoy the fruits of affluence. During the depression years the poor had not been so invisible. The New Deal was a massive effort to restore millions of people who once knew some degree of economic security and were confident of the future. The Second World War clearly restored them and also laid the basis for a greater gross national product and an economy of abundance and expanded wealth. But this new affluence, combined with international concerns, served to distract Americans from the evidences of rural and urban poverty.

By the mid-fifties the American people had drifted into a mood of complacency and self-satisfaction—at least so it was with those Americans whose moods and status at that time filtered through to the Establishment and decision-makers in general. They could be stirred by very few issues other than the President's health. They might be moved by articles about education but only insofar as it related, for example, to competition with the Russians— rarely about education as a possible means of social mobility out of low-income origins.

This mid-fifties mood stretched even into the period of the recession of 1957–1958. In those months 5 million out of 67 million workers were unemployed, but the overall feeling was that this could not be compared with the gravity of the Great Depression, when a higher proportion and many more millions were afflicted with joblessness. The unemployment of the late fifties was viewed as "spotty," and the administration was rather to be congratulated for not being panicky about such localized troubles. After all, in accordance with the ethos of those years, America had become a land of abundance.

For some of us, the current war against poverty began in the campaign of 1960, when John F. Kennedy provoked the nation's conscience about chronically jobless miners in West Virginia and others like them in such areas as the Upper Peninsula of Michigan; about the high unemployment rates in Pittsburgh, New Bedford, Fall River, and Scranton. Black and white steelworkers and autoworkers—along with those in dependent industries, not to mention the communities in which they were concentrated—were skidding downward into poverty or had already reached it. The rural South and Appalachia had long since been packaged out of collective memory.

Kennedy's election made possible the eventual passage, in 1961, after at least two Eisenhower vetoes, of a depressed-areas bill long championed by the Senate's economist, Paul Douglas of Illinois (his own state's southernmost thirty counties were an underdeveloped, low-income region). The original 1961 provisions of Senate Bill S.1 (a mark of the priority placed on the issue) included far more than the final legislation: for example, the doubling of surplus food distribution, and the extension of unemployment compensation to men and women who had exhausted their eligibility for regular jobless insurance funds. The ultimate law, creating the Area Redevelopment Administration (renamed the Economic Development Administration in 1965), provided for liberal loans to build new factories and offices for the creation of new jobs, and grants and loans for public facilities to provide the "infrastructure" for such factories and offices. For the first time, a training program for unemployed and underemployed workers would pay allowances to such men and women. This provision became the precedent for the larger training efforts created by the 1962 Manpower Development and Training Act, the second major milestone toward the eventual anti-poverty program. Like many congressional leaders, President Kennedy came to the conclusion that both the Area Redevelopment Act and the Manpower Development and Training Act were limited in scope and effectiveness. The first statute, for example, was written in almost complete ignorance of the extent of urban ghetto unemployment and "sub-employment." Cities with untold numbers of potentially employable poor persons, such as Los Angeles, Detroit, and New York, were not eligible for the job-creating provisions of the Area Redevelopment Act since that law required a very high unemployment rate for a *total* labor market area—not just a Central City within such an area—as a condition for economic development assistance. Few people in Washington were aware of the possibility that in a *section* of a labor market area with a few hundred thousand people (such as in central and eastern Los Angeles, which includes Watts), unemployment could be as high as 15 to 20 per cent. The *total* labor market area—also known as "Los Angeles," but encompassing more than that city—was enjoying a low *average* jobless rate of 5 or 6 per cent, and was therefore ineligible for assistance for job development under the Kennedy program.

That program, along with others developed in the early 1960's, was thus not addressed to all the problems subsumed under the general rubric of "poverty." Hence the Grand Design of an Economic Opportunity Act that was subsequently passed under Lyndon Johnson's leadership and administration. This was the same administration which became bogged down in the Grand Mistake in Southeast Asia, to such an agonizing extent that it could not (or would not) provide guns overseas and "butter" for everyone at home.

Wealth and Poverty Issues in the Future

In the decade ahead, the discussions and debates about income, wealth, and poverty in the United States will include the following kinds of questions:

1. Should poverty be defined strictly in terms of monetary income, as opposed to some qualitative formula which takes into consideration styles of life as well as material possessions?

2. Which social categories should be eligible for "guaranteed income" programs? Under what conditions? How will such programs affect the opinions and behavior of individuals and groups on the margin of eligibility but not receiving such assistance?

3. Will the "war against poverty" programs (apart from the issue of whether they are run from one agency exclusively concerned with the poor, or by more general government departments) be necessary as permanent features of national policy? Or are they temporary mechanisms (albeit long-term, e.g., for ten years) for assimilating previously neglected social groups into the "main current" of the American political economy? As an illustration of this general question, how long will there be a need for a Head Start program?

4. If and when the processes of education, economic development, and urban growth, to cite only three, are improved to raise the life chances of today's poor, what will be the role of community action organizations which were originally formed to "organize the poor"?

5. In any systematic, thorough analysis of shifts in income distribution, will it be possible to determine the impact on that redistribution, if any, of the various programs—public and private —that have become associated with the war against poverty?

6. Should there be some type of special program to aid the men

and women who work year-round, full-time, but nevertheless re-main in poverty? Or should the low-wage industries and occupa-tions in which most of them work be required to provide adequate income?

7. Do we need new policies and programs designed to cope with the continuing migration of the rural poor to the large cities which are typically ill-equipped to absorb smoothly such popula-tions? Will the American people and their representatives ever commit themselves to a policy of regional economic development, the creation of New Towns, and the racial desegregation of housing as indispensable long-term solutions to this challenge?

8. Will the lower socio-economic status of black Americans become defined more in terms of the traditional patterns of dis-crimination and prejudice ("racism")—or more in terms of the educational, health, and social-psychological handicaps inherited from those patterns? And as the general population of blacks becomes more and more differentiated itself in terms of wealth, income, and poverty, what new explanations will be proffered for whatever lower status continues to characterize Negroes vis à vis whites? The answers to these questions will, in turn, determine the types of proposed solutions to any black-white status differences.

9. Will measures of individual and family income, by them-selves, be sufficient as indices of change in the access to national wealth enjoyed by different parts of the American population?

10. At what point does the ostensible conflict between personal affluence and the public good become so blatant that American taxpayers will finally consent to a drastic overhauling of their tax system in order to restore and maintain that public good?

The issues surrounding income and wealth will obviously con-tinue to be an intrinsic part of our social concerns. The contro-versies involved may become even more aggravated than they are today despite—or because of—the predicted rise in "average" family purchasing power and the expected dramatic improvements in our standard of living. This is so for two reasons:

1. Even if we do not change the quantitative measure of the "poverty line," that is, the level of income which denotes who is poor (taking family size and location into account), many millions of Americans will still exist on incomes below that level. Unless

radically new shifts in public policy take place, this will be especially true of elderly individuals, isolated rural residents, and fatherless families in the central city ghettos. These groups may be a declining proportion of all Americans, but in a growing population, small percentages can mean large numbers.

For example, even with social security benefits more than four million Americans over sixty-five are poor. This excludes beneficiaries who are not yet sixty-five but receive retirement benefits, and more than another million elderly persons not receiving any social security benefits at all.

The number of poor fatherless children in the central cities of the Big Metros (those with more than one million inhabitants) actually increased from 1960 to 1968—from 768,000 to 1,222,000. Despite the hue and cry about the vast amounts of welfare dollars being spent on "dependent children," the *rate* of poverty among all children without fathers changed very little during the same period. The very cities which have produced rapid growth in individual and family income *in general* have failed somehow to distribute "economic opportunity" throughout all urban families. No solutions are yet on the horizon.

2. Suppose we do raise the quantitative measure of the "poverty line" as part of the continuing American pattern of converting past desires and luxuries into necessities. Many families and individuals will nevertheless experience a feeling of relative deprivation. A sort of "moving level of discontent" seems to be a constant in a society that simultaneously (1) professes a sincere belief in egalitarianism and (2) produces rapid rates of income growth that result in a further widening of the range of income distribution, as discussed above.

Part of the resolution of such a dilemma may lie in the direction of achieving what Richard Titmuss has called for: a shift from economic growth to social growth. Social growth will be achieved when, for example, our society spends proportionately more on the educationally deprived; when improved, decent housing construction is developing at a far greater rate for the poor than for the wealthy; when preventive medical care is available to all, and not just curative facilities for the few; and when universal personal self-respect and dignity replace race and class arrogance and shame.

Part 1

OTHER AMERICAS: PAST AND PRESENT

DEXTER KIMBALL'S pre-depression article stands in contrast to the apathy of that period, for it was aimed explicitly at the broad subject of poverty and made no attempt to disguise the fact of its widespread existence. Kimball cites the economist Irving Fisher's estimate of 76 million Americans living in poverty, using the Department of Labor's budget figure of $2,400 for a family of five as the minimum for a decent standard of living in 1928. Kimball strikes some ringing words in his statement that "we are committed to an effort to build a civilization where the want, misery, and vice that follow in the wake of compulsory poverty shall be unknown . . . if we have the will to do so we can put poverty behind us even as we have relegated slavery to the past."

Four years later, Franklin D. Roosevelt was elected President in the midst of an economic crisis of gigantic proportions. By 1937, Roosevelt, re-elected by an even greater margin, was still directing a nation stricken by low-paying jobs and high unemployment. His second Inaugural Address, reprinted here, made famous the reference to one-third of the nation ill-clothed, ill-fed, and ill-housed. Alluding to his administration's first term at combatting the depression, Roosevelt proclaimed on that cold and wet

January day: "We refused to leave the problem of our common welfare to be solved by the winds of chance and the hurricanes of disaster."

The New Deal helped to stave off revolution and greater depths of despair, and the Second World War took the United States out of low rates of economic growth. But the events and policies (and the lack of them) of the quarter-century after the 1937 Inaugural Address resulted in conditions that prompted Michael Harrington's *The Other America* in 1962. Not an original piece of research but rather a much-needed popularization of government and scholarly reports, Harrington's book was a sharp jolt to many policy-makers, among them John F. Kennedy. Hence it was credited with having inspired the New Frontier's dream of a War Against Poverty.

Building Up a Country to Reduce Its Poverty

by Dexter S. Kimball

THE MOST insistent cry that has gone up from the human heart
through all the ages has been a prayer to be relieved from the
drudgery of unremitting and ill-requited toil, and to be enabled to
enjoy some of the good things of this life. To the vast majority
of the countless men and women who have preceded us this
longing has been a vain hope that has colored their ideals of
existence here and led them to picture the future life as one of
idyllic ease and comfort.

The attainment of even an approximate realization of this
dream of universal well-being was denied to all of the old handicraft civilizations that have preceded us. It does not appear to be
possible to create by handicraft methods sufficient worldly comforts to support a civilized nation without having the larger part
of the population work as menials with little or no mental
development.

This was clearly recognized by thoughtful men of the past.
Plato accepted and defended slavery as a necessary principle in
civilization and Aristotle praised it as a desirable institution in the
organization of the State. The national ideals of all nations have
always been and always will be governed by their necessities, and

they rise in quality only as the nation can conquer its environment.

Of the new industrial forces that have brought about our present high American standard of living, the first was the improvement in machines that brought about the so-called industrial revolution. Up to that time the tool had always been an adjunct to the skill of the worker, but this improvement made the worker an adjunct to the machine, and the semi-automatic and the automatic machine became possible. The second was the steam engine which gave man, for the first time, an abundant supply of power. The third was the development of electrical machinery, which is an ideal way of transmitting and applying power. The fourth was the development of machinery and of apparatus for transmitting intelligence, such as the telegraph and the radio. These last have greatly accelerated the speed of the industrial machine and added greatly to its efficiency. And, last, modern science has made a great contribution both to the necessities and comforts of life to be manufactured by old methods; and, in the case of chemical science, by opening up new fields of production of its own.

Of course there are other contributing factors—such as great natural resources, an inventive and energetic people, and, on the whole, fairly friendly relations between employer and employe. But in the last analysis our national prosperity rests primarily upon men and machines.

Judged by any standards, we have made great economic advances. The first census, taken in 1850, gives the per capita wealth of this country as $383. Today the per capita wealth is nearly $3,500. Allowing for all difference in purchasing power of money this is a prodigious gain. Our total wealth is about $400,000,000,000 and the national income about $90,000,000,-000 a year. These are in themselves impressive figures, and when we consider the brief time in which this wealth has been created, they are startling. But simple per capita wealth is not a fair criterion of actual well-being.

Professor Irving Fisher, discussing this question recently, stated that for the 76,000,000 people composing the "poorest" class the average income in 1926 was $2,300 per family of five, or $132 below the minimum family budget of the Department of Labor. It will readily be seen from this that the majority of our people still live very close to the margin of decent and healthful living.

And it should be remembered that these are average figures. A great many families live considerably below this level.

On the other hand, it is pointed out that the average wage is increasing, though economists differ as to the rate of increase. After reviewing several of these statements, Professor Fisher remarks that "the best estimates show an increase in real income of 36 per cent in 1926 over 1921 for the nation as a whole," which he characterizes as "the most astonishing gain in real income yet shown by any nation," and states further that "if this rate of gain continues for the period 1927-31 inclusive, poverty will virtually be abolished in this country."

Granting that we can make such a gain, I do not believe that poverty will be abolished so quickly. It should be remembered that these figures are average figures. Even with our present high prosperity there is much poverty, due to unemployment and other causes, and we probably shall have to lift our averages somewhat higher before the lowest levels are raised above the danger line. But these figures are encouraging. They show we are at last coming to grips with the grim spectre of want, and for the first time in human history hope dawns of an existence where cold, hunger and rags will be practically unknown.

What likelihood is there, then, for improving our industrial technique so that this hope may be realized?

First, as to machinery. No doubt we can yet go a considerable distance in machine production along many lines—in fact, we are still making much progress in so-called time-saving machinery. I am well aware that there are those who view with alarm any extension of machine production and express the fear that we may finally be dominated by the machine. Such conjectures, however, come from those who are wholly ignorant of machine production and its limitations. It has limitations that are quite definitely fixed by the law of diminishing returns. We have already reached a limit, apparently, in some trades. In shoemaking, for instance, we may make more efficient machines, but the limits of mechanization appear to have been reached. There is room in other lines, however, for vast improvement.

In the operation of our machines and factories great gains in efficiency are yet to be made. The average efficiency of operation of our entire industrial organization is probably lower than we suspect. Much is being done to remedy this, and we are much better informed about the science of organization and management than we were twenty-five years ago. But much yet remains to be done.

Possibly the greatest single factor in our prosperity is our supply of power. Dr. Fred Low estimates that the total capacity of all prime movers (that is, power-producing machines, such as steam engines) in the United States is 750,000,000 horsepower. If this machinery were called upon to operate at full capacity it would furnish every man, woman and child in this country physical service equivalent to that of 150 slaves. And all the able-bodied men in the world working from sunrise to sunset could not perform the labor now being done by power-operated machinery in this country. No other country has such a supply of power in proportion to population. And we are adding at a rapid rate to our power supply through oil and coal burning power plants and by harnessing water power.

The size of some of these undertakings is noteworthy. At Niagara Falls single water turbines generate 70,000 horsepower, and at the Brooklyn Edison plant, a single turbo-generator, steam driven, develops 107,000 horsepower. The new State Line power house of the Chicago Edison Company will have an ultimate capacity of 1,350,000 horsepower and will house one unit that will develop 140,000 horsepower alone. These gigantic power-producing machines can be appreciated only by being seen in operation.

The efficiency of these great plants is astonishing. A few years ago it required 6 or 7 pounds of coal to produce 1 horsepower per hour. These new installations will require but one pound of coal per horsepower hour. Here, at least, is one productive factor that can still be greatly extended and which, more than any other perhaps, will hasten the economic millennium.

We probably cannot look for very great improvement in machinery for generating and applying electricity. This is already highly developed and highly efficient. We can, however, expect to see much higher voltages used in the transmission of electric current, which will make available more distant water falls and enable us to generate power at more advantageous points, thus saving much of the present high cost of transporting fuel. Nor can any great advances in the art of communication be expected. Time and distance have already been eliminated by the telegraph, the telephone and the radio. Any further gains in this direction will be negligible—just as reducing the time of crossing the Atlantic by a few hours is of no real consequence, compared with the reduction of time already attained.

But we may look for great extension of the use of those facilities which indirectly accelerate our industrial machinery. What scientific research may do to raise the economic level by bringing forth new products or processes we may only imagine. But certainly the future holds new discoveries of great value. Synthetic chemistry is still in its infancy, and we may yet see palatable foods produced this way.

In addition to the direct gains that may be made through the development and extension of these productive factors there are several others of an indirect nature that have a large bearing upon the problem. The first is the general problem of waste. We are proverbially the most wasteful of people. This waste is of two general kinds; personal and industrial. Personal waste of food and of clothing due to change of style and personal pride, and the careless waste of the everyday things of life in this country constitute a great loss which, if it could be checked, would help to raise our economic level. There is little hope, I fear, for improvement along this line for it is a national weakness affecting both rich and poor alike.

Industrial waste, however, is already being attacked with marked success. That which is due to poor management has already been widely surveyed and advertised in the business world. The economic gains that are possible through the reduction of types and sizes of manufactured products has been very fully set forth by Secretary Hoover and constitutes one of his greatest contributions to the industrial life of this country. The report on waste in industry made by the American Engineering Council during his Presidency of that organization is a classic document that has been translated already into several foreign languages. Here is a field where great economic gains are possible and in which we may expect to see marked progress.

Another industrial waste which is often overlooked is the work expended in manufacturing and distributing products that are of no economic value and which are of no value artistically. Our homes and stores are filled with manufactured articles that are "made to sell" and which do not profit us physically, mentally or spiritually. Of course, no one would wish to reduce the output of truly artistic products. But if we should devote all of our productive capacity to products that are essential and truly artistic we probably should not know what to do with them, the volume would be so great.

Great economic gains could be made by a better understanding of the flow of money from industry to the worker, in the form of wages, and from the worker back to industry, through the purchase of the products he has made. If this flow of money were well understood and could be controlled so that wasteful and ill-advised projects could be prevented and the peaks and valleys of our curve of industrial production could be ironed out, losses due to unemployment could be reduced. Today unemployment is one of the principal causes of want.

Here is a spectacle for the economist to explain: Warehouses filled with goods which the very people who walk the streets unemployed sorely need, while the factories through which they might earn money to purchase these goods are shut down.

Our economic progress, both in production and distribution, will be hampered so long as our legislators are poorly informed concerning industry and finance. The old days of handicraft where one man's opinion was as good as another's have gone. The majority of our national problems are industrial, economic and technical, requiring special knowledge for their solution. Yet Congress spends long months upon an Agricultural Relief bill, which the President vetoes as being economically unsound. We shall have such unsolved problems as Muscle Shoals before us indefinitely as long as we try to settle them by town-meeting methods.

How shall we bring to bear upon these great industrial problems of national importance the same special skill and intelligence that has created modern industry and which is daily solving similar problems quickly and efficiently? If democratic government fails us it will not be for lack of patriotism, but because of our failure to apply specialized skill and knowledge to these difficult industrial problems which beset our National Government.

Lastly, one of the greatest hopes of abolishing poverty lies in a

more enlightened view on the part of those who are responsibl
for industry. There is an ever growing sentiment that industr
should be primarily a means of supporting life and not solely
source of personal or corporate profit.

Not only must we raise our average income, but we must til
the gradient of our wage line so that there will not be so great
difference between the maximum, the minimum and the averag
wage.

As a nation we are committed to an effort to build a civilizatior
where the want, misery and vice that follow in the wake of compulsory poverty shall be unknown. I fully believe that if we have
the will to do so we can put poverty behind us even as we have
relegated slavery to the past.

The Inaugural Address, 1937

by Franklin D. Roosevelt

MY FELLOW-COUNTRYMEN:

When four years ago we met to inaugurate a President, the Republic, single-minded in anxiety, stood in spirit here. We dedicated ourselves to the fulfillment of a vision—to speed the time when there would be for all the people that security and peace essential to the pursuit of happiness. We of the Republic pledged ourselves to drive from the temple of our ancient faith those who had profaned it; to end by action, tireless and unafraid, the stagnation and despair of that day.

We did those first things first.

Our covenant with ourselves did not stop there. Instinctively we recognized a deeper need—the need to find through government the instrument of our united purpose to solve for the individual the ever-rising problems of a complex civilization.

Repeated attempts at their solution without the aid of government had left us baffled and bewildered. For, without that aid, we had been unable to create those moral controls over the services of science which are necessary to make science a useful servant instead of a ruthless master of mankind. To do this we knew that we must find practical controls over blind economic forces and blindly selfish men.

From the *New York Times*, January 21, 1937.

We of the Republic sensed the truth that democratic government has innate capacity to protect its people against disasters once considered inevitable—to solve problems once considered unsolvable. We would not admit that we could not find a way to master economic epidemics just as, after centuries of fatalistic suffering, we had found a way to master epidemics of disease. We refused to leave the problems of our common welfare to be solved by the winds of chance and the hurricanes of disaster.

In this we Americans were discovering no wholly new truth; we were writing a new chapter in our book of self-government.

This year marks the one hundred and fiftieth anniversary of the constitutional convention which made us a nation. At that convention our forefathers found the way out of the chaos which followed the Revolutionary War; they created a strong government with powers of united action sufficient then and now to solve problems utterly beyond individual or local solution. A century and a half ago they established the Federal Government in order to promote the general welfare and secure the blessings of liberty to the American people.

Today we invoke those same powers of government to achieve the same objectives.

Four years of new experience have not belied our historic instinct. They hold out the clear hope that government within communities, government within the separate States, and government of the United States can do the things the times require, without yielding its democracy. Our tasks in the last four years did not force democracy to take a holiday.

Nearly all of us recognize that as intricacies of human relationships increase, so power to govern them also must increase— power to stop evil; power to do good. The essential democracy of our nation and the safety of our people depend not upon the absence of power but upon lodging it with those whom the people can change or continue at stated intervals through an honest and free system of elections. The Constitution of 1787 did not make our democracy impotent.

In fact, in these last four years, we have made the exercise of all power more democratic; for we have begun to bring private autocratic powers into their proper subordination to the public's government. The legend that they were invincible—above and beyond the processes of a democracy—has been shattered. They have been challenged and beaten.

Our progress out of the depression is obvious.

But that is not all that you and I mean by the new order of things. Our pledge was not merely to do a patchwork job with second-hand materials. By using the new materials of social justice we have undertaken to erect on the old foundations a more enduring structure for the better use of future generations.

In that purpose we have been helped by achievements of mind and spirit. Old truths have been relearned, untruths have been unlearned. We have always known that heedless self-interest was bad morals; we know now that it is bad economics. Out of the collapse of a prosperity whose builders boasted their practicality has come the conviction that in the long run economic morality pays.

We are beginning to wipe out the line that divides the practical from the ideal, and in so doing we are fashioning an instrument of unimagined power for the establishment of a morally better world.

This new understanding undermines the old admiration of worldly success as such. We are beginning to abandon our tolerance of the abuse of power by those who betray for profit the elementary decencies of life.

In this process evil things formerly accepted will not be so easily condoned. Hard-headedness will not so easily excuse hard-heartedness. We are moving toward an era of good feeling. But we realize that there can be no era of good feeling save among men of good-will.

For these reasons I am justified in believing that the greatest change we have witnessed has been the change in the moral climate of America.

Among men of good-will, science and democracy together offer an ever-richer life and ever-larger satisfaction to the individual. With this change in our moral climate and our rediscovered ability to improve our economic order, we have set our feet upon the road of enduring progress.

Shall we pause now and turn our back upon the road that lies ahead? Shall we call this the promised land? Or shall we continue on our way? For "each age is a dream that is dying, or one that is coming to birth."

Many voices are heard as we face a great decision. Comfort says "tarry a while." Opportunism says "this is a good spot." Timidity asks "how difficult is the road ahead?"

True, we have come far from the days of stagnation and despair. Vitality has been preserved. Courage and confidence have been restored. Mental and moral horizons have been extended.

But our present gains were won under the pressure of more than ordinary circumstance. Advance became imperative under the goad of fear and suffering. The times were on the side of progress.

To hold to progress today, however, is more difficult. Dulled conscience, irresponsibility and ruthless self-interest already reappear. Such symptoms of prosperity may become portents of disaster! Prosperity already tests the persistence of our progressive purpose.

Let us ask again: Have we reached the goal of our vision of that fourth day of March 1933? Have we found our happy valley?

I see a great nation, upon a great continent, blessed with a great wealth of natural resources. Its hundred and thirty million people are at peace among themselves; they are making their country a good neighbor among the nations. I see a United States which can demonstrate that, under democratic methods of government, national wealth can be translated into a spreading volume of human comforts hitherto unknown—and the lowest standard of living can be raised far above the level of mere subsistence.

But here is the challenge to our democracy: In this nation I see tens of millions of its citizens—a substantial part of its whole population—who at this very moment are denied the greater part of what the very lowest standards of today call the necessities of life.

I see millions of families trying to live on incomes so meager that the pall of family disaster hangs over them day by day.

I see millions whose daily lives in city and on farm continue under conditions labeled indecent by a so-called polite society half a century ago.

I see millions denied education, recreation and the opportunity to better their lot and the lot of their children.

I see millions lacking the means to buy the products of farm and factory and by their poverty denying work and productiveness to many other millions.

I see one-third of a nation ill-housed, ill-clad, ill-nourished.

It is not in despair that I paint you that picture. I paint it for you in hope, because the nation, seeing and understanding the injustice in it, proposes to paint it out. We are determined to make every American citizen the subject of his country's interest and concern, and we will never regard any faithful law-abiding group within our borders as superfluous. The test of our progress is not whether we add more to the abundance of those who have much, it is whether we provide enough for those who have too little.

If I know aught of the spirit and purpose of our nation, we will not listen to comfort, opportunism and timidity. We will carry on.

Overwhelmingly, we of the Republic are men and women of good-will, men and women who have more than warm hearts of dedication, men and women who have cool heads and willing hands of practical purpose as well. They will insist that every agency of popular government use effective instruments to carry out their will.

Government is competent when all who compose it work as trustees for the whole people. It can make constant progress when it keeps abreast of all the facts. It can obtain justified support and legitimate criticism when the people receive true information of all that government does.

If I know aught of the will of our people, they will demand that these conditions of effective government shall be created and maintained. They will demand a nation uncorrupted by cancers of injustice and, therefore, strong among the nations in its example of the will to peace.

Today we reconsecrate our country to long cherished ideals in a suddenly changed civilization. In every land there are always at work forces that drive men apart and forces that draw men together. In our personal ambitions we are individualists. But in our seeking for economic and political progress as a nation, we all go up—or else we all go down—as one people.

To maintain a democracy of effort requires a vast amount of patience in dealing with differing methods, a vast amount of humility. But out of the confusion of many voices rises an understanding of dominant public need. Then political leadership can voice common ideals, and aid in their realization.

In taking again the oath of office as President of the United States, I assume the solemn obligation of leading the American people forward along the road over which they have chosen to advance.

While this duty rests upon me I shall do my utmost to speak their purpose and to do their will, seeking Divine guidance to help us each and every one to give light to them that sit in darkness and to guide our feet into the way of peace.

The Unknown and Unseen

by A. H. Raskin

THE OTHER AMERICA: Poverty in the United States. By Michael Harrington. 191 pp. New York: The Macmillan Company.

BEHIND THE GLITTERING facade of America's "affluent society" lies a ghetto of loneliness and defeat populated by the poor. It is an invisible land, even though it has millions of inhabitants and its streets are often those we walk. It is a modern poor farm for the rejects of the economy and of society—men, women and children maimed in spirit and dragging out their lives at levels beneath those necessary for human decency.

This is the angry thesis of Michael Harrington's study of poverty in a nation that prides itself on having built the highest standard of living in the world and on having done most to assure economic justice for all its people. Mr. Harrington, who began being angry ten years ago when he was ministering to Bowery derelicts as a member of the staff of The Catholic Worker, makes no pretense to detachment. His book is a scream of rage, a call to conscience. He considers it scandalous that so much social misery should survive in a nation with a technology adequate to provide every citizen with a decent life.

His study is not meant as a dissent from the thesis so illuminatingly expounded by John Kenneth Galbraith in "The Affluent Society" that our economic thinking must now be geared to solving the problems of opulence rather than those of want. Mr. Harrington cheerfully embraces the Galbraith notion that today's poor are the first minority poor in history, the first poor not to be seen and thus the first poor the politicians can afford to ignore. But he has no sympathy for Mr. Galbraith's belief that what we have left in the way of poverty can be overcome by an individual case approach or by attacking "islands" of unemployment or social neglect.

His skepticism stems from a conviction that the structure of our welfare state, with its hitching of public and private social-security systems to wages, is calculated to provide the least help for those who need it most. He estimates—and the basis for his estimates is likely to draw violent challenge from less impassioned analysts—that 40 million to 50 million Americans now live as internal aliens in a society bent on forgetting their existence.

In this quarter of the population he puts the needy, aged and the sick, the workers rendered useless by technological change, the unskilled in an industrial netherworld exempt from minimum-wage protection, the undereducated adolescents stripped of aspiration, the uprooted farm workers now equally unwelcome in urban slums, the victims of racial discrimination and a broad range of other economic outcasts.

Handicapped by lack of schooling and lack of skills, they stand not to benefit by automation and other industrial progress but to experience a deepening of exile. Not only do they not share in the fruits of the higher productivity improved technology permits, but they find themselves further disadvantaged by the freeze-out of the unskilled and semi-skilled work on which they once relied.

To Mr. Harrington, there is a culture of poverty that makes the poor different from the rich in ways that transcend money. "Everything about them, from the condition of their teeth to the way they love, is suffused and permeated by the fact of their poverty. * * * They need an American Dickens to record the smell and texture and quality of their lives. The cycles and trends, the massive forces, must be seen as affecting persons who talk and think differently."

Mr. Harrington does his best as stand-in for Dickens, with strong overtones of Jeremiah. He writes with sensitivity and perception as well as indignation. The Council of Economic Advisers might say, with justice, that he has overdrawn his case as to both the size and intractability of the problem. That is no indictment. The chroniclers and celebrants of America's upward movement are plentiful; it is good to be reminded that we are still a long way from the stars. Without the will to see through the wall of affluence and recognize the brotherhood of the impoverished stranger on the other side, we are unlikely to muster the corrective energy essential to render false this parting Harrington thrust:

"At precisely that moment in history where for the first time a people have the material ability to end poverty, they lack the will to do so. They cannot see; they cannot act. The consciences of the well-off are the victims of affluence; the lives of the poor are the victims of a physical and spiritual misery."

Part 2

THE ANATOMY OF INCOME AND THE NATURE OF POVERTY

THE FIRST ARTICLE in this section, published in 1938, discusses the need for more precise information about the bottom third of the nation which had been identified by FDR a year earlier. Ten years later, Richard Neuberger—at the time a crusading journalist, later an Oregon state legislator and a United States Senator—told how a household of five attempted to make ends meet on $250 a month, 40 per cent of that amount for food alone.

A clear-cut, unambiguous discussion of the low-income population appeared in 1950, written by the Harvard economist Sumner Slichter. Much of his data was based on 1948 information which revealed that nearly ten million families (with nine million children) were trying to live on less than $2,000 a year. More than six million of these families were in the nonfarm category. And two-thirds of these nonfarm Americans were (a) disabled or sick family heads; (b) in broken families; or (c) elderly family heads. Another problem, the connection between poverty and the family headed by a female, has persisted in the two decades since Slichter's facts and figures. Twenty years ago such families made up about 24 per cent of all the nonfarm poor families; today they constitute more than 30 per cent. With the aged, they are an increasing proportion of the nation's low-income population. It seems that only the younger, male-headed families (black as well as white) are the chief beneficiaries of America's economic "progress."

It is noteworthy that Slichter omits any reference to *low wages* as a factor in the creation or maintenance of poverty, especially for the other one-third of the nonfarm poor population, the working poor. For Slichter the problem was essentially one of inadequate welfare for unemployable unfortunates.

The two articles by Herman Miller, the succinct analyst of the Census Bureau, are important as correctives to generally accepted opinions. The first one, "Is the Income Gap Closed? No!," dispels the comforting myth that incomes are becoming more evenly distributed. In this 1962 article Miller cited Arthur Burns (one of Eisenhower's chief economic advisers—and now one of Nixon's) and Paul Samuelson (a Kennedy consultant) for their mistaken notion that such redistribution was occurring. Miller's analysis was one of the first to indicate that while nonwhite incomes were improving substantially, so were the incomes of whites. The result was that white-nonwhite differentials were relatively unchanged; in fact, in certain categories they were worse. But this relationship must be evaluated in the light of one of Miller's other observations, based on his careful analysis: ". . . this nation may soon be faced with an increase in the disparity of incomes caused by the existence of a large block of untrained and unwanted men."

Miller's second article is reprinted here because it reminds us of the inconvenient fact that poverty is not an objectively existent phenomenon: the criteria used to define it have changed, and will change, over time. "Standards of poverty are culturally defined." Suppose we do "eliminate poverty" by 1976—a year symbolically chosen by Sargent Shriver, the General of Lyndon Johnson's War Against Poverty. To quote Miller, by then "The chances are that we will lift our standards a little higher, open our belts another notch, and still find a large number of families living under what will then be considered substandard conditions."

Robert Bendiner's 1968 article should have been written, and its message recognized by government poverty warriors, a long time ago. Bendiner stresses that today's poverty has proven to be much harder to deal with than that of the 1930's. Much of it cannot be solved merely by pumping more money into those entry points in the social system that result in the demand for more highly skilled employees. Moreover—and this reinforces Herman Miller's view—changing criteria emerge. One new aspect is the belief, philosophy, or ideology that it is irrelevant to say how much worse things used to be; the critical issue is how much *better* they could be if only we would inspire ourselves—and were inspired by great leaders. Finally, Bendiner catches the recurring theme of our current concern with the elimination of poverty: the urban variable. It is in the cities that the pressure to fight poverty is primarily generated.

More Data Sought on the Poorest Third

by John H. Crider

WASHINGTON

HOW CAN A family live on $471 a year? That question puzzled many citizens this week after the National Resources Committee estimated in a report that the average income of the poorest third of Americans—that is, the mean income of the least fortunate 13,000,000 families and single individuals—was $471 in 1935-36.

In offering economic data in support of President Roosevelt's frequent references to the "underprivileged third," the committee focused attention on the manner of life of those Americans whose existence in many cases borders on starvation and disease. About 30 per cent of this lowest-income group, whose highest income was less than $780 a year, had received some assistance from a relief agency during the year.

The writer has just returned from a visit to a large apple orchard near Charlottesville, Va., where he found a number of families living on less than $450 in cash income per year. These low-income families, mostly of the "mountain white" class, are now largely "on relief," according to an apple grower who employs them, but a few of the stalwarts still try to make their way without assistance from the government or private charity.

A number of the non-relief families in the vicinity received

$350 or less in cash per year. These families can grow vegetables for their use during the Winter and eat what they can from the ground during the Summer. During the week they eat "fat meat," which can be brought for around 10 cents a pound, and on weekends a chicken is killed for a holiday "feast."

An orchard foreman who receives about $450 in cash per year has a wife and five children, drives an automobile, and seems to fare healthfully on that sum. However, he pays no rent. A patch of cultivated ground, a cow and some chickens were presented by his employer. The wife aids by sewing.

The term "income" in the National Resources Committee study means money income from all sources plus "the money value of the occupancy of owned homes and of rent received as pay and— for rural families—of home-grown food and other farm products used by the family." Thus the foreman who received $450 in cash plus his home and a large part of his food would be considerably above the $471 average for the lowest-paid third.

Actually, if a family of four had to buy all of its food, the lowest amount for which an "adequate diet" could be obtained in 1935 would be about $435, according to data on scientific diets prepared by Rowena Schmidt Carpenter and Hazel K. Stiebeling of the Bureau of Home Economics of the Department of Agriculture.

On the other hand, if a family of four was in desperate straits it could live on an "emergency diet" for about $270 a year; but such a diet, these home economists warn, cannot insure good health over an "indefinite period." This "emergency diet" includes one pint of milk daily for each child and a cup of milk for each adult; eggs once a week, meat (usually a meat and cereal combination) and fish twice a week, and bread at every meal. A relatively small quantity of vegetables and fruit also would be included.

The study of consumer purchases by the Bureau of Home Economists shows that the highest average monthly rental paid by village families in the $250 to $499 annual income class in any region of the United States was $9 in the 1935-36 period. The same study showed that the same income group paid not more than $15 per year for clothes in eight North and South Carolina counties (white farm families only).

If the average American farm village family expenditure for clothes in the class averaging $471 was, say, $30, the total for food, clothing and rent on this scant basis would come to $408. This would leave about $63 for heat, medical care and other necessities, plus any recreation.

While the Bureau of Home Economics surveyed village consumer expenditures for the lower income classes, the Bureau of Labor Statistics of the Department of Labor made a companion survey of urban spending habits which reflects the higher cost of living in cities.

The urban study took in many who were outside the lowest income groups. It showed that the median family income of non-relief families (of income up to "well over $3,000 for a few families with several earners") ranged from a low of $460 for Negroes in Albany, Ga., to a high of $2,015 for New York City whites.

The average monthly rent of these urban non-relief families ranged from $6 for the Negroes in Albany, Ga., to $42.71 for the families studied in New York.

It is this difference in costs in various parts of the country which makes it virtually impossible to state the cost of living for the country as a whole. All living-cost items vary in different regions, and so no one scale can be said to be universally adaptable for the nation.

The National Resources Committee, in its report, stressed the need of further studies of income distribution.

"Those concerned with the living standards of the people need more accurate information on the extent to which shortage of income brings poverty damaging to health and happiness," the report said. "Law-making bodies striving to apportion taxes equitably and without damage to the processes of industry need to know what will swell or deplete the stream of income. Business men require more abundant and reliable data on the probable demand for their products in order to stimulate and meet that demand."

The Battle of the
Family Budget

by Richard L. Neuberger

PORTLAND, ORE.

A SIX-CENT spurt in the price of hamburger a few weeks ago was particularly unwelcome to Martha Andrews. Martha is a 28-year-old housewife with a husband, Ted, aged 34, and three small children—Ted, Jr., aged 8; Jane, 2, and Robert, 7 months. While Ted was off fighting in Europe with General Patton's Third Army his mouth watered for Martha's baked hams and veal roasts. However, meat loaf, hamburger patties and spaghetti with meatballs have become the regular diet in the wartime housing unit in which the Andrews live, and that is why the rise in the cost of hamburger from 42 to 48 cents a pound at the corner butcher shop did such damage to Martha's budget.

The Andrews are an average American family. Ted earns $250 a month pumping gasoline at an independent service station and garage four or five miles east of Portland, on U.S. 30 along the timbered shores of the Columbia River. This is $75 more than he earned at the same work before he went to war in 1942. Of the three children, two were born after Ted returned from the Army with a medical discharge early in 1945.

From the *New York Times Magazine,* January 11, 1948, copyright © 1948 by The New York Times Company.

For a time the rising cost of living merely inconvenienced the Andrews. Now it has passed far beyond the casual stage. Ted is not sure what the family would do if it had a serious illness. A small legacy left by Martha's parents is down to $350 and that is their only reserve. Half a dozen Series E war bonds were cashed to pay for Christmas presents.

The Andrews take some comfort from the fact that practically all their friends seem to be in a similar predicament. Martha is certain of that from her conversations with other housewives who live in the housing project which was occupied by Henry J. Kaiser's shipyard workers during the war. She also gets letters from her married sister in Spokane, and Ted hears occasionally from men with whom he served in the Army.

All these sources indicate to the Andrews that their experience is by no means unique in this period of the highest prices in American history. Indeed, Martha says, "I suppose there must be millions of families all the way across the United States in just exactly the same boat. If they can keep afloat I guess we can, but it's getting harder all the time."

How have the Andrews made out thus far? What fate do they think 1948 holds for their strained and battered budget?

It is easy to tell where the money goes today. The two chief items are food and rent. Forty-four per cent of the monthly income, or $110, goes for food; rent, including light, heat and water, is $49.50. And the remaining $90.50 of Ted's salary seems to disappear like a snow man in the noonday sun. Ted insisted on having a telephone installed when the new baby was on the way: this costs $2.75 for a four-party line. He spends $16.50 a month to carry his GI life insurance policy. The family has no car, and transportation for Ted to and from work comes to $9. They budget $15 a month for medical care and prescriptions and the total is nearly always spent.

All of this comes to over $200 and still some big items must be taken care of. So far as clothing is concerned, Martha improvises all she can. Jane is very much a little girl but she wears slickers, "Dr. Dentons" and overalls which her brother Ted, Jr., long ago outgrew. Martha paid $20 to a crippled friend with sewing skill to make an old coat into a trim suit, complete with the "new look." Ted wore his GI shoes to work until the uppers split away from the composition soles, and then had to count out $15.50 for a new pair which would withstand grease and gravel.

With five $500 deductions, including his own, Ted Andrews' income taxes are small. He pays $42 a year to the Federal Government and $6 to the State of Oregon. Ted says he has no complaint about taxes, but he and his wife resent the high prices that keep them from saving. "After a few dentist's bills and other odds and ends," says Ted, "we don't even have enough left when the month is over to pay for a week's summer vacation seventy-five miles away at the beach."

Martha allocates $25 for food each week. Last week she spent $24.89, in this way:

Meat	$7.00
Milk (9 quarts)	2.07
Cheese	1.00
Eggs (3 dozen)	2.13
Bread (7 loaves of 1½ lb. each)	1.47
Staples (sugar, coffee, flour, etc.)	2.25
Fruit (canned and fresh)	3.00
Vegetables (canned and fresh)	3.00
Margarine (3 lbs.)	1.32
Baby food (canned)	.72
One qt. ice cream	.43
Ted's contribution to coffee-and-soup fund at garage	.50

Before the war, with less money, Martha was able to serve leg of lamb or even prime ribs for Sunday dinner and some kind of meat or fish the other six nights. Now she buys roasts only occasionally, and on at least two evenings a week the principal course consists mainly of rice, macaroni or noodles. Many months ago Ted cut out the irregular indulgence of a hot lunch at the diner across the highway from the garage. He and the other workers bring sandwiches and make coffee or heat canned soup over a hotplate.

Only on Sundays does Martha serve ice cream to her family.

Otherwise they finish the principal meal with fresh fruit from the grocery store or peaches canned at home. At breakfast only the children get the juice of fresh oranges; the parents drink canned juice, which is cheaper. Eggs are the great luxury all enjoy; it was to enable Ted to start for work with two fried eggs under his belt that, nearly a year ago, the Andrews gave up butter. The one time that Martha entertained the other wives in the housing unit she served a big golden omelet and homemade applesauce.

Martha says all the culinary skill taught her by her mother has vanished in the onrush of inflationary food prices.

"I used to be famous for meat loaf," she tells me. "Everyone raved about it. The recipe was my mother's. But now I have to fill the meat loaf so full of bread crumbs or rice to stretch the hamburger that it has no resemblance to the original. Thanksgiving Day also upset some notions which had lasted since childhood. Even on the farm turkey was a delicacy—yet Ted and I treated ourselves to a Thanksgiving turkey because it turned out to be only a few cents more a pound than hamburger."

She is indignant at warnings from the Government not to waste food. "How many families do they think are able to waste any food at these prices?" she asks, her dark eyes flashing. "That Thanksgiving turkey lasted us a whole week. We had it roasted, warmed over, served in cold slices, creamed and made into hash, croquettes and soup. I don't believe I threw out enough of that turkey to fill a coin purse."

High prices have forced on the Andrews many economies. They get books at the public library instead of buying them at a bookstore. Except when a jovial customer has thrust a pack in his direction, Ted has not smoked a cigarette since the end of 1946. A pipe satisfies his taste for tobacco. Martha puts up her own jams, jellies, fruits and vegetables. She and other housewives in the Vanport Housing Project even buy jars and lids in big quantities to get them cheaper. During the summer months Ted, a six-footer who was star tackle in high-school football, often spends a Sunday helping cultivate a near-by truck garden along the Columbia bottomlands. Then he comes home laden with heads of cauliflower, bags of peas and ears of golden corn.

Martha cuts the children's hair, washes her own and gets a

permanent but once a year, and then at a beauty school for less than half the regular price. Ted postpones his haircuts as long as he can; when he finally does get one, it is from a beginner at a local barber college for 40 cents instead of at a commercial shop for $1.

The high cost of hamburger and bread long ago ruled movies out of the Andrews budget. However, Ted discovered that by joining the Portland auxiliary police force he could get into shows free, and occasionally he sends Martha into a movie which he tells her is really "colossal," while he stays at home with the children. He and Martha can't go together because they can't afford a baby-sitter. Teen-aged youngsters in the neighborhood want 50 cents an hour.

In his spare moments at the garage Ted works with the two mechanics. Within the next nine or ten months he expects to be tuning up motors and straightening out bent fenders. Then his salary will jump to $300, or perhaps even $350. However, he believes the increase will do him no good "unless somehow prices are brought into line." The worst of it is, says Ted, is feeling that he is on a treadmill. "At these prices," he says, "you can't build or buy a house, you can't get an automobile, you can't save for a vacation, you can't even put away some money for your children's education. That's the worst of the whole thing. We're just standing still. We can't get ahead of the game. Prices eat up every cent I earn."

The Andrews are resentful of economic conditions in general but their resentmnt is channeled in no particular direction. They didn't like it when in September their rent was raised $7 a month. The units of their housing development are of flimsy construction and the squeak of boards in the apartment next door is clearly audible in the Andrews home. But their special interests do not shape their whole philosophy. A member of the Auto Mechanics Union, Ted believes organized labor "made it tough on the white-collar fellow by getting pay boosts the white-collar fellow had to help pay for, without any assistance from a union of his own." Ted also thinks business profits are too high and that "the rich man is getting richer."

Ted and Martha are registered as Republicans, principally because they were brought up in rural Oregon, which is predominantly Republican. Ted worked on a farm until he and Martha, the daughter of a German-born wheat rancher, were married in 1938. They moved to Portland a few months later and Ted greased cars while Martha was a member of a championship girls' swimming team.

The Andrews voted a straight Republican ticket in November, 1946. They admit they are disappointed, for they thought even then that prices had risen far higher than they should. "We hoped the Republican Congress would bring down the cost of living," says Martha. "Instead, prices are worse now than they were at the time of the election—much worse. I don't know how we will vote this year, but I'm sure it will be for the party we think will do the most to end these fearful prices."

There doesn't seem to them to be anything they can do directly. "I thought at first that buyers' strikes might be the answer to high prices," says Ted. "That was all right when it came to automobiles, radio sets, new refrigerators and even shoes and clothes. But you can't save on food when you have three little children. I believe I'd buy my children milk with the last dollar in my jeans, even if it was 43 cents a quart instead of the 23 it is now."

Ted and his wife have strangely conflicting fears. On the one hand, they fear that inflation may get further out of bounds, that prices will go higher. Ted predicts that his next raise will simply keep him where he is now. Yet the Andrews also fear a deflation, the possibilities of a crash. "If we have another big depression, where will I be?" Ted asks.

When they express these fears, Ted is grim and his wife somber. Yet, on the whole, the Andrews are not a gloomy or melancholy family; in fact, they are quite the contrary. The three children are chubby and cheerful. The parents likewise are in excellent health. Martha, straight and trim, still can flash 100 yards through the water in 66 seconds. And Ted, when he takes a rusty set of clubs and rides on the trolley to a public golf course, can negotiate eighteen holes in the low eighties.

Ted had hoped to study civil engineering at Oregon State College, but the $90 a month of the GI Bill of Rights was not enough to feed five mouths at 1946 prices, let alone those of 1948. Ted overcame that disappointment, and now he takes solace in the belief that some day he will be an expert auto mechanic.

Despite their fears, Ted and his wife are hopeful that both the luxuries and necessities of life will again be available at prices which make sense and that the adjustment will come before the country suffers permanent economic damage.

The High Cost of
Low Incomes

by Sumner H. Slichter

IN 1948, the most prosperous year in the history of the country, nearly ten million American families had cash incomes of $2,000 a year or less. The condition of such families concerns the entire country. For one thing, these families contain about nine million children, and the small income of the family may deprive the children of fair opportunity. Moreover, low incomes are frequently the result of low productivity; if the productivity of these families could be raised, the whole country would have more to consume. Apart from these considerations low-income families contain a high proportion of people hard hit by misfortune, and all humanitarian peoples want to do what they can for the unfortunate.

The situation of the non-farm low-income group, numbering about 6,300,000 families, is probably more difficult than that of the farm families, so this article will center on impoverished people living in towns and cities. Three principal questions stand out: Who are these families and what are the reasons for their low income? What kind of lives do they lead? What can be done about the problem of low incomes?

Over two-thirds of the low-income families fall into one of three large groups: (1) families whose head has been disabled by accident or disease; (2) broken families—that is, families headed by women because of widowhood, desertion, or divorce; and (3) families whose head is 65 years of age or more.

The exact size of the first group, headed by persons permanently disabled for long periods, is not precisely known, but it numbers well over a million. These are persons of working age who at one time were members of the working force but now are totally disabled for an indefinite period. The second group, headed by women who have lost their husbands, includes 1,500,000 families. More than one-third of these families have no earners. The third group, headed by older persons, includes 1,700,000 families—more than one-fourth of all non-farm families with incomes of less than $2,000. About half of these families have no income earners among their members.

In addition to these three major groups, there are many other kinds of low-income families. Some families are in the low-income class only temporarily—because they are starting new businesses or have experienced business losses, or because the chief earner has been temporarily disabled. Then, too, the low-income families naturally include many headed by persons who are incompetent, or misfits, or maladjusted, and who have trouble in getting and holding jobs. The misfits include persons with low intelligence who require so much supervision that they are hardly worth employing and persons who suffer from phobias and complexes of various sorts and do not easily fit into an organization.

Included among the misfits are many alcoholics. Information about their numbers is not reliable, but a recent conference on alcoholism in Chicago concluded that about 1,300,000 alcoholics are regularly employed. Of course, not all alcoholics are in the low-income class, but alcoholism frequently results in low income.

What kind of lives do the low-income families lead? Here is the part of the population, of course, where hardship is concentrated. The best measure of this fact is the high proportion of low incomes absorbed by expenditures on food. Nearly three-quarters of the income of non-farm families receiving less than $1,000 a year and nearly half of the income of families in the $1,000-$2,000 class goes for food—in comparison with about one-third for the average-income non-farm family.

Nevertheless, many of these families are not so badly off as one might suppose. In the first place, there is a general tendency for people to understate their cash incomes. In the second place, many families have resources apart from cash income, particularly in food and in shelter of their own houses. Also, the low-income families are smaller than the average. In addition, such families tend to be concentrated in the smaller cities and the rural non-farm areas, where, as a rule, it is easier to live simply and cheaply than in a large city.

In fact, the low-income families have a surprising amount of property. This probably reflects the fact that at some earlier time —before the family head retired or died or was disabled—these families were better off. At any rate, almost half of such families own their own homes, and about three out of four of these homes are owned mortgage-free. Over one-fourth own an automobile— of sorts—and the ownership of United States Savings Bonds and savings accounts is equally frequent. In 1948, over one out of four of these families purchased such goods as furniture, radios, refrigerators, washing machines, or television sets.

What can and should be done about the problem of low-income families? Since there are many causes of low income and many kinds of families in the low-income group, there is no panacea. Many of those persons who have suffered severe disabilities can learn new work or, in a few cases, new ways of doing their former jobs. In 1948, 53,000 persons were rehabilitated under the joint Federal-state retraining program, but there are about 1,500,000 persons in need of retraining. Great expansion of retraining programs is indicated.

Many disabled persons are prevented by illness from holding jobs and some of them are not able to learn new ones. In nearly all of these cases public or private assistance is needed. The Federal Government now helps the states that provide assistance to the blind and to families having dependent children, and last summer the House of Representatives passed HR 6000, which provides for grants to the states for assistance to permanently and totally disabled persons not covered by existing programs. It was estimated that this program would help about 200,000 totally disabled persons.

If there are dependent children in the family of the disabled worker, help may be given under the Federal-state program of aid for dependent children. In July, 1949, about 540,000 families were being assisted under the program by an average monthly payment of more than $70. Federal participation in aid to dependent children is not as liberal as Federal participation in old-age assistance or aid to the blind. The Advisory Council on Social Security, appointed by the Senate Finance Committee of the Eightieth Congress, has recommended that this difference in Federal help be eliminated.

A long-range program dealing with the problem of disability should include insurance against the loss of income because of temporary or permanent disability. Under present conditions the problem of temporary disability can be handled best by the states, and New York and several other states already have started such schemes. More important is the insurance against disability of indefinite duration (say six months or longer), or so-called "permanent" disability.

Many insurance experts do not believe that it is practical to write such insurance because the possibility of getting an income for many years, and perhaps for life, creates too powerful a temptation to malinger. Others believe that total and permanent disability is an insurable risk provided it is required that the disability be medically demonstrable.

The Advisory Council on Social Security has recommended that the present old-age and survivors' insurance plan be broadened to cover insurance against permanent and total disability, and such insurance is included in the social security bill passed by the House of Representatives last summer. The insurance would be limited to persons who have been in the labor force for at least ten years and whose disability can be medically proven.

In nearly two out of three of the broken families, the wife or one of the children is gainfully employed. The proportion of widows or divorced mothers and of children between 14 and 17 years of age who are in the labor force has increased substantially since 1940. Hence the maintenance of a high demand for labor is particularly helpful to members of broken families. While certain jobs are not good for children, children of 14 and over are likely to be helped by some employment if it does not interfere with education.

In the main, however, the income problem of broken families

must be solved in ways other than by employment of the mother or children. Where there are dependent children in the family, the help can be obtained through the Federal-state program of aid to dependent children.

Nearly four out of five broken families have lost their chief breadwinner by death. Hence, a great step would be taken toward reducing destitution if the Federal old age and survivors' insurance plan were extended to the 25 million jobs not now covered. The benefits also need to be made larger and eligibility requirements more liberal. At present the average primary benefit (on which survivors' benefits are based) is only about $26 a month.

Two changes in the law would be particularly helpful to families broken by the death of the chief breadwinner. One would raise the benefit of the first dependent child or of a dependent parent to three-fourths of the primary benefit. The other would permit widows of deceased workers to begin drawing benefits at the age of 60 instead of 65. Widows caring for a minor child of the deceased worker draw benefits now.

The largest class of low-income families comprise those in which the breadwinner is retired. Consequently, measures to meet the needs of these families offer the most promising way of attacking the broad problem of low incomes. Three changes would be particularly useful: (1) raising the usual retirement age in industry, (2) modifying the so-called "work clause" in the present Federal pension laws, and (3) providing a more generous Federal pension system.

A large proportion of persons 65 or over are quite capable of continuing their occupations, so the practice of some companies of retiring all employes at the age of 65 is quite unnecessary. Furthermore, it increases the number of low-income families, and thus aggravates the problem of low incomes. Studies of the Social Security Agency show that most retirements occur against the will of the worker. The problem of low-income families would be substantially reduced in importance if the retirement age in industry were made 68 or 70 instead of 65. In addition, the output of industry would be raised, and the standard of living of the country as a whole would be improved.

The present Federal old-age pension law contains a peculiarly vicious work clause. It is designed to prevent persons from drawing pensions who are also receiving income through employment. The law provides that a pension recipient who earns $15 or more a month shall lose his pension so long as his earnings equal or exceed that amount. The obvious effect is to discourage beneficiaries from supplementing their pensions by useful work.

A more sensible arrangement would be to permit pensioners to earn a fairly liberal amount, say $75 a month, without losing their pensions, and to provide that for every dollar above $75 a month earned by the pensioner a dollar would be subtracted from his pension for that month. This would encourage retired workers to help themselves.

The third change—to extend and liberalize the present old-age insurance scheme—is the most promising way of dealing with low incomes among retired workers. As has been pointed out, the plan at present covers only about three out of five jobs. It should be made virtually universal. In addition, the benefit payments should be raised to about 50 per cent of a man's earnings before retirement. This would eliminate much of the problem of low-income families. The present pension payments of $26 a month for persons without dependents and $40 for persons with dependents are far below a decent level.

In addition to these direct measures, there are numerous indirect ways to help low-income families—some important, others less so. Since a high proportion of low-income families have their savings in Government savings bonds, one form of help to them (and to many other families as well) would be for the Government to issue a savings bond payable in a fixed amount of purchasing power rather than a fixed number of dollars. Persons who bought Government savings bonds in 1943, 1944 or 1945 have lost a large part of the purchasing power which they put into those bonds. Small-income families wishing to save should not be compelled to gamble on whether the price level will rise or fall.

Another kind of indirect help would be the removal of economic barriers to opportunity. More abundant scholarships to young persons of demonstrated ability would be one way to do this. Setting limits on the initiation fees that men must pay in order to join unions would also help. Fortunately, most unions are opposed to high initiation fees, but a minority charge $100 or more. An amendment to the Taft-Hartley Act should impose a maximum $25 initiation fee for admission to any union which is granted exclusive bargaining rights or which is permitted to establish a union shop.

Still another form of help would be modification of the Government program of supporting the prices of farm products. Because low-income families spend a high proportion of their cash incomes on food, the price-support program, which now includes wheat, corn, pork, butter, eggs, potatoes, cheese, apples, pears, concentrated orange juice, lard and other commodities, is especially burdensome to non-farm families with low incomes. The so-called Brannan Plan of agricultural aid has grievous faults—in particular, it undertakes to support farmers' incomes at too high a level—but it would have the important merit of letting farm products be sold at free-market prices.

The most important indirect aid of all is encouragement of technological research, because it is from a rise in all incomes that more adequate support can be given the low-income groups. Not only does technological progress raise the incomes of all classes, but it has had the important result of reducing the proportion of unskilled jobs and of increasing the proportion of jobs that require semi-skilled or skilled workers. Between 1910 and 1940, for example, common laborers dropped from 36 per cent to 26 per cent of the labor force. Converting of common-labor jobs into semi-skilled or skilled jobs reduces the proportion of workers receiving low pay and helps people rise out of the impoverished class.

These measures—direct and indirect—to aid low-income families are of great importance, not only to the persons immediately concerned but to the nation as a whole. They would raise the contribution of the low-income families to production, and thus diminish the extent to which these families are supported at the expense of the rest of the country. Broadening and liberalizing social insurance would reduce the dependence of low-income families upon relief, and thus reduce—though not eliminate—the possibility that help for the low-income groups could become a corrupting influence in politics.

Most important of all, good arrangements for meeting the problems of low-income families would raise the esteem in which the American economy is held both here and abroad. Critics of

American economic institutions have been forced to admit that these institutions are remarkably efficient and give the country an unmatched standard of living, but they insist that this highly efficient economy neglects human needs.

As a matter of fact, few other countries distribute as large a proportion of income on the basis of need as does the United States. Income distributed on this basis was about $11 billion in 1949, and was about three times as large relative to all personal incomes as in 1929.

Nevertheless, a rich and successful economy such as that of the United States must be expected to look out for the nonproducers or low-producers more adequately than do the less efficient economies. Arrangements for meeting the problem of the needy more generously will show the critics of American institutions that this economy is the most efficient in the world.

Is the Income Gap Closed? "No!"

by Herman P. Miller

A MYTH has been created in the United States that incomes are becoming more evenly distributed. This view is held by prominent economists of both major political parties. It is also shared by the editors of the influential mass media.

Arthur F. Burns, chief economist for the Eisenhower Administration, said in 1951 that "the transformation in the distribution of our national income * * * may already be counted as one of the great social revolutions in history." Paul Samuelson, one of President Kennedy's leading economic advisers, said only last year that "the American income pyramid is becoming less unequal." Several major stories on this subject have appeared in The New York Times, and the editors of Fortune magazine announced not long ago that "though not a head has been raised aloft on a pikestaff, nor a railway station seized, the U. S. has been for some time now in a revolution."

What are the facts about trends in income distribution in the United States? Nobody questions that real incomes have risen for most of the population and that even those who have been left behind enjoy a far higher level of living than most people in other parts of the world. Since the level is so high and conditions

From the *New York Times Magazine,* November 11, 1962, copyright © 1962 by The New York Times Company.

are still improving, why consider the gap between the rich and the poor? Isn't it enough that the amount of income received by the poor has gone up substantially? Why be concerned about their share?

The reason is that "needs" stem not so much from what we lack as from what our neighbors have. Except for those rare souls who have hitched their wagons to thoughts rather than things, there is no end to "needs." So long as there are some people who have more, others will "need" more. If this is indeed the basis for consumer behavior then we obviously cannot ignore the gap between the rich and the poor, however high minimum levels of living may be raised.

Has there been any narrowing of the gap between the rich and the poor?

If we stick to the figures the answers are clear, unambiguous, and contrary to widely held beliefs. The statistics show no appreciable change in income shares for nearly twenty years. The heart of the story is told in the chart on page 58 which comes from data in U.S. Government publications available to all. The figures were obtained by ranking families from lowest to highest according to income and totaling the amount of income each group received. Not shown is the share received by the top 5 per cent—large because their incomes are so much larger than the others. In 1960, the top 5 per cent made over $16,250, whereas the lowest 20 per cent made less than $2,800 (about $55 a week). During the thirties and the war years there was a distinct drop in the share of the income received by the upper-income groups. The share received by the wealthiest families dropped from 30 per cent of the total in 1929 to 21 per cent in 1944. Since that time it has not changed significantly.

Now let us look at the bottom of the income scale. In 1935, the poorest 20 per cent of families received only 4 per cent of the income. Their share rose to 5 per cent in 1944 and has remained at that level ever since. The stability of the shares received by each of the other fifths is equally striking.

These figures hardly support the picture that many Americans have been given about the equalization of incomes in our society.

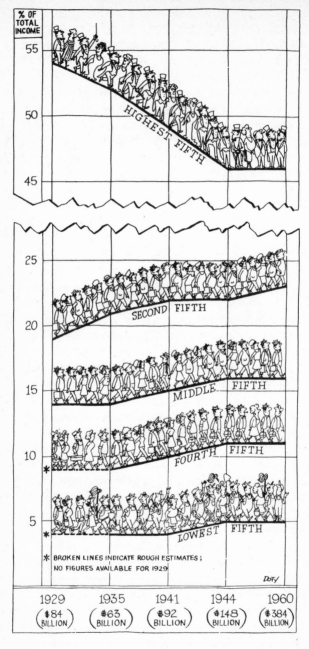

% OF TOTAL INCOME

55

50

45

HIGHEST FIFTH

25

20

SECOND FIFTH

15

MIDDLE FIFTH

10

FOURTH FIFTH

5

LOWEST FIFTH

* BROKEN LINES INDICATE ROUGH ESTIMATES;
NO FIGURES AVAILABLE FOR 1929

DOTY

1929	1935	1941	1944	1960
($84 BILLION)	($63 BILLION)	($92 BILLION)	($148 BILLION)	($384 BILLION)

The changes that took place ended nearly twenty years ago and they largely involved a redistribution of income among families in the top and middle brackets.

The figures cited are for income before taxes. Since the wealthiest families pay a large share of the taxes, we might expect their share to be smaller on an after-tax basis. It is, but not by as much as one would guess. In recent years the wealthiest 5 per cent received 20 per cent of the income before taxes and about 18 per cent of the income after Federal individual income tax payments were deducted.

Are white-non-white differentials narrowing?

The narrowing of income differentials between whites and non-whites (mainly Negroes) is sometimes cited as evidence of a trend toward equalization. Surely one would expect a change here in view of the major relocation of the Negro population in recent years.

Migration and technological change during the past twenty years have altered the role of the non-white from a Southern farm wage worker or sharecropper to an industrial worker. Twenty years ago, four of every ten unemployed non-white males in the United States worked either as laborers or sharecroppers on southern farms. At present, less than two of every ten are employed in agriculture and about half work as unskilled or semi-skilled workers at non-farm jobs.

The change in the occupational status of non-whites has been accompanied by a marked rise in educational attainment, proportionately far greater than for whites. In 1940, young white males averaged four years more of schooling than non-whites in the same age group. Today the gap has been narrowed to one and a half years.

Despite all these changes that have occurred in the past decade, the earnings differential between whites and non-whites has not changed. The average wage or salary income for non-white workers was about three-fifths of that received by the whites in 1950 and in 1960. (See chart on page 60.) Prior to 1950, there was a substantial reduction in the earnings gap between whites and non-whites; but this was largely due to war-induced shortages of un-

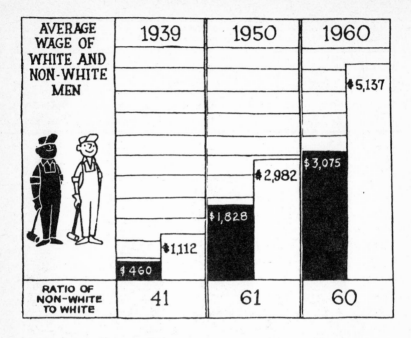

AVERAGE WAGE OF WHITE AND NON-WHITE MEN	1939	1950	1960
			$5,137
		$2,982	$3,075
		$1,828	
	$1,112		
	$460		
RATIO OF NON-WHITE TO WHITE	41	61	60

skilled labor and government regulations designed generally to raise the incomes of lower-paid workers.

Are occupational differences narrowing?

One of the most widely and strongly held views regarding income distribution concerns the narrowing of earnings differentials among occupations. The prevailing view holds that the decrease in the earnings gap between the skilled and unskilled in the United States is part of a historical process that has been going on since the turn of the century.

Recent trends in income differentials between skilled and unskilled workers are shown in the chart opposite. These figures represent the average wages and salaries received during the year in the major occupation groups in which men are employed. Women are excluded because their earnings are highly influenced by the fact that a large proportion of them are intermittent workers who do not work at full-time jobs.

MEN'S WAGES OR SALARIES BY OCCUPATION

$	PROFFSSIONAL AND MANAGERIAL WORKERS	CRAFTSMAN	SEMI-SKILLED FACTORY WORKERS	SERVICE WORKERS AND LABORERS
6500	1960			
6000				
5500				
5000		1960		
4500				
4000				
3500	1950		1960	
3000		1950		
2500			1950	1960
2000				1950
1500	1939			
1000		1939	1939	
500				1939

PER CENT CHANGE				
1939-60	230	316	325	290
1939-50	96	160	172	180
1950-60	68	60	56	39

There was not too much variation among occupation groups in the rate of income growth during the entire 20-year period. But when we look at the growth rates for two different periods, 1939-50 and 1950-60, striking differences are revealed.

During the forties, the lower-paid occupations made the greatest relative gains in average income. Laborers and service workers (waiters, barbers, janitors and the like) had increases of about 180 per cent; craftsmen had increases of 160 per cent; and professional and managerial workers, the highest paid workers of all, had the lowest relative gains—96 per cent.

During the past decade the picture has been reversed. Laborers and service workers made the smallest relative gains, 39 per cent;

craftsmen had increases of 60 per cent; and the professional and managerial workers had the greatest gains of all, 68 per cent. Evidently, the trend toward the narrowing of the income gap between the high-paid and the low-paid workers has stopped during the past decade and even seems to be moving in the opposite direction.

The facts show that our "social revolution" ended nearly twenty years ago; yet important segments of the American public, many of them highly placed Government officials and prominent educators, think and act as though it were a continuing process.

The stability of income distribution, particularly during the fifties, could be related to the fact that the decade was dominated by an administration that was committed to stability rather than change. The Kennedy Administration, on the other hand, has shown a keen awareness of the need to cope with our pockets of poverty.

The President has pressed for and obtained legislation intended to raise the levels of living of the poor; extension of unemployment insurance benefits, Federal aid to dependent children of the unemployed, liberalization of social security benefits, increase in the minimum wage and extension of its coverage, Federal aid to revitalize the economies of areas with large and persistent unemployment. These measures would also tend to reduce income inequality, other things being equal.

In opposition to the political factors that now seem to favor equalization, we face some very stubborn economic factors that seem to be headed in quite the other direction. For many years now unskilled workers have been a declining part of the American labor force. This fact has been documented over and over again; but during the past decade there appears to have been a significant new development.

In the decade 1940-50 and again in 1950-60 only one nonfarm occupation group for men—laborers—declined in number, at a time when all other groups were increasing. Laborers had the greatest relative income gains during the forties when they were in short supply but the smallest relative gains during the fifties when their supply far exceeded the demand. Now the unskilled are finding it increasingly difficult to locate jobs and many who are employed live in constant fear of being replaced by machines.

It is now generally acknowledged that the American economy has been plagued by relatively high unemployment since late 1957. According to the Joint Congressional Economic Committee, which has studied the problem in some detail, it is still premature to attribute this unemployment to technological changes; but there can be no doubt that many thousands of unskilled workers have been permanently displaced by machines and that this trend will continue. Moreover, some economists disagree with the committee's view that our current difficulties in the employment field stem largely from shortages in aggregate consumer demand rather than from technological changes in the economy.

It is conceivable, to many who have given the matter serious thought, that in the absence of remedial action, this nation may soon be faced with an increase in the disparity of incomes caused by the existence of a large block of untrained and unwanted men. Unless we are careful, we may then discover that our "social revolution" not only has been marking time for nearly twenty years, but is beginning to move backward.

Our 398 Millionaires—
A New Breed

by Alvin Shuster

WASHINGTON

IT WAS EASY in the old days to tell the millionaire from the rest of us. He had that private railroad car, courted Lillian Russell and assorted French actresses, imported chefs from Paris to prepare 20-course meals to be served on gold plates, swam in pools of white Venetian tile or Carrara marble, built "cottages" with 110 rooms and 45 baths and owned a Nile steamer just in case he went to Egypt.

Not so the millionaires of today. They live well but, for the most part, quietly, without the flamboyance of their predecessors. A few even live in the house with the 100-foot lot they bought 15 years ago before they hit it big. With a few exceptions, most are a little shy about it all. And even though one of their kind reached the White House by popular demand, many still feel ill at ease when publicly identified as "a millionaire."

Accordingly, it's difficult to calculate just how many of the breed are around these days. But the Internal Revenue Service, which naturally keeps its statistical eyes on such things, has just disclosed that the club is growing; 398 taxpayers had incomes of at least $1,000,000 for 1961.

From the *New York Times Magazine*, September 15, 1963, copyright © 1963 by The New York Times Company.

This was 92 more than in 1960, and the highest number since the record 513 in 1929 when the stock market hit its catastrophic peak. By 1932, the number had fallen to 20. But the millionaires fought back. In 1944, the figure inched to 62 and, by 1954, leaped to 201.

The income reports turned out by the service's experts who peeked at the returns obviously mention no names—it's against the law to reveal that kind of information. So the service is not very helpful to those who would like to follow in the precise footsteps of the present-day 400 (minus two). The Government may put out plenty of "how to" books ("How to Control Bedbugs") but you are on your own when it comes to trying to pinpoint just how to become a millionaire.

There are some facts around, of course. The experts tell you where most of the millionaires earned their money, how many got tax refunds, whether they paid alimony, whether they were big givers to charity, how sick they were, how many dependents they have, what states they hail from, and other such tidbits.

Surprisingly, they also tell you that there were 17 taxpayers with adjusted gross incomes of over $1,000,000 who paid no income tax at all for a variety of legitimate reasons.

Obviously, the 398 are not the only millionaires in the country. There's a difference between "wealth" and "income" and there are probably thousands worth more than a million who reported less in income. Their wealth was in property, or businesses, or stocks, or jewels, or tax-exempt local bonds, among other assets. For example, 16,600 taxpayers reported they got dividend checks in 1960 totaling more than $50,000. This means, assuming a 4 per cent return on their dough, that they had stocks valued at more than $1,000,000.

A neat package of facts about these thousands is impossible to come by. But perhaps a lesson or two can be learned from the preliminary figures on 1961's "over-a-million" 398 and from the more detailed figures on 1960's 306.

California, which has now edged New York for the population title, falls short on millionaires. New York had 84 in the club in 1960, while California, with 17, sits fifth behind Delaware with 23, and Pennsylvania and Illinois with 22 each. Texas reports 15, but this is clearly misleading: a Texas oilman can pocket

27½ per cent of his profits as depletion before he even begins to figure his income.

Nineteen states, including the newest, Alaska and Hawaii, had none. And if there were any big winners in Las Vegas that year, you couldn't tell it from the tax returns. Nobody in Nevada reported an income over a million dollars.

How did the 398 do it? "Mr. Average Millionaire" in 1961 showed an adjusted gross income of $1,907,165. Most of it—59.8 per cent or $1,140,000—came from capital gains, buying low and selling high stocks, real estate, or other property. By earning the majority of his income this way, he kept more than if he "worked" for it and earned a salary. Capital gains are never taxed at more than 25 per cent under present law, while the rates on other income go up to 91 per cent.

Of the 1961 group, 137 "didn't work"; they showed no income from salaries and wages. And those who did get pay checks averaged "only" $48,800 a year, a piddling 3 per cent of their total reported take.

Next to capital gains, the biggest money-maker for these millionaires was dividends. Some 35.7 per cent of the average income, $681,300, came in dividend checks—a huge portfolio of stocks his mother left him or he managed to build up himself. Thus 95.5 per cent of the total income came from just two sources—capital gains and dividends.

But Mr. Millionaire had some losses, too. He reported an average business setback of $35,000. Don't fret. Tax experts say few millionaires lose money because of the fortunes of fate. The tax laws provide incentives for "losing ventures" and some of the losses may have come from racing stables that never seem to produce winners.

Apart from helping describe in general terms how he makes his money, the bare statistics also show a few other things about the millionaire taxpayer.

Some, for example, would appear to be moonlighting. The 1961 figures show that 58 of them in effect had "more than one job." Actually, they show that that many get social security tax refunds, because the tax was withheld at more than one source. Presumably these men were drawing salaries as officers or directors from more than one company.

As for their ages, 100 of them were over 65 in 1960.

As for their families, they had an average of four exemptions, about the same as ordinary people.

As for their married lives, 10 of them paid alimony averaging $24,000 a year each. And this doesn't reflect any huge multi-million dollar lump-sum divorce settlements.

As for their bad luck, 77 reported casualty and theft losses: uninsured jewels stolen, uninsured race horses dying, an uninsured yacht sunk. This totaled $1,220,000.

As for their big hearts, they gave an average of 15 per cent of their incomes to charity. But there was one, in 1960, who gave less than $100, and 14 others who gave less than $500.

As for their bookkeeping, 63 paid too much in advance; five of them got tax refunds totaling $127,000,000, and the 58 others applied the surplus, totaling $2,900,000, to their next year's tax bills.

And, as for their health, 12 had medical deductions of over $10,000. (A taxpayer has to have medical expenses over 3 per cent of his gross income before he can take any deductions, so this means that those 12 had medical costs of at least $40,000.)

But perhaps the most amazing of all to the layman are the 17 in 1961 who made more than a million dollars and paid no tax at all. Presumably these are men of inherited wealth who escaped taxes through a loophole known as "unlimited charitable deductions." In simple terms, they donated the equivalent of their incomes to charities under a rule that says you can deduct all such contributions without limit if you have been giving away an amount that equals most of your income in the past 8 to 10 years.

What happens is that a millionaire gives away a piece of property that originally cost very little, but deducts the value of it at today's prices. This could be real estate or securities in his family for years. For example, one taxpayer had an income totaling almost $20 million in the three years beginning in 1958, yet he paid no income tax.

Thus, through a variety of methods, particularly with the help of the lower capital gains tax, millionaires in general have managed to get their tax rate down considerably. In 1961, the experts figure, the effective tax on total income of "Mr. Average Millionaire" was 27.6 per cent. This is only a little more than the average tax bill of individuals in the $20,000 to $50,000 income group.

Indeed, the most heavily taxed people in the country are those with incomes of $500,000 to $750,000. The typical taxpayer in that group, with income mostly from salaries rather than investments, is the only one who pays out more than 50 per cent in Federal taxes.

In short, if at all possible, become a millionaire.

New Definition of Our "Poor"

by Herman P. Miller

"YE HAVE the poor with you always." So it says in the Bible—and so it is. The proof can be found right here at home. We are told that in this, the richest of all countries, 40 per cent of the families live in poverty or deprivation. In fact, that is the title of a recent study, "Poverty and Deprivation in the U.S.—The Plight of Two-Fifths of a Nation." This is no phony Communist propaganda, nor the wild charge of a radical reformer. It is hard-boiled statistical "fact" as presented by Leon Keyserling, chief economic counselor to President Truman and former head of the Council of Economic Advisers.

Does it seem strange that we should now be talking about the plight of two-fifths of our families when even during the Depression only one-third of the nation was ill-housed, ill-clothed and ill-fed? The amount of goods and services per capita has doubled since the early thirties. How then can we have a larger proportion of our population living at substandard levels? The answer is quite simple: it all depends on how high you set your standard. Let us consider a specific case.

If you remember the Depression, you are almost sure to remember Harlan County, Kentucky. It was the scene of many bloody mine-union battles during the thirties. Harlan County was poor then and it still is. It has been officially designated as a depressed area, eligible for Federal aid because it suffers from chronic unemployment.

The best sign of its poverty is the fact that people are leaving in droves. About one-third of the people who lived there in 1950 were gone by 1960. And those who remained did not live well by any means. Two-thirds of the homes are substandard. Half lack baths, inside toilets and other conveniences that we regard as essential for modern living. One-fourth of them even lack running water. By present-day American standards, they are poor, poor, poor.

But, when we probe a little deeper, 88 per cent have washing machines; 67 per cent have TV; 45 per cent have a telephone, and 59 per cent have a car. (Some families who have washing machines but no running water, carry water from a well to the machine to get their clothes washed.)

It is quite evident, therefore, that even in this poor American community, we find many of the trappings of an affluent society. Many of the cars may be jalopies, but even a jalopy costs $500 or more a year to operate. The TV sets may not be the latest models, but the fact that they are there at all points to an immediate distinction between the American poor and the starving poor in India or China.

The term poverty connotes hunger; but this is not what we mean when we talk about poverty in America. According to Keyserling's definition, an American family faces stark poverty if its income is under $4,000 and it is deprived if it has an income of less than $6,000. I have no quarrel with this definition—nor do I endorse it. My own preference is to define the poor as families in the bottom fifth of the income distribution. In 1960, these families had incomes of under $2,900, and in 1951, their incomes were under $2,000.

In 1890, a study was made of poverty in London—"Life and Labor of the People." It showed that about one-third of the people lived in poverty. During the Depression, a similar study was made in the United States. It also showed that about one-third of the people lived in poverty. Recent statistics for American cities also point to the conclusion that about one-third of the people have incomes insufficient to maintain a decent level of living. Do these facts mean that conditions are not getting better?

Of course not. No one in his right mind will deny that even the poor are living longer and better than ever before. The painfulness of earning a living has been reduced in more ways than we can measure. And it has improved more for manual workers than for those who are higher paid—vacations with pay, more adequate safety devices, better medical care, mechanization of routine work, air conditioning and so on.

The clear meaning of these findings is that as incomes go up, "needs" also go up—evidently in such a way as to leave a large proportion of the population at substandard levels. Today, it would be unthinkable to be without electricity. Why, you couldn't even watch TV! But as recently as 1920, 99 per cent of American farms lacked electricity and more than half of nonfarm families were without this "necessity." Even at the time American farm boys were donning their World War II uniforms, two-thirds came from homes that lacked electricity and 80 per cent had never known the luxury of having a toilet inside their homes. Like everyone else they griped about the Army, but many were living it up for the first time in their lives.

Poverty is nothing to joke about. It is real, serious and important. But it is also one of those emotionally charged words that can trap us if we are not careful. Much needless soul-searching can be avoided if we recognize at the outset that there is no objective definition of art or beauty. Standards of poverty are culturally determined. They can be arbitrarily defined for a given time and place. But they vary from place to place, and they differ from time to time in any one place.

Prof. Dorothy S. Brady, one of the world's leading authorities on income distribution, wrote: "When faced directly with the problem of determining [poverty] for a given time and place, the theorist will deny the possibility of a unique answer and the propagandist will settle for one of many solutions if the result suits his purpose." The prophetic wisdom of this remark is most clear when we see the way in which politicians and propagandists manipulate income figures to meet their particular needs.

Unless we are content to sit around speculating about the problem, we must turn to statistics to give body to our thoughts.

Who are the American poor? How did they get that way? How have their characteristics changed with the passage of time?

There are many reasons for poverty; but some are much more important than others and they appear with remarkable regularity in the studies that have been made. The key fact to notice in the figures below is how little the characteristics of the poor have changed in the past decade. Of course, this does not mean that those who were at the bottom in 1951 were still there in 1960. If we could put tags on people and follow them through life we would surely find that some who were higher up on the income scale in 1951 have dropped down in relation to others because of retirement, widowhood, divorce, illness and many other factors.

Conversely many who were at the bottom in 1951 have undoubtedly moved up. This would be particularly true of young couples who were just starting out ten years ago. On the average, however, it seems quite clear that the *same kinds of people* that are now at the bottom of the income pyramid were also there ten years ago, as shown in the following figures.

These are the percentages of poor families who were:

	1951	1960
Aged	31	31
Without a worker	25	28
Broken families	23	24
Nonwhite	21	21

Even these few figures present a very graphic picture of three factors that are traditionally associated with poverty, in addition to outright unemployment or failure to work for other reasons. Other factors not shown, but equally important, are lack of education and occupational skill. And many of the bottom-income families suffer from a combination of all these traits.

Let us consider the first group, the aged. Since most of them are in retirement, it is to be expected that their incomes will lag behind those of the working population. Many, of course, have their homes paid for or are living on savings which are not reflected in their current incomes. (We all know some elderly people whose income is only $1,000 a year but who manage to get to Florida every winter by drawing on their savings.) But, these are undoubtedly the exceptions rather than the rule.

Most of the aged depend on Social Security or other pensions, and while these have gone up, they have not risen sufficiently to keep them on a par with the rest of the population. Younger men can always take on a second job when they feel that they are falling behind—and millions do. They can also send their wives out to work—and millions do that, too. But the aged have no such option and so they tend to fall behind in a booming economy. In view of this fact, it is surprising indeed that the aged have not increased as a component of the bottom income groups.

The economic problems of broken families—whether through divorce, desertion, illegitimacy or the death of a husband—are not too dissimilar from those of the aged. In a very large proportion of these cases, there are young children in the home and so the mothers are unable to work because they must take care of them. And even when they do work, many are employed in low-paying jobs because of their lack of training, skill or experience or else they can only work part-time because of family responsibilities.

Of the nonwhites, the great majority are Negroes. Over all, they represent only about 10 per cent of all families; but they are 21 per cent of the bottom income group. Much has been written and said about their plight. There are undoubtedly many factors that keep the Negro at the bottom but there can be little doubt that racial discrimination is a key cause.

Only recently, President Kennedy's Council of Economic Advisers prepared an estimate of the economic loss to the nation resulting from racial discrimination in employment. This study showed that if the education and training of the Negro population were fully utilized by the elimination of racial barriers in employment, our national product might rise by as much as 2½ per cent a year. In 1961, this would have placed $13 billion more in the hands of people who are now concentrated in the bottom income groups. These wasted skills amounted to almost one-fourth of the total that we spent for national defense in that year.

And this monetary loss in national income is, of course, only a small part of the total social cost that results from discrimination.

When we add the costs of higher crime rates, poor health, urban renewal and many other problems that stem directly or indirectly from discrimination, the amount becomes astronomical.

In considering what can be done about the people at the bottom, we recognize that we are not all equally endowed with good health, intelligence, creativity, drive and the like. In any society a premium will be paid to those who are most productive. The individual can legitimately demand from a democratic society that he be given the chance to develop his God-given talents to the utmost and that he then have the same opportunity as everyone else to use those talents. But society, in turn, must place a floor beneath those who fall to the bottom so as to minimize their suffering.

On the first point, we still have a long way to go in America. There is still much evidence of discrimination, neglected talent and the transmission of poverty from one generation to the next— although the picture is not all black. Millions of immigrants who came to this country with only the clothes on their backs have lived to see their children outgrow the filthy slums of the Lower East Side, Hell's Kitchen and other such spots. But there is still a long road ahead, particularly for Negroes, Puerto Ricans and other minorities.

On the second point, we have much to be proud of. In 1929, 70 per cent of our families and individuals had incomes below the $4,000 (in 1961 dollars) that Leon Keyserling calls the poverty line. That number has been more than cut in half and we are told that at our current rate of progress only about 10 per cent of the population will be below that line in 1977.

Does this mean that we will virtually eliminate poverty in the next 15 years? The historical evidence points strongly against such a conclusion. The chances are that we will lift our standards a little higher, open our belts another notch and still find a large number of families living under what will then be considered substandard conditions.

The Bureau of Labor Statistics has estimated that the cost of a "modest but adequate" level of living (excluding taxes) for a working-class family of four persons in New York City was about $4,000 in 1947 and about $5,200 in 1959 (both figures in terms of 1961 purchasing power). In other words, the "modest but adequate" level of living rose by exactly 28 per cent in this 12-year period. At that rate of growth, a working-class family will need nearly $7,000 (1961 dollars) to get by in New York City in 1975; and a very much larger amount if we allow for normal inflation and taxes.

Do these figures seem unreasonably high? Well, they are no more unreasonable than our present standard of living would have seemed at the end of World War II. We have come a long way from that bleak day in January, 26 years ago, when President Roosevelt told the nation in his second inaugural address: "I see millions of families trying to live on incomes so meager that the pall of family disaster hangs over them day by day."

We still have families like that, to be sure. We always will. But abject poverty of this type is dwindling and when we speak of the millions of poor today we mean something entirely different.

Poverty Is a Tougher Problem Than Ever

by Robert Bendiner

IF THE Johnson Administration's war on poverty is ever substantially successful, in spite of a reluctant Congress and a competitive war in Asia, history will have to credit the President with
as great a social and political triumph as any brought off by
his mentor and idol, Franklin D. Roosevelt. For the poverty of
the sixties, though less extensive by far than that of the thirties, is
proving considerably harder to deal with. It is, in fact, the poverty
that the New Deal scarcely touched—congenital, chronic, and
now all the more galling to its victims because of the opulence
that surrounds it on all sides. More than that, the *avowed* objective now is not merely relief and amelioration, as it was when
Roosevelt took office 35 years ago, but the very eradication of
poverty.

So great indeed is the difference between the two periods that
the most casual comparison will show why popular attitudes
toward the poor have changed, why the poor themselves have
moved from resignation to the fringes of rebellion, and why their
plight calls for more fundamental approaches than were ever
dreamed of in the New Deal philosophies.

Although one-third of all Americans, even by President Roose-

velt's conservative estimate, were "ill-housed, ill-clad, ill-nourished" in the years of the Great Depression, there was less talk
of poverty in the abstract then than there is now—and much
more specific talk of making jobs, giving relief and priming the
national pump. For that earlier decade was a period of emergency, with all the excitement that a great crisis generates and
an intense nationwide preoccupation with the immediate. Now in
the sixties, it is "pockets of poverty" that are talked about—
deeper and more extensive perhaps than the phrase suggests, but
pockets nonetheless—in a landscape of plenty. And it is poverty
itself that is the object of attention rather than the poor.

The contrast, in terms of national attention, is roughly the difference between the destruction of a coastline by slow erosion
and a dramatic assault on it by a tidal wave. The erosion may be
more deadly in the long run but, except for those who live on
the disappearing coast, it will excite only the far-seeing, the ultra-
sensitive, and the "cranks," whereas all the resources of the state
will be poured, with the blessings of the public, into the proclaimed disaster area left in the wake of the wave.

Just so, the shrinking minority who now live in the "pockets
of poverty" do not evoke in the general public or in the run of
politicians the kind of passionate interest that practically all politicians in the dramatic thirties were obliged to display toward the
poor on pain of seeing their public careers brought to an untimely
end. The coolness of the 90th Congress toward the Office of
Economic Opportunity and all its works is a far cry from the style
of political debate in the early thirties.

Then a Representative Cross from Texas, of all states, could
make his tremulous colleagues shudder with talk of "the French
Revolution with its guillotine, its Dantons and Robespierres" and
warn them that "when the storm breaks, it will be too late, and
there will be no cellars in which to hide." Huey Long could shake
the nation and make even the triumphant Roosevelt Administration jittery with his plans to recarve the economic pie so as to
"Make Every Man a King." And Dr. Townsend could send
tremors of alarm through politicians who expressed doubts about
his scheme to give $200 a month to every American over the age
of 60.

Today's poor, by contrast, are viewed by most politicians with impersonal detachment. Congress evinces no qualms whatever about taking a stern, even self-righteous, attitude regarding welfare, showing a keener interest in controlling riots than in controlling rats. Few candidates for office feel obliged to make their pitch any more to those below the officially recognized poverty line. And only four years ago a Presidential nominee other than Mr. Johnson could boldly observe that people were poor because they had either "low intelligence or low ambition."

Altogether it is reasonable to suggest that the current drive against poverty is neither politically nor economically inspired, then, but essentially a "cause," a moral crusade, with all the strength and weakness that such crusades are likely to have.

But while this moral concern is the driving force of those who are on the outside looking in, very different sources of power are operating within the dark pockets themselves, where the poor seem to be slowly waking from a torpor, sensing for the first time that they have been locked in a needless misery and that just beyond them are the good things of life they see on television, in advertising and, tantalizingly close, in shop windows. Both drives are significant in giving poverty and the war on poverty a wholly different coloration from that of the thirties, and each rates a little further examination.

The current campaign against poverty owes its begining not to any sense of national urgency but to the coincidence that a book entitled "The Other America," by Michael Harrington, fell into the hands of that omnivorous reader, President Kennedy, soon after he had seen, as though for the first time, the gaunt face of poverty in that particular pocket called West Virginia. To be sure, Kennedy had among his advisers several who were keenly aware of the problem and were preparing to press their view on him in any case. But as it happened, he needed no convincing and was planning to advance a major program at the time of his death.

Harrington's thesis was that too much had been made of the country's affluence, as though the poverty of 25 per cent, or even 20 per cent, of Americans was a minor problem, especially since some of them had jalopies and even washing machines (often without running water). "Shall we say to them that they are better off than the Indian poor, the Italian poor, the Russian poor?" Harrington asked with the fervor of an old-time Socialist. "I should put it another way. I want to tell every optimistic and well-fed American that it is intolerable that so many millions should be maimed in body and spirit when it is not necessary that they should be. My standard of comparison is not how much worse things used to be. It is how much better they could be if only we were stirred."

Just as President Kennedy had been stirred, so was his successor, who had known poverty at first hand and who had an active desire to go down in history as the President who completed and extended the work of the New Deal. Harrington's book had a surprisingly good sale, other authors and magazines took up the theme, and soon the poor found themselves not only the subject of major Federal legislation but for the first time since the Depression a focus of interest for social idealists in search of a cause.

But where social movements in the thirties saw the plight of the poor as a measure of the need for changing the entire economic system, few of today's workers on the anti-poverty front take any such drastic view. They are moved not by the messianic hopes of ideologists but by a wistful idealism not unmixed with guilt. For the question of poverty now, at least in the big cities, is tied to the question of race to a degree that would have seemed fantastic in the thirties, when at least hardship, if nothing else, was integrated.

"During the W.P.A. days, the day of relief, when every one was undergoing the economic crisis of the nation," Ralph Ellison has said, "there seemed to be a closer relationship between Negroes and whites and between Harlem and the rest of the community." It is typical of the more guilt-ridden present that Mayor Jerome P. Cavanagh of Detroit, citing the example of West Germany's payments to the victims of Nazism, should call on the Federal Government to establish the principle of "reparations" to the Negroes "for the deeds of past generations and of our own."

The fact that Negroes actually represent only one-fifth of those in the country who are technically defined as poor—that is, with incomes below $3,000 for a family of four—is immaterial. So is the fact that nearly half the poor families of the country live in rural areas. The steam for the drive on poverty is being generated in the cities. It is there that hundreds of thousands of people whose parents in the thirties were sharecroppers on Tobacco Road, without sufficient knowledge of the world to be desperate, have seen the fruits of middle-class life and want them —immediately.

It is the migration of these 1.5-million Negroes since 1950 that has made most, though by no means all, of the difference between the problems posed by poverty in the two decades. To the wretched tenant farmer of the pre-civil-rights South, rumors and reports from the Harlems of the north were easily converted into dreams of an earthly paradise, complete with jobs, money, schools, electricity, indoor plumbing and human dignity. When it all turned out to be squalor and the misery of supporting a family of seven on $65 a week, paradise receded, leaving an intolerable vacuum. And if that was true even for the lucky ones who consistently took home a low wage, how about the ones who soon discovered that in the economic scheme of things they were doomed to be last hired, first fired?

Families, unstable enough to begin with, broke up at an accelerating speed, but the disappearance of fathers did nothing to reduce the swiftly mounting birth rate. On the contrary, sex became often enough a source of income for abandoned mothers and for youth one of the few indulgences to be afforded. Testifying last year before a United States Senate subcommittee on urban problems, a 30-year-old grandfather and veteran of most of New York's state prisons explained that he had the first of his illegitimate eight children when he was 15 and his daughter had her first at the age of 12. Sex, a more literary witness explained, "was the most we had," and everyone knew all about it from the age of 6. "By the time we were 13 we knew it was a great anodyne, you know, before you got to heroin."

While the Southern parents of these witnesses and thousands like them knew little of the material things they were missing in American society, their children quickly learned all about them. Claude Brown, author of "Manchild in the Promised Land," explained: "We knew the things that were in the offing, what was out there to be had. It is like our parents' generation didn't have TV, we had it. We came up in school and read the same comic books others were reading. They showed us the same magazines, even though they didn't include us in them. . . . We knew what the good life was supposed to be. . . ."

They heard, too, from their teachers about the "American Dream," but those who had come to school without breakfast because there was no food at home were not sufficiently inspired by such fiction to listen to it any longer than the law demanded. Becoming dropouts, they thereby made certain what had before been merely probable—that their share in the dream would be no more than the possibility of a lucky break in the numbers game, or perhaps what could be had from a successful and not too risky crime. Given this preoccupation with the acquisitive, a not un-American emphasis, it is understandable that many impoverished and embittered black Americans came to resent, on the one hand, those middle-class Negroes who have "made it" (they were among the major targets in the Detroit violence) and, on the other hand, those hippie fugitives from the white middle class who affect to despise the very objects of materialism that deprived black youths will smash windows to acquire.

At least 11 per cent of all Americans live in families whose income qualifies them for public assistance even under state laws, a standard notoriously short of indulgence. Another 9 or 10 per cent are a shade above that desperation level but still below the $3,000-a-year poverty line. It is this latter group, owning an occasional television set or a household appliance admittedly beyond the dreams of an Egyptian fellah or a Balkan peasant, who have induced some redefining of poverty.

They are the "psychological poor," who manage to eat enough to keep going but who suffer as keenly as those below them on the economic ladder because they have so little hope of ever enjoying what the rest of American society routinely enjoys—12 years of schooling for their children, sanitary plumbing, medical care outside of impersonal factory-like clinics, and an occasional jaunt out to the country in bumper-to-bumper traffic.

What is so different about these "psychological poor" of the sixties from the poor of the thirties, to whom resentment was likewise no strange emotion? Indeed, the *nouveaux pauvres* created then by the collapse of the economy were much more aware of what they were missing in the way of bourgeois refinements than those who have never enjoyed them, the genteel poverty of "reduced circumstances" being, after all, among the hardest forms of the curse to endure.

The difference, quite simply, is the difference between a feeling of *temporary* exclusion from the good things of one's society and deprivation as a permanent, even hereditary, way of life. To be sure, many of the temporarily dispossessed in the days of the Depression did give way to despair—too old, too tired or too discouraged to pick up the pieces and start all over again—and their lot was tragic. But there were more who either were certain that with the recovery of the economy their fortunes would rise again or who were perfectly prepared to join some movement or other for trading in that economy for a newer and more workable model. In short, there was hope and spirit, or at the very least the feeling of being in the same boat as half the population of the country.

However low in the mind a jobless man might get, trudging from one shabby employment office to another—and I can testify to the lowness—he did not have to feel that, thanks to some inherent inferiority, he was an exile in his own country, forever fixed in a second- or third-class status. And everywhere he turned there were vivid reminders that the Depression was as bad or worse for others: a mushroom colony of improvised shanties in a vacant lot, a breadline of shabby men waiting impassively along the wire fencing of a shabby building, a row of empty storefronts recalling a departed way of life.

Even the popular culture of the day reflected the great common experience in which he shared, and it took out a little of the sting. Over the radio he could hear Eddie Cantor chirping that what with potatoes being cheaper, "Now's the Time to Fall in Love." He might be reassured by Ethel Merman and Rudy Vallee that "Life Is Just a Bowl of Cherries." Or he could at least feel a bond with all those who sang "Brother, Can You Spare a Dime?" And if he read at all, or even watched the newsreels on Bank Night at the movies, he couldn't help knowing something about the Dust Bowl, the Okies and the sharecroppers.

Above all, the entire apparatus of Government was giving evidence every day in the week that those in high places knew the straits he was in and were trying to do something about it. The President himself came on the air from time to time to confide in him, as no President had ever done before, and to explain what it was he hoped to do. If a man was not himself in the ranks of the W.P.A., the P.W.A. or the C.C.C., he had a friend or relative in one or another of them and knew what those agencies were up to.

And for a time he could not avoid seeing on all sides that sign and symbol of his Government's interest, the blue eagle of the N.R.A. Not only did that bird proclaim the will to National Recovery from shop windows, food packages and factory rooftops, but it rode aloft on banners carried in gaudy parades through the streets of cities by Mayors, industrial tycoons, trade-union presidents and folk heroes from Hollywood and Broadway—all to advise their countrymen that in the great campaign for recovery, "We Do Our Part."

To the dispossessed of the thirties, none of this brought joy perhaps, but the atmosphere was one in which the solidarity of disaster did provide a certain warmth—and strength. The contrasting bitterness of the dispossessed today is both striking and understandable. It is one thing to be caught out in the rain with a thousand others and another to be left there while everyone else has gone home to dry off.

Conversely, the comfortable find it increasingly hard to recall the discomfort, the further removed they are from it. This relativity factor in poverty is no less real for being psychological and is both a brake on action by the "haves" and a source of bitterness to the "have-nots." Certainly it feeds those smug reflections on the "rich poor," which run all the way from Will Rogers's famous boasts about our being "the only nation in the history of the world that ever went to the poorhouse in an automobile" to John Jacob Astor's philosophical reflection that a man who has a million dollars is as well off as if he were rich.

While Government *was* doing things in the thirties, it must be pointed out that, except for direct emergency relief, its activity was not aimed at those in the greatest need but at those in need who were most vital to a quick restoration of the economy—the trade-union member, the big-market famer, the skilled worker, the small pensioner. As it happened—and one will be as skeptical on the subject as his nature dictates—these were also the ones who in spite of hard times still had a large measure of political leverage, who indeed made up the backbone of the Administration's electoral support. Those who had no such leverage—the share-croppers, tenant farmers and migratory workers, the chronically and congenitally poor of the city slums, lacking both the vigor and the organization to exert political pressure—these were helped very little and in a fundamental way not at all.

It is the children and grandchildren of these same long-sufferers who are the hard core of the problem today. The extent to which this is not just figuratively but also literally true is a dismal phenomenon now being faced for the first time: hereditary poverty. What has been regarded for millennia in the Old World as a fact of life, to be meekly accepted as one's divinely ordained lot on earth, has not traditionally been viewed as part of the American Way, but on the contrary a gross violation of the spirit of Horatio Alger.

Now, however, a United States Senate Committee can report in passing that ". . . poverty in America has been changing in nature. The American frontiersman knew poverty as he struggled to build a society sufficiently productive to offer a more abundant life. The immigrant knew poverty as he entered a new land and pre-pared his children to move upward in the economic and social scale. In both cases poverty was a transition stage to better things. Poverty in modern America tends to be a permanent state, con-centrated among certain disadvantaged groups and in many cases continuing generation after generation."

This is what the technicians mean by *structural* poverty as opposed to the *cyclical* variety that hit so many Americans in the thirties. It has little to do with general prosperity or lack of it, because, prosperity or no, there is nothing to do for those whose unskilled services are no longer needed, who cannot acquire new skills for lack of education, and whose lack of education stems in turn from the atmosphere of neglect, apathy and ignorance which their parents' poverty has imposed on them. They are poor, it has been said, not because they are just starting out to be rich but because they have already been rejected—or feel they have, which amounts to the same thing.

Obviously this kind of poverty calls for different approaches from those that seemed applicable to the hardships of the fallen *bourgeoisie* in the thirties. They had to do with lifting the entire economy. But, as Galbraith and others have pointed out, general prosperity now not only fails to help those trapped in the "pockets" or those who are poor because they are individually handicapped but actually deepens their misery and increases their bitterness.

All of which brings us to two attitudes on the subject of poverty which are gaining a degree of acceptance now and which would have been unthinkable 35 years ago. Both serve to give the whole question an emphasis sharply different from anything we knew in the days of the Depression.

The first is that since the poverty of the "structurally poor" is scarcely of their own making, and since they have so few chances to escape through their own initiative, they are as much entitled to a voice in plans for improving their lot as any other element in the citizenry. In principle the Office of Economic Opportunity and other Government agencies recognize that claim, and elsewhere their spokesmen increasingly assert it as a matter of right. They represent their constituents, as it were, on community anti-poverty boards, and before legislative committees, much as lobbyists represent war veterans, chiropractors or oil promoters. And they cover professional gatherings, whether invited or not.

Crashing a recent conference of the American Medical Association on health care for the poor, a delegation from a Chicago Negro slum marched up to the platform and demanded a voice at the gathering on the ground that the matter concerned them. "You are interfering with our efforts to help the underprivileged," said the irate chairman, thereby setting up the retort obvious: "We *are* the underprivileged." Under pressure from the assembled doctors, the chairman allowed the poverty delegates five minutes to denounce the health care facilities in their district, after which they triumphantly filed out.

If today's spokesmen for the poor are for the most part a pragmatic lot, with an eye on what can be had here and now, the dispossessed also have would-be champions of a more revolutionary bent, just as they did in the thirties. But there are differences. Devotees of the New Left, determined to steer clear of the fatal dogmatism of the Old, carry individual whim to the point where programs are consumed in personal anarchy and a passion for disorder passes for democracy. If the Old Left in its procedures too often suggested Kafka, the New—witness last fall's

National Conference for New Politics—often recalls nothing so much as the trial of the Knave of Hearts in "Alice in Wonderland."

More fundamental, the left could seriously envision a forced change in the whole economic order in the thirties, when a quarter of the working force was idle, when the poverty wave had engulfed a third of the population and was imminently threatening more than that, and when new economic orders were very much in vogue elsewhere in the world. Today's left has less a program for revolutionary change than a fondness for using revolutionary rhetoric and tactics to extract immediate concessions from the Establishment.

It is possible that the New Left will in time settle down to a more systematic approach to whatever goals it decided upon, but so far it would seem to have considerably less influence on events than the Popular Front had in the thirties—and extremely little in the campaign to abolish poverty. It is worth noting that the most comprehensive and detailed program to this end, the "Freedom Budget" for massive Government investment, comes not from the New Left but from such representatives of the relatively Old (and Mild) Left as A. Philip Randolph and Leon Keyserling.

The other major change in attitude which I suggest has occurred raises an equally basic question: Since much of the remaining poverty is of the "case" variety for which jobs are not the prescription—roughly 50 per cent of the poor are scarcely in the job market at all—why not face facts and simply subsidize the victims out of their poverty?

Certainly a return to the public-works programs of the thirties is not the answer for this very large segment of today's poor, handicapped as they are by age and health. Even for the young and healthy, but poorly educated, Government-provided employment is not the obvious answer it once was. For there is clearly less need for huge pools of unskilled manpower than was the case in the preautomation days of the Depression. By and large, I was told by a former official in the poverty program, such projects would employ the wrong people—"they wouldn't do much for the poor, just mean double time for the building trades."

Clearly this was not true in the thirties, when scores of thousands of highly skilled men were idle. With all the loose charges of "leaf-raking" and loafing, P.W.A. contributions to Hoover Dam, Triborough Bridge and a whole new sewage system for Chicago went all but uncredited, not to mention such other fruits of indolence as the aircraft carriers Yorktown and Enterprise. The injustice of the criticism was caught fairly enough by a contemporary cartoon showing two lady tourists gazing at a plaque indicating the New Deal origin of a magnificent bridge. "And to think," one of them says in astonishment, "they did all of this while leaning on shovels."

But that was a time when the unemployed ran as high as 25 per cent of the nation's working force. The first order of business was clearly to get them back to work and restore the nation's buying power. What we are faced with now is an unemployment rate of less than 4 per cent and a growing number of *unemployables,* people who never will have either buying power or decent lives unless something is done to *give* them income while educating their young to the point where they can earn their own.

What public-works programs were to New Deal critics, namely a red rag, current proposals for subsidizing the poor out of their poverty are to critics of the present Administration—or will be if the proposals get beyond the talking stage.

The schemes vary in amount and in mechanics. At their most stringent is Milton Friedman's "negative income tax," which would guarantee each family 50 per cent of minimal needs, calculated on the poverty threshold figure, in exchange for *all* further welfare assistance. This plan of Senator Goldwater's economic adviser would seem to offer the poor only a freer choice of how to spend their lack of money. But through several gradations of generosity, coupled with provisions designed to encourage the recipients to work if possible, the negative income tax proposal at its peak is offered as a way to eliminate poverty altogether. For $11-billion a year, which is well under 2 per cent of the gross national product, the entire bottom fifth of the population could be lifted once and for all over the threshold of poverty.

If this is deemed too ambitious, there are several schemes on tap to grant Government family allowances, such as Canada and other nations have long provided. Generally these would be paid for by eliminating the present income-tax deduction for dependents, so that the poor, who don't pay taxes, would net $10 or so a month for each child, while those who do pay taxes would in effect foot the bill.

These proposals, none of which, again, stem from the New Left, are mentioned here not with any idea of judging them or even discussing their merits but merely to highlight the overriding difference between the two decades. What was done 35 years ago was done out of weakness and the demands of an emergency. What is proposed now stems from strength and a growing, though hardly pervasive, sense in the country, if not in Congress, that social decency requires it. For the first time in the long history of man it is possible here and now to wipe out this most venerable plague. And the decision, at last, is more philosophical than economic. As in the thirties, war at the end of the decade has all but eliminated cyclical poverty, while leaving the structural variety untouched. The difference is that the structurally poor know now what their forerunners in the thirties could not know —that their plight is wholly unnecessary.

In this respect the poverty of the sixties in America differs not only from that of the thirties but from that of every period and every society that has gone before. It was all very well for feudal serfs to accept an animal-like poverty as the decree of Providence, or for the Puritans to regard it as a confession of sloth and a mark of disgrace. It was understandable even for the Rev. Henry Ward Beecher, on a yearly income that would be $75,000 in today's currency, to rail at do-gooders in the Gilded Age who thought it hard for a man to support a family of five on a dollar a day. Not pretty but understandable. Because none of these nor any of their contemporaries could eliminate poverty even with the best will in the world.

We can. And that fact poses for us a moral question that no people has yet had to decide—certainly not the Depression-ridden Americans of 35 years ago. To execute the required programs would scarcely tax our ingenuity, but to make the required decision, so hostile to the Puritan tradition—that will not be easy.

Part 3

WEALTH:
ITS POTENTIAL USE
AND MISUSE

THIS SECTION DEALS with the potential uses and misuses of our national wealth and income, and begins appropriately with a 1945 article on "Our Fear of Abundance" by Walter Reuther. World War II had just ended. While most Americans were pre-occupied with the challenge and romance of helping Europe toward recovery, the Auto Workers' leader was reminding us of the need to modernize our railroads, to eliminate slums and substandard housing by utilizing the mass-production techniques and other technical know-how we had developed during the war, to change the face of rural and urban America—and simultane-ously to raise the incomes of the workers involved in such a grand endeavor.

Apparently we did little in the way of heeding Reuther's ad-vice. One year later, in "This Is a World I Never Fought For," Richard Neuberger told how million-dollar race tracks were touted while ex-GI's could not find materials to build a home. "The money-making orgy of 1946 is bad enough; . . . the general indifference to it is infinitely worse."

In the middle of Eisenhower's second term (1958), Leon Keyserling's essay on what might be, "Next Step—A 600 Billion-Dollar Economy?," held up another picture of how we could be using our productive machinery and fiscal instruments. Keyserling argued that if we pursued a 5 per cent growth rate policy, an America in 1964 could have the facilities, and a well-paid corps of teachers, to speed our scientific progress and furnish a college education for every qualified person seeking it; provide enough hospitals and medical care to improve vastly the health of all men, women, and children; and rehouse ten million of their families, not to mention the doubling of the average Social Security benefit to the aged.

Our Fear of Abundance

by Walter P. Reuther

THERE IS a widespread failure in Congress and with the public to appreciate the domestic implications of Japanese surrender. There is a general reluctance to confront the problems of transition from war to peace. If we do not face them soberly and soon we run the risk of creating a situation potentially as explosive and damaging as the atomic bomb.

Uncritical use of the term "reconversion" is itself a clue to the "normalcy" temper of our thinking, in and out of Washington. We regard the next few crucial months almost exclusively as a period of relaxation or abolition of controls, of an automatic kicking over of wartime traces and return to some status quo ante.

Congress apparently intends to ignore the sound recommendations for action contained in President Truman's recent message. There is every indication that whatever slapdash emergency measures the Congress may contrive we intend to rely almost solely on what J. A. Krug of the War Production Board has called "the natural resilience of the economy" to lift us out of the doldrums of contract terminations and mass layoffs. We are gambling on the effect of a combination of pent-up demand for civilian goods and a backlog of savings to prevent a tailspin into deflation.

This "coming in on a wing and a prayer" economics rests upon too many unwarranted assumptions. The first is that there is

From the *New York Times Magazine*, September 16, 1945, copyright © 1945 by The New York Times Company.

somewhere and something to go back to. Yet there can be no return to the balmy Palm Beach climate of the Nineteen Twenties —unless we are willing to take with it the inevitable aftermath of depression. And, if I am correct in my appraisal of the average American's present mood, there will be no easy road back to the serfdom which made outcasts of millions of unemployed in the Thirties.

As for the "resilience" of our economy, it proved insufficient to stabilize boom conditions or to turn the corner of the slump. It could not convert from peace to war production without Government prodding. And there is good reason to assert that, left to its own devices, it will be unequal to the task of converting another boom, if one arises, into continuing prosperity.

The third assumption, existence of a vast reservoir of savings which will immediately spring into action as purchasing power, is equally untenable. Most of the billions of dollars in war bonds are held either by corporations and financial institutions or by individuals and families in the upper-income brackets who habitually save a great proportion of their income. Those billions, therefore, will not prove a source of demand for consumer goods. Where will that demand come from? The rest of wartime savings, held by lower-income families, must serve to absorb the shock of reduced hours, down-grading, lower-paying civilian jobs and unemployment. It will be used cautiously, dribbled out for necessities, not expended confidently and lavishly to confirm optimistic predictions of another lush era.

Thus our dilemma is a real one. It cannot be solved by hymns to Free Enterprise or by efforts to turn back the clock to the halcyon days of Harding. The road leads not backward but forward, to full production, full employment and full distribution in a society which has achieved economic democracy within the framework of political democracy. We shall not attain these positive goals by a single-minded concern for the contract-termination pains of business or by grudging, belated and negative action calculated to take care of the "human side of reconversion." Necessary as are such measures as adequate unemployment insurance they remain poultices applied to an inflamed surface; our real ills lie deeper, temporarily forgotten during an ersatz wartime prosperity, but arising now to plague us again.

We suffer, to put it briefly, from what Thorstein Veblen called the "inordinate productivity" of the machine. We have mastered technology and possess a complex, high-octane B-29 production machine. But our productive genius has always been stalemated by our failure at the distributive end. We have found it impossible to sustain a mass purchasing power capable of providing a stable market for the products of a twentieth-century technology. This disparity between our B-29 technology and our huffing and puffing Model T distributive system led to the crash of 1929 and ushered in a period of unprecedented waste of human and material resources—a waste estimated at 200 billion dollars in potential goods and services.

In the light of this diagnosis we see how precarious must be any post-war boom. We see, moreover, that the chief intent of national policies during the transition must be not merely to cushion the change-over to supposed normal ways of doing business, but rather to remedy the central flaw of our economy, wiping out the fitful succession of boom and bust, feast and famine, and providing stable mass distribution of the goods and services made available by mass production.

Any program designed to accomplish this end will require action along two lines: full use of our industrial plant and, secondly, a wage-price policy capable of creating and maintaining an effective demand for the products of that plant at capacity output.

In behalf of the United Automobile Workers thrown on the scrapheap by the closing of the Willow Run bomber plant, I recently proposed a plan providing for continued operation of that plant and of the thousands of other Government-built war facilities which can be turned to the use of peace.

This plan, published by Willow Run Local 50, UAW-CIO, and now under consideration by Government officials, recommends conversion of publicly owned war plants to the mass production of modern railroad equipment and low-cost housing.

Government authorities similar to the Tennessee Valley Authority would be set up in housing and transportation, and under their jurisdiction a survey would be made of the $20,000,000,000 in war facilities, the vast bulk of which is public property, financed by the War Bond investments of millions of Americans. Most of these plants have a high peacetime utility. They are ultra-modern and contain the most efficient machine tools and equipment.

It is important to emphasize that most of these plants can

readily be converted to production of civilian goods, just as plants were retooled for production of war matériel under the defense and war programs. Certain private management spokesmen will protest that this is not so; the same cry was raised in the fall of 1940 when I presented, on behalf of the technicians and production workers of the automotive industry, a plan to utilize its plant and equipment for the mass production of warplanes. Yet three years later, in testimony before the Truman Committee of the United States Senate, K. T. Keller, president of the Chrysler Corporation, admitted that 89 per cent of Chrysler's machines had been converted to war production—and could be converted back to civilian production.

What was true of Chrysler was true also of General Motors, Ford and minor producers. The will to change corporate habits and to renounce a profitable civilian business simply wasn't there. After Pearl Harbor the Government had to move in and force conversion.

After determination of the facilities adaptable to the program these housing and railroad equipment authorities would place them in production either through direct operation, through lease to private manufacturers or through lease to workers' producer cooperatives. In each case the plant would be operated as part of the total program and its management would conform to three standards: an equitable wage pattern, a good low-cost product and protection of the Government's investment.

This program holds the promise of stimulating our whole economy through the progressive introduction of the most modern rolling stock and the proportionate retirement of obsolescent equipment. Use of roller and ball bearings, of aluminum, magnesium and diesel power will increase the payload (just as important in freight car as in air transport) and will permit the radical scaling down of rail rates. As for housing, the same mass production miracles which have made us a nation on wheels can place a modern, durable, healthy house within the economic reach of the common man. Airframe, aircraft engine, magnesium, aluminum, electrical equipment, forge, foundry and other Government-owned war plants can be utilized in the mass production of complete homes, including all fixtures, complete bathroom, kitchen, garbage disposal and air conditioning units, electric dish washers and other appliances—all designed and constructed as integral parts of the house according to the latest standards of convenience and efficiency.

By giving the construction industry a public utility status, by fostering cooperative and Federal housing projects, by working through a technical commission under the Housing Authority to revise and implement building codes and eliminate slum housing the entire vicious circle of primitive methods and restrictive practices in the building industry can be broken.

Anyone familiar with technological advances made in the automotive industry cannot regard such a promise of low-cost prefabricated housing as visionary. These advances have been accelerated throughout industry in the last four years as a result of the pervasive demands of war. We have but to mobilize for peace the resourcefulness and technical know-how which put the B-29 in the skies over Tokyo and sent the atomic bomb crashing into Hiroshima—and we can wipe out the slums and sub-standard housing, both rural and urban, which sap the health and dignity of millions of American families. We have spent billions to destroy cities. Let us be lavish in the equally challenging and more creative assignment of building homes and rebuilding cities here in the United States, a victorious but poorly housed democracy.

The railroad and building industries are two vital areas of our economy which have not kept pace with technological advance in the past decades and whose practices are geared to scarcity rather than to that abundance which is now both physically possible and socially imperative.

In the building industry outmoded construction techniques, inflated land values (often based on illegal but highly profitable use of slum property in violation of unenforced health and building codes), a multiplicity of small dealers and middlemen and high interest rates on capital have combined to create high unit costs and general instability and have made home ownership either impossible or impractical for a majority of American families.

In both industries only aggressive government action can cut through the tangle of inertia and vested interest and initiate sorely needed reforms. Housing and railroad equipment authorities would provide the administrative machinery to effect these changes.

The war has demonstrated to the American people that full employment is possible. They will not readily be convinced by conservative economic theorists that a return to peace must mean a return to a "normal float of unemployed" and "no help wanted" signs. Existence of a vast industrial empire of government-owned war plants, most of them adaptable to peacetime production, serves to dramatize, to focus more sharply than ever, the dilemma of American capitalism.

The proposals I have advanced deal chiefly with housing and transportation, but throughout industry the issue is the same: back to monopoly, to operation at a fraction of capacity, to cherished and (to a few) profitable habits in a scarcity economy —or forward to full use of resources, full employment and an equitable distribution of the products of our labor? We cannot dodge that issue. If the right answer is too long delayed Willow Run and the other giant plants of World War II will stand idle as rotting monuments to our fear of abundance—but our free way of life may well lie in ruins around them.

Physical plant and technical skill will avail us little if the complex process of production and distribution is impeded by an inequitable and unrealistic policy regarding prices and wages. The chief objective of that policy must be a general rise in the wage level without a concomitant rise in the price level.

The issue, viewed here from another perspective, is the same: will industry, in its search for profits, find them by exacting a high price per unit of a limited output, maintaining an artificial scarcity, pocketing the returns on advancing technology and shutting millions out from employment and a stake in the preservation of the system? Or will industry, following the most respectable economic theory, pass on to labor its just share of the benefits of technical progress in the form of higher wages and seek its profits in capacity production for an expanded market?

Fantastic war profits, before and after taxes, and favorable Government tax policy place most American corporations in an unusually strong position for adopting the high-wage, high-volume approach now, setting the pattern which will shape our peacetime economy. But there are ominous signs emanating from the oracles of government stabilization policy which suggest that the emerging pattern is just the opposite.

Sixty-five industries reporting to the War Production Board have revealed the volume of production at which they feel confident of breaking even in peace-time operations. Of the sixty-five, fifty-one stated that they could operate without loss at less than 70 per cent of capacity output. The break-even rate for the automotive industry is 55 per cent. Add to these figures the fact that the NWLB has held labor in the vise of the Little Steel Formula despite rocketing living costs, while the OPA has shown a disposition to grant price rises on flimsy evidence or none, and we have the elements of the post-war wage-price structure: low wages, high prices, high profit per unit, few units. The picture can be developed further: deficient purchasing power, shrinking markets, rising unemployment, a growing conviction on the part of those whom industry has thrust aside that the game of free enterprise, played at their expense, isn't worth the candle. It is to be hoped that we do not drift this far toward disaster.

There is, as we have said, an alternative: reduction of unit cost by high-volume production and constant technological innovation, enabling the masses of workers to get their bigger cut out of a larger pie and providing industry with an expanding market.

There are two other main items in a desirable wage policy for peace: industry-wide wage agreements based on the principle of equal pay for equal work, regardless of geographical area, and the introduction of guaranteed annual wage systems through collective bargaining between labor and management. The first will protect labor from exploitation as a pawn in the competitive struggle; the second will place responsibility for continuity of employment where it belongs—with employers—and will minimize the need for Government intervention.

The logic of these two demands is simple. Competition, to be socially acceptable in a society which pretends to be at one remove from the jungle, must be founded upon the relative efficiency of management techniques, productive skills, technological improvements and the resulting superiority of product. As for area differentials the solution lies in raising low living standards, not in maintaining depressed conditions. General Motors does not charge less for a Chevrolet in Birmingham, Ala., in deference to the lower standards of the South. Senator Bilbo receives as much for his services to democracy as do Senators Wagner and Vandenberg. UAW members in the South will not accept less for their sweat and skills than the auto workers of Michigan.

The guaranteed annual wage proposal represents a challenge to management to sponsor the greatest "back to work" movement in the history of labor relations. To business men who have been known upon occasion to boast of their ability to meet payrolls and who in times of strikes and picket lines are extremely vocal about the "right to work," the annual wage proposal says, in effect, "You can't have your cake and eat it too; if private enterprise wants to stay private it has to stay enterprising. If you won't accept a continuing commitment to employ, the Government will have to move in."

But the annual wage offers a positive alternative to Government intervention. Besides being a powerful incentive to maintain capacity operations and a spur to labor morale and productivity through removal of lay-off fears, it offers the expectation of a continually growing market by placing pay checks regularly in the hands of the millions of American workers who are the great consumers of the products of this country's assembly lines.

These are the bare bones of a minimal program for making America as prosperous in peace as she has been formidable in war. The flesh and blood must come from our unswerving will to plan and work together for peace and abundance just as we joined forces for death and violence. To assert that planning to fulfill the promise of American life in an economic as well as a political sense must degenerate into tyranny is to utter a counsel of despair and to resign ourselves to drift and ultimate disaster.

If we fail our epitaph will be simply stated: we had the ingenuity to unlock the secrets of the universe for the purposes of destruction but we lacked the courage and imagination to work together in the creative pursuits of peace.

"This Is a World
I Never Fought For"

by Richard L. Neuberger

SOMEWHERE IN THE U.S.A.

IN MY home town a sports syndicate is building a $1,000,000
track for horse racing. The promoters recently announced with
pride that it would be ready for pari-mutuel wagering by August.
Few townspeople seem to think it ironic that while hammers fall
and planks are sawed at the race track, veterans with HH priori-
ties tramp from lumber yard to lumber yard vainly trying to buy
construction materials for homes.

The race track symbolizes to many of our former fighting men
a public attitude they never expected to find on their return from
the wars. "Everything for the boys" was the motto as long as the
battle raged. Today, loan companies and automobile sales agencies are putting up elaborate new buildings—with the approval
of the Civilian Production Administration, it might be added—
but veterans encounter difficulty getting the tiniest screw or sim-
plest window frame for bungalow or cottage.

In defense of my home town, I think what is taking place there
is only a symbol, too—a symbol of a national determination to
make all the money one can just as quickly as possible. Why
build a home for a veteran when you can erect a barbecue stand

From the *New York Times Magazine,* July 28, 1946, copyright © 1946 by
The New York Times Company.

which will clear $500 a week? What contractor can make as much putting up a small house as he can outfitting a cocktail bar?

"All over the United States," says H. V. Simpson, executive director of the West Coast Lumbermen's Association, "there is what amounts to a riot of new construction on race tracks, dance halls, road houses, night clubs, saloon halls, gambling joints, pool-rooms and other spots that compete for 'sucker money' now in circulation by the billions. No other kind of construction in the Pacific Northwest and elsewhere has taken so much material and labor away from the supply necessary for veterans' housing."

Social workers report that the local divorce rate is the highest in history. They attribute many of the divorces to the fact that veterans are forced to double up with parents and in-laws. More marriages are ended each day than begun. "Double or nothing is a bad bet," said a domestic relations court judge, himself a veteran of Anzio beachhead. "Our soldiers and their wives need homes of their own. Otherwise, more wartime marriages are going to be wrecked by family strife."

But you can't build a house without two by fours, door jambs and plumbing fixtures. A cynical official of the Federal Housing Authority refers to a veteran's HH priority as "only a hunting license and by no means a buck in the bag."

I stood with an Air Corps sergeant who had flown the Hump to China, watching nails driven and foundations dug on a row of $12,000 summer homes at a beach resort along the Pacific Ocean. "If you're a veteran," said the sergeant wrathfully, "you can't get materials for a little $4,000 three-roomer. That's all I can afford. But if you're a banker or slot-machine operator, you can put up an eight-room house at the beach to live in three months out of the year. I don't think that's what I flew the Hump for. In fact, I know it isn't."

In my town—and I repeat that conditions in my town are indicative of conditions in the United States of America rather than unique—city authorities regretfully evicted a veteran's family of eleven living in a basement. It was contrary to the building code, the officials said. A week later a dozen firemen were injured battering down the double doors of a gambling den to put out a fire in the business district. The gambling den and the double doors were illegal, too.

My wife and I toured the town looking for an apartment. Where the door was not slammed in our faces, we were told, "You've got to sign a promise you haven't any dogs or children." Three landlords would rent to us if we paid $250 to "decorate" the apartment. Another wanted $100 cash for himself. We could occupy a one-roomer elsewhere if we bought for $500 an assortment of dilapidated furniture worth one-fifth that amount.

At one place where the "No Vacancy" sign was shoved under our noses, a prominent pin-ball machine operator moved in the following week. I asked one rental agent if he gave any special consideration to veterans. "How can I, Buddy?" he answered with surprising frankness. "That $300 discharge money you fellows get from the Government doesn't go very far."

While guns boomed and warships plowed the seas, no speech about the welfare of "our boys in service" could be too flowery. Politicians outdid themselves in promises. Houses valued on the tax rolls at $5,000 in our town are being sold for $15,000 to veterans in desperate search of a place to live. The State Planning Commission contends that many of these veterans will be unable to maintain payments and interest charges, and will lose the homes as well as their first deposits.

To keep down the price of homes, veterans asked local assessors and the Tax Commission to reappraise for tax purposes any house put on the market at more than its actual value. Real estate agents were shocked by so brazen a proposal. Needless to add, it was not adopted.

My wife and I bought an acre on the edge of town. FHA officials estimated that it might be another year before we could begin to build, perhaps a year after that before the house could be fully completed. Two years! I remember being at Whitehorse with the United States Army Engineers and facing the prospect of an Arctic winter in tents. Barracks for 3,000 soldiers were built in two weeks.

This was the experience of men in uniform all over the world. They saw barracks, camps, bases and airfields constructed in jungle and muskeg almost between dawn and dusk. Yet, now that they are back in the United States, the men who accomplished these miracles must wait years to move into a little cottage or duplex.

Few soldiers have come home to large incomes. Many whom I know are earning less than $200 a month. Yet the cost of living soars constantly. Everyone in business has seemed intent on smashing the OPA. No labor union is content with the last pay boost. The game of grab becomes more intense. Business uses pay raises as an excuse to demand higher prices; labor uses higher prices as an excuse to demand pay raises. No one dares to say, "This far and no farther!"

The man home from war is one of the principal victims of this whirling spiral. Despite all the bragging about our generosity to service men, the Baruch report has shown that we give less mustering-out pay than Canada or Australia. The soldier's $300 goes for his first outfit of clothes. Many soldiers have returned to jobs unworthy of the experience they gained in service. A former Air Corps major, a much-decorated pilot, is running a trolley car. An infantry master sergeant has found a job ushering at an amusement park.

Business men complain that they could not make money because of the OPA. Practically all the business men I know have ordered new automobiles, they and their wives made trips last winter to Miami and Palm Springs, yet they talk with chagrin of what strikes have done to their investments in the stock market.

When first he comes home the soldier is apart from the reckless spending and money-making mania that grip the land. This detachment does not last for long. "I could get back my old job as a garage mechanic," said a thin young man in whose buttonhole the pin emblematic of the Purple Heart gleamed. "The job would pay $45 a week. That isn't enough for me and my family to live on at these prices. I've got three children. So I'm getting a line of punchboards instead. If I can get in solid with a beer distributor, I'll clean up $150 a week. That's more like it."

Nor does the desire for quick money always stop with punchboards. More than 25 per cent of the men being admitted to prison in the State of California wore their country's uniform in the war so recently concluded. The last two men on trial for their lives in this town, facing charges of first-degree murder, were veterans of World War II.

"The rich get richer," a sailor said to me, "and the fellow who was in service gets the royal run-around."

The glamour of the uniform is wearing thin. An Indian, member of a tribe whose warriors greeted Lewis and Clark as they paddled down the Columbia River, walked into a hamburger stand near my home town. The Indian wore his khaki blouse, with the discharge insignia sewed on the breast, but the man behind the counter snarled, "Beat it! Can't you see the sign? Can't you read? No native trade here."

The red-skinned soldier, graduate of the Indian School at Chemawa, was not bitter. He merely said, "One would think that this dreadful war would have taught people something about tolerance and understanding. It is disappointing that so few have learned the lesson taught by Hitlerism."

Devotion to the cause of the returning heroes is often confined to lip service. The Legislature of my State passed many resolutions extolling the deeds of our soldiers overseas. It also passed a law making it as difficult as possible for those soldiers to re-establish voting rights. Registration requirements were tightened; mobile registration booths, traveling out into rural and working-class districts, were abolished. I asked one of the legislators why this was done. "Heck!" he said. "Most of you fellows got so much propaganda in the Army that you're all indoctrinated with Roosevelt's ideas now."

Of course, greed and selfishness are not the whole story. I have met storekeepers who risked their economic future to trade with Japanese-Americans back from the Italian and Philippine battlefronts. Railroad engineers refused to follow the strike call until they had pulled troop trains into camp. A real-estate agent in our town closed up the offices of all doctors and dentists who went into military service. "The offices stay shut until you return home," the agent told his tenants, despite the fact that a loan company interested in the building ownership was not pleased.

But such incidents are the exception rather than the rule. And more shocking even than the examples of injustice, it seems to me, is the lack of outrage over them. People who are told of a race track under construction while veterans can obtain no building materials look at you skeptically and wonder why you are so riled up. Several ask when the pari-mutuel windows will open; they want to place a wager.

The four small children of a soldier suffocate when the chicken coop in which they are living catches fire. Newspapers of the same day tell of hotel rooms and apartments filled by delegates to numerous conventions. And no one is indignant.

People used to be stirred by a man with a sense of outrage. Now they seem merely disturbed. I sat in a meeting where a plea was voiced for the relief of starving Europe. The group was advised that any donation could be deducted from income taxes. An Army chaplain got to his feet. Air Corps wings and three battle stars glistened on his blouse. "If I hear again that money to keep a child from dying can be subtracted from tax returns I'm going berserk," the chaplain said, "I have seen some of those children die and I don't like that kind of plea."

The chaplain strode out; people looked at each other, embarrassed, and the speaker continued to emphasize over again the blessings of tax deductions.

We have proved ourselves capable of sacrifice and heroism. America's record in the war is studded with tales of the nobility of man to man. Many soldiers perished so that a comrade might be spared. Yet the nation capable of this devotion is also apparently capable of indulgence, without blush or shame, in a reckless orgy of spending, gambling, high living and frivolity while the rest of the world suffers and many of the men who did the fighting are without adequate homes or worth-while jobs.

The war was grim and dreadful, yet perhaps we shall look back upon it as sort of a golden age when we were concerned about our brothers. The money-making orgy of 1946 is bad enough; but, I repeat, the general indifference to it is infinitely worse. To people who shrug their shoulders at stories of injustice and gouging I should like to cite the philosopher who said that acceptance of evil exceeded evil itself.

Next Step— A 600-Billion-Dollar Economy?

by Leon H. Keyserling

WASHINGTON

DURING THE recent political campaign President Eisenhower and others spoke sharply of a trend toward "spendthrift government." While spending should not be a partisan issue, it is a proper subject for discussion because it involves great issues of public policy. Since practically all economic activity is galvanized by spending, the economist asks this question: Are we today, as a nation, spending as much as we should?

I believe we are spending too little. A steady increase in government spending, and even more so in private spending, are essential parts of an over-all policy to build our national strength. This, in my opinion, became apparent more than a year ago when Russia launched the first sputnik, and when we in the United States resolved to make a reappraisal of our entire performance as a nation.

In our heart of hearts we knew why we were lagging in primary military strength, science, education, and many other things. It was not because we lacked the material potentials to do much better. It was because we were not trying hard enough to marshal these potentials.

Now the need for harder effort should be still more apparent. The announcement of the new Soviet seven-year plan aimed at increasing production by 80 per cent by 1965 is a grim warning to us. The Soviet economy has been growing more than 10 per cent a year, almost five times our national average since the Korean war. We cannot grow as fast as the Soviets because we are already much more highly developed. But we cannot cope with their military and especially their economic efforts if we acquiesce in the long-term expansion of our total economic strength at less than half the rate which we could reasonably maintain.

But thus far, despite the ferment in the Middle East and in the far Pacific, and the Soviet economic challenge now being added to the military challenge, the promised rethinking of our economic performance has not been translated into sufficient action. Today we remain content with a defense strength far below the minimum judged essential by most experts. We put forward new economic plans for the Middle East and elsewhere, but these plans are scaled tragically short of the need. We have not significantly intensified our efforts in science, education, health services, or many other cardinal elements of our total strength for the long pull.

There is one root cause of all of these shortcomings. It is the erroneous belief that our economy "cannot afford to do more." We are still trying to "protect" our economy by scaling down our demands upon it in accord with its relatively low actual rate of performance. We have not yet learned that we could afford what we *must* have, if we lifted our economy's actual performance closer to its great potentials.

This "protective" or defensive psychology neither protects nor defends adequately, because it is too narrow in scope. To be sure, the indication that we have reversed another recession without sinking into a depression refutes the old Marxist dogmas. But it does not meet the Soviet challenge nor our needs abroad or at home.

A more positive approach is required. We should not relinquish what "we cannot afford" until we first explore what we could really do if we tried hard enough. To illustrate: The size of our economy was about $440,000,000,000 in 1957. This means that this was approximately the volume of all goods and services produced in that year. This included all our products, agricultural and industrial, the schools, roads and hospitals built, the defense weapons forged, and all services performed for compensation by everybody from the preacher to the sweeper.

If we grow in the future—and we can and should—at the average annual rate of about 5 per cent which was achieved in some previous peacetime years without inflation, we would reach an economy of more than $600,000,000,000 in size in 1964. This would mean a total production of goods and services more than one-third greater in volume than in 1957. This huge increase would be available for wise utilization, in accord with our priorities of need.

But this rate of growth will not come automatically. While there are some top limits, the progress of a nation, like that of an individual or a business, depends upon the vigor and wisdom of policies and programs. The immense needs of wartime led us to adopt programs conducive to an absolutely maximum rate of economic growth. This averaged 8 to 10 per cent a year—too high to be sustained over many years. As already indicated, in some periods other than wartime we grew almost 5 per cent a year without inflation. This might be called a high rate of sustainable economic growth for peacetime. In other periods, including the last few years before the most recent recession, we grew at less than half this rate. Since the Korean war the annual growth has averaged only a little better than 2 per cent.

The choice now is between the competing sets of policies and programs which would yield in future the high growth rate for peacetime or relative peacetime (about 5 per cent a year), or the low growth rate (less than half of this). Let us now see why the high growth seems imperative for the years immediately ahead.

One reason for choosing the higher rate (the Russian challenge aside) is that if actual production does not expand rapidly enough to utilize fully our growing labor force and our rapidly advancing technology, more workers and plants become idle. This happened during the recent years of low growth, even before the recession, and it brought on the recession itself. Hence there is no ground for complacency in the mere checking of the recession, when most forecasters agree that our average rate of economic growth during the few years ahead is likely to be low. This would continue a very high level of chronic unemployment.

By far the main reason for the high growth rate is positive and immensely heartening. A great nation, even more than a family or a business, is more concerned with what happens over a span of years than in just one year. So, let us make a contrast between the results of the high and the low growth rate, not for the year 1964 alone, but rather in the aggregate for the seven-year period from the end of 1957 to the end of 1964.

The aggregate seven-year difference in our total national production would be about $400,000,000,000, or almost equal to our total production last year.

For the seven-year period as a whole, the low growth rate, and the consequent economic slack, would result in almost 11,-500,000 more man-years of unemployment than the high growth rate.

The high rate would enable us to serve adequately our vast and growing public needs. For, over the aggregate seven-year period, the high rate would automatically yield at least $70,000,-000,000 more Federal, state and local public revenues, even with some reduction in taxes, than the low rate would yield.

This differential in public revenues would not impose an additional strain upon our economy. It would merely reflect the $400,-000,000,000 differential in national production, from which public revenues are derived. These higher revenues could, between now and 1964, finance a vast expansion of outlays for national security and international economic cooperation, in line with expert judgment of needs. In addition, they could finance vast increases in domestic public programs.

These—coupled with the much larger private efforts which high economic growth would permit—could by 1964 build an America with the facilities and well-paid teaching staff to speed scientific progress, and to furnish an education through college to every qualified person who sought it; provide enough hospitals and medical care to improve vastly the health of all Americans; rehouse about 10,000,000 American families; double average social security benefits, and add greatly to our national resource base.

Even with these expanding public programs, the high over-all economic growth rate would provide, during the seven-year period as a whole, about $6,200 more in average private income for all American families than the low growth rate would provide.

Our whole system of private business enterprise would correspondingly benefit. Expanding public outlays also expand private markets. And when these expanding public outlays are financed out of economic growth, rather than out of higher tax rates, the net benefit to private enterprise is especially high. For the seven-year period as a whole, the $400,000,000,000 differential in total national production, resulting from the high growth rate in contrast with the low one, would involve a differential of about $75,000,000,000 in private business investment opportunity. It would mean a differential of about $62,000,000,000 in business and professional incomes.

Objections to a high rate of economic growth are, I believe, unwarranted. The first usual objection is that a 5 per cent annual growth rate is unrealistic, when contrasted with an average of only about 3 per cent during the past half century. But this half-century "average" includes periods of recession and even depression. Furthermore, this half-century "average" makes no allowance for this fact: over the decades, our productivity or output per man-hour has expanded at an *accelerating* rate. The "Rockefeller Report" on the American economy accepts the 5 per cent growth rate in future as attainable and highly desirable. And recent productivity figures are most encouraging.

The traditional argument that the 5 per cent growth rate would be inflationary is based upon a serious lag in much of our economic thinking. To be sure, the wartime growth rate of 8 to 10 per cent a year was accompanied by much inflation. That inflation, of the "classical" type, resulted because the demands of consumers, business and Government exceeded our top productive capabilities. But the new inflation has been taking place while our productive resources have been substantially idle, and while total demand has been deficient rather than excessive. In consequence, the "classical" inflationary remedies, designed to slow down our economy further and to reduce total demand, have been applied in the wrong context, with unfortunate results.

In truth, there has been nothing really "paradoxical" about rising prices in a retarded or recessionary economy. Just as an automobile consumes more gas per mile when running too slowly than when running at the most efficient speed, so an industrial plant or our total economy operates inefficiently when running too slowly. This may be reflected in rising costs per unit of production, including labor costs. Prices are then lifted.

Sharp changes in business expectancies, and prevalent uncertainties about the economic outlook, are also conducive to price fluctuations. The recession has caused very sharp cutbacks in business investment in plant and equipment. This might well cause inflationary shortages or bottlenecks when an adequate growth rate is resumed. In contrast, a high and steady rate of economic growth promotes price stability.

For example, price increases during the years of high economic growth between 1947 and 1953 averaged much less than during the year immediately preceding the most recent recession, when our economy was practically static. The recession and its aftermath have brought on an even more rapid increase of many basic prices.

Another idea is that we are already so affluent that we should primarily place stress upon redistribution of actual production, with less going into private consumption and more going into essential public services. There is much merit in the proposition that our sense of values, in using what we now produce, needs to be greatly improved. But historically, a high growth rate has facilitated improved distribution, while a low rate has usually been accompanied by regressive distribution. Similarly, improved distribution encourages a high growth rate, while faulty distribution retards the whole economy.

The sizable reduction of poverty depends far more upon private economic expansion than upon public services. And it would be impossible, both economically and politically, to attend to our huge unmet public needs through higher tax rates rather than primarily through higher tax revenues resulting from larger total production. Moreover, why should we meet our needs on one front only at the sacrifice of our needs and aspirations on others, when we clearly can achieve large gains on all basic fronts?

The unique genius of the American economy is its ability to combine economic growth with wiser utilization. This combination is not only the source of our strength at home; it is also our great non-secret weapon throughout the world. For even if we were to reach the apogee of affluence at home, what next? Should we then withdraw into an island of plenty amid oceans of deprivation? Or should we then produce still more and use it around a world still struggling with starvation?

The Russians, through dictatorial methods which we should not copy, have assigned so large a part of their total national production to the things they need most, or think they do, that they have been able to catch up with us in science, education and military strength in the form of economic assistance to others, despite a present production less than half of ours. What would happen throughout the world if their total production should come to approximate ours?

The sharpest protest against a high rate of economic growth is that the changes in policies and programs needed to attain it would impair our traditional balance between enterprise and the Government. Instead of attempting to answer this argument on ideological grounds, let us look pragmatically at what we need to do to maintain a high rate of economic growth. It will be seen that the proposed changes would further dedicate both our private and our public instruments of freedom to the ends which freedom should serve.

This is what I think needs to be done, specifically:

(1) The President, in his annual Economic Reports to the Congress, should set forth a "National Prosperity Budget," furnishing short-range and long-range over-all targets for production and employment. These should be based upon sufficient use of our manpower, skills and technology to square with an annual growth rate of about 5 per cent.

The targets would not be nearly so high nor so detailed as in wartime, but all of the programs of the Federal Government itself, impacting upon the economy, and the President's economic recommendations to the Congress, should be consistent with this "Prosperity Budget." This would merely apply to Government the coordinating methods used by large and successful private businesses. The Congress should enact legislation consistent with the "Prosperity Budget," or consistent with Congressional revision of the "Prosperity Budget." The Employment Act of 1946 envisages this procedure, but it has not been sufficiently used.

(2) The Federal Budget should be derived from the "National Prosperity Budget." In accordance with what a high-growth-rate economy can afford, and to meet the needs set forth earlier, we should gradually lift Federal spending to an annual rate of about $96,000,000,000 by 1964, contrasted with less than $74,000,-000,000 in the President's original budget for the fiscal year 1959.

This would enable us gradually to increase national security outlays by the amounts called for by qualified experts, and to expand annual per capita Federal outlays for international economic assistance to a 1964 level about two-and-a-half times the 1959 level contemplated in the original 1959 budget. Over the same period, we should gradually expand annual per capita Federal outlays for resource development, public assistance and labor and manpower more than 50 per cent, for health services about four times, for housing about five times, and for education more than ten times.

With all of these increases, the Federal budget would be about 16 per cent of a $600,000,000,000 economy by 1964, while a much lower Federal budget in recent years has averaged about 17.5 per cent of a much smaller national economy. This means that the burden of the Federal budget by 1964 would be much less than in recent years.

(3) All tax policy should be guided by the "National Prosperity Budget." "Taxation for revenue only" promotes less economic growth, and therefore yields less public revenues, than taxation geared to activating the high potentials of the whole economy. We have long needed revisions in the tax structure, to place more purchasing power in the hands of low-income families, and to encourage investment. Monetary policy also needs revision in the light of economic growth requirements.

(4) We need large social security expansion, and much-improved farm income programs, not only for reasons of equity, but also to help keep consumption in line with expanding production potentials. The specifics of these programs should be derived from the "National Prosperity Budget."

It has already been shown, in dollars and cents, how private enterprise would benefit by the high rate of economic growth which the "Prosperity Budget" would encourage. But how would private enterprise be joined in the "Prosperity Budget" process?

In contrast to wartime practice, the "National Prosperity Budget" would have no *mandatory* force upon the powerful private groups in our economy. But it would necessarily contain over-all *advisory* targets for private investment and consumption. It would also provide an evaluation of price and wage and profit trends in terms of these targets.

Recent experience has once again proved that our kind of economic system cannot solve its problems of price stability and economic growth through reliance solely or mainly upon Government fiscal and monetary policies to correct maladjustments. Private and public economic adjustments must constantly reinforce and supplement one another. This effective blend of private and public action remains an outstanding test of our system's effectiveness.

And just because the great virtue of our system is that it is based upon consents rather than fiat, the goals set for private enterprise in the "National Prosperity Budget" should not be "handed down from above" by Government. Instead, they should be developed through constant consultation with industry, labor, agriculture and other powerful forces in our economic life. Much of the fact-finding and research now being carried forward under the aegis of Government, especially in the economic field, is already based upon machinery for this kind of representative and nation-wide participation.

However, not nearly enough progress has yet been made toward building the institutional devices for the needed governmental and business cooperation, which would not only improve private economic policies by bringing them closer to a national perspective, but would also improve public economic policies by bringing them closer to the practicalities of business action. For example, the Council of Economic Advisers should resume and expand its consultation with business and other private economic groups (and with state and local public groups) on a systematic basis. Well-prepared agenda for such meetings should be circulated in advance.

Even now, when the President's Economic Reports are sent to the Congress, their evaluation by the Joint Economic Committee and by other Congressional committees benefits by the advice of private economic groups who are called upon to testify. But this comes too late in the whole process. Testimony bearing upon the crystallized program of the President cannot take the place of a genuine sense of participation in its formulation.

All this does not mean that the public interest and the private interest are the same thing, or that Government can really be a "partner" with industry or labor or share its sole responsibility for representing the public as a whole. Nonetheless, some middle way must be found between the virtual merger of public and private action which necessarily occurred during wartime, and the opposite extreme which fails sufficiently to recognize that, while there are many segments in our economic life, there is in the final analysis only one America.

While we are not at war, we are nonetheless in a struggle filled with challenge and danger. In such times, there can be no doubt that leadership within our private enterprise system would rise increasingly to the opportunities offered for participation in the development, evaluation and improvement of a "National Prosperity Budget."

Perhaps most important, the "National Prosperity Budget," commencing as a tool of leadership, would ultimately educate and inspire the citizen-at-large, the ultimate voice in a democracy.

By full use of our fantastic and ever-increasing productive power, we could do more than meet our national security needs. We could also within a decade or two achieve so much plenty at home, and add so much to plenty elsewhere, that the economic problem of shortages of important things—existing since history began—might be virtually ended here and reduced to manageable proportions overseas. Then, the higher values of peace and goodwill, cultural development and intellectual strivings could come to engage more fully the efforts of mankind. This is the true nature of the challenge to America.

Part 4

MORE THAN DOLLARS: HOUSING, HEALTH, AND JUSTICE

ALTHOUGH WE tend to define poverty by means of a dollar income cutoff, we cannot pretend that nothing but dollar income is involved—hence the selections here on housing, health, and justice. According to Charles Grutzner's article of June 1958, "A Home Is a Strain to 7 of 10 Families," a survey by the National Housing Conference revealed that this high proportion actually could not afford a three-bedroom house at minimum prices, assuming the rule-of-thumb that no more than one-fifth of a family's income should be spent on shelter. The difficulties of home purchase and ownership for low-income families are even greater, for the principle followed in the housing industry for this group is only one-seventh of family income. Of course, we know what happens in the great overemphasis on home-ownership: families with children buy older houses, often with substandard facilities, and skimp "on other things to spend a disproportionately large share of income on housing."

William Lee Miller and Thomas Appleby's 1965 article on the controversy over urban renewal and its meaning for the poor is an attempt to correct the frequent criticism about the federal bull-dozer destroying a poor but happy slum neighborhood to make way for the construction—years later—of unaesthetic office build-ings and luxury town houses for the rich. Despite such allega-tions as their being nothing but legalized (or fireproof) slums, the public housing projects begun under the New Deal, according to Miller and Appleby, provided decent shelter for "hundreds of thousands of families that simply was not available before, and which the 'free market' was simply not going to provide." But public housing and urban renewal were oversold to the general public and probably to their direct beneficiaries (victims?). When these programs turned out not to be a cure-all for our social problems, everyone began hollering. As if they had a crystal ball, Miller and Appleby wrote in their 1965 article that "one day the same thing may happen with the 'war on poverty.' "

The 1946 article on the "Battle of Hunger" by Dr. Ancel Keys was chosen for several reasons, the most obvious one being that currently the anti-poverty spotlight has turned to the problem of malnutrition among America's poor. Dr. Keys concentrates on the *effects* of various degrees of starvation, as revealed in careful experiments with volunteer conscientious objectors during World War II. In addition to expected physiological consequences (such as decline in temperature, dehydration, shrinkage of the heart, and drop in pulse rate), there are other pathologies: the individual loses his desire or will to perform physical and mental tasks, and his resistance to diseases drops. And here is the punch line that is so apropos the modern scene: *Apathy and listlessness, both mentally and physically, probably helped to prevent the outright violence that otherwise might have occurred.*

Equally relevant to today's scene is the observation by Dr. Keys that the victims of malnutrition cannot be cured overnight, or in a few months, through some miracle injection of vitamins or pro-tein concentrates. ". . . It is months, probably many months, before the full level of vigor and work capacity can be regained." It must be added that a human organism malnourished from con-ception through childhood probably can never be raised to a normal level of physical and mental activity. More recent research indicates that poor diets can irretrievably injure an infant's brain cells—and no amount of compensatory nourishment or education will raise the child's mental capacity. The ageless issue of "motivation," therefore, cannot be resolved until persons of equal *nutritional* input (as well as equal socio-economic status) are placed in similar "opportunity structures" to determine their responses to those opportunities. This is not to deny at all that there are variations in motivation, and that these variations have an impact on socio-economic mobility.

Ten years later, in 1956, Howard Rusk, in "The State of the Union's Health," was able to report a 1944–1954 decline in our illness and mortality rates as the result of better nutrition, better housing, and the general increase in personal income—"everything that has created a continuing rise in our standards of living, but particularly scientific advances in medicine and the availability of more and better medical care." This glowing account was correct because it was based on aggregate averages. Rusk's observation that "our country is currently at the greatest peak of 'health' in its history" was typical of that period in our social history in which *overall* images and *general* data obscured the "Other America" of the apparently invisible poor. Rusk himself has been acutely aware of the health problems of *specific* subcategories of America's total population—for example, the aged—but his article is an example of how the *statistical average* became a kind of hallucinatory drug to many students of the social scene, blinding them to the exceptions that did *not* prove the rule.

In 1964, Justice Arthur Goldberg ("Equal Justice for the Poor, Too") was in the vanguard of judicial and other sensitive authorities who pleaded for a legal system that would provide effective legal services for all Americans, regardless of ability to pay. It is not only that lawyers are not easily available to the poor; there are, in addition, differences in *de facto* treatment by the courts themselves and by other agencies of government which "have not brought their ingenuity sufficiently to bear on these crucial areas of equal justice."

A Home Is a Strain to 7 of 10 Families

by Charles Grutzner

SEVEN OUT OF ten American families can not afford to own the cheapest new three-bedroom house available in their communities, the National Housing Conference has reported after a nation-wide survey.

But renting a three-bedroom apartment is more expensive generally than home ownership, according to the same survey. And in most cities there are few, if any, three-bedrom apartments for rent.

The answer for many families with children has been the purchase of older houses, renting undersized or substandard accommodations, or skimping on other things to spend a disproportionately large share of income on housing.

The Housing Conference analysis used the rule of thumb that a family should not spend more than one-fifth of its income for shelter. This is considered high. Many housing and welfare experts believe low-income families should not spend more than one-seventh of income for shelter.

The lowest price reported for a new three-bedroom house was $8,990, in a Long Island development sixty miles from New York. The highest minimum price for a house of the same size was $15,000, in Rochester. The national median was $10,990, in Fall River, Mass.

From the *New York Times*, June 29, 1958, copyright © 1958 by The New York Times Company.

Data for the study were obtained from real estate and business editors of daily newspapers in twenty-nine cities. The original data, based on Jan. 1, 1958 prices, indicated Phoenix, Ariz., as the place where a new home could be bought most cheaply—for $8,295. But a recheck in April showed that the builder was no longer constructing that model, described as "a small, stripped-down home," because it was unpopular. The minimum price for its successor was $9,950.

The Housing Conference estimates that a family requires an annual income of at least $6,409 to be able to carry the $10,990 home that was the national median. It estimates that 28.5 per cent of American families had that much income.

It was estimated that a New York family should have income of at least $6,350 to afford the cheapest new home in a distant suburb. An income of $4,864 could carry the $8,990 home in Norfolk, but a family in Erie, Pa., should have a $9,564 income to justify purchase of the cheapest new house, priced at $14,500. But in Rochester an income of $9,215 would justify purchase of the minimum new house at $15,000.

Varying taxes and utility costs were said to be responsible for the non-parallel relationship of required income to home prices. For instance, it was estimated that purchase of a $12,500 home in Long Beach, Calif., would require an annual family income of $8,561, while a Kansas City family could buy a home at the same price on an income of only $7,058.

The survey findings are detailed, along with rental costs in the same cities, in the 1958 Housing Yearbook. The volume was published last week by the National Housing Conference, a non-profit organization of individuals and public-interest groups concerned with better housing. It provided a forum last week, at its thirty-seventh annual meeting in Washington, for the widest public discussion held so far among Congressmen, Federal housing and redevelopment officials, and housing experts on the 1958 housing measure that is nearing debate on the Senate floor.

The conventional resolutions, adopted by 400 delegates, gave strong endorsement to the major features of the housing bill sponsored by Senator John Sparkman, Alabama Democrat, and went even further in a few instances in proposals for more public housing and urban renewal.

The yearbook is available at the conference's permanent head-quarters, 1025 Connecticut Avenue N. W., Washington. It contains a review of housing since passage of the first United States Housing Act in 1937 and a "prescription for achieving a well-housed America." The formula was prepared by Lee F. Johnson, executive vice president for the last fourteen years, who is leaving that post to become executive director of the Denver Housing Authority on Tuesday.

Other features of the yearbook include an account of how the Newark Housing Authority pioneered in facing the problem of troublesome and socially troubled families, which is now a major unsolved difficulty in New York and some other cities. Louis Danzig, executive director in Newark, describes why and how that agency set up in 1953 a tenant relations division. The Public Housing Administration first looked askance at it, but now fully approves it as part of the management function.

Mr. Danzig's report tells how the authority changed some policies, devised new techniques for dealing with problem families and halted the flight of desirable families.

A nation-wide survey of the slum-clearance and urban-renewal program reports that the number of cities with authorized projects increased in the last two years from seventy-three to 128 and the total number of projects from 110 to 193. The report concludes that "urban renewal has quit creeping and taken a few strides toward the ultimate goal of sound cities from coast to coast."

The prices quoted by the National Housing Conference run about $3,000 less than those bought across the nation with mortgages guaranteed by the Veterans Administration.

A recent report by the Veterans Administration said the average new home bought last year with V. A.-guaranteed financing was priced at $14,335. The average price for used homes bought with V. A. guarantee was $12,100.

"You Shove Out the Poor to Make Houses for the Rich"

by William Lee Miller
and L. Thomas Appleby

A FACULTY member of Amherst, visiting Yale recently, looked around at the very impressive rebuilding of the center of New Haven and, after the manner of professors, was not impressed.

"Where are the Negroes who used to live here?" he asked. "They push the poor people out and put up these luxury apartments and fancy stores and office buildings. Urban renewal means Negro removal."

This is one of the more pungent criticisms of urban renewal expressed nowadays by liberals, reflecting their disenchantment with a tool for social reform which they themselves sponsored. It is criticism that hurts, because the welfare of hundreds of thousands of slum-dwellers—not to mention the future of our cities—depends on continued public support for the renewal program. These allegations must, therefore, be refuted as they arise, and fortunately the city of New Haven, Conn., can supply most of the evidence to do so. (There are also criticisms from the right,

From the *New York Times Magazine*, April 11, 1965, copyright © 1965 by The New York Times Company.

of course, about government interference with "freedom" and subsidies for "uneconomic" uses of land; but civic-minded people have long ago agreed that a great many human needs are not going to be served at all by a free market left entirely to itself.)

The urban renewal program came into being as Title I of the Housing Act of 1949. The idea was that the Federal Government would pay two-thirds of the cost (prohibitive for any private agency or for government at a lower level) of buying, clearing and reselling slum land.

This meant a greater use by local governments of "eminent domain." Whereas before they had taken private properties for public *use* (a highway or a school), now they could take private properties for a public *purpose*—to eliminate slums and urban blight. The Federal Government made it possible to tear down one set of private properties (tenements, flop houses, run-down businesses), to compensate the owners and to resell the land to another set of private developers and owners for office buildings, housing projects, hotels and business "plazas."

The program has since spread, prospered and been improved by further legislation—especially by the 1954 Housing Act, which provided for commercial redevelopment, rehabilitation of existing buildings and comprehensive urban planning. To date, $4.7 billion has been provided for renewal projects which are dramatically visible in the center of many cities from Boston, Hartford and Pittsburgh to San Francisco. The Federal Government is now spending at the rate of $700 million a year on the program and the President's housing message proposes that this be raised to $750 million—which is still not nearly enough, according to most people in the field.

New York City has spent the largest amount, but its program in the past has emphasized clearance almost to the exclusion of rehabilitation, and is still far too small for the staggering and unique problems of the great metropolis. The top four cities in total urban-renewal spending are New York (population 7.7 million), Chicago (3.5 million), Philadelphia (2 million), and New Haven, Conn. (152,000). New York has spent $109 million. If it had had a program of New Haven's scope, it would have spent more than $1.5 billion.

But even in New Haven some liberals, like that Amherst professor, are uneasy about urban renewal. They charge that tax-payers in effect subsidize the erection of fancy apartment build-ings like University Towers (which has a swimming pool and rents to match), Madison Towers and the soon-to-be constructed Crown Towers. The answer, of course, is that there is no subsidy, because the cleared land is sold at market value, and also that those are valuable properties which help to make a beautiful city and markedly increase its tax base. Rebuilding New Haven's center has already added over $9 million to the tax list of this medium-sized city—$2.9 million last year alone. Furthermore, we want the people who live in those apartments to stay in the city. We need them and the money they spend.

The liberal critic, however, may say that this answer only confirms his worst fears. "You have shoved out the poor to make homes for the rich," he claims. "You may help the city's finances, but what has happened to the people who used to live on Oak Street?" (Oak Street, once New Haven's most notorious slum, has been wiped away by urban renewal and replaced by those Towers and by a highway connector, among other things.)

There are two answers to this. One is defensive—that those displaced are better housed today than they ever were. The second is more positive—that without urban renewal the problems of the destitute who once lived on Oak Street would not have become the visible responsibility of the community that they are now. Urban renewal is a weapon the community needs to meet that responsibility.

The defensive argument is based on statistics showing that the overwhelming majority of people displaced by urban renewal—the removed Negroes—have moved into better housing; that a lot less slum now exists. Today there simply isn't as much "sub-standard" housing in New Haven as there was when Oak Street existed.

But are the people who lived on Oak Street and in other re-newal areas now paying a higher rent than before? This is another sore point with liberals. The answer is yes—they are, on the average, paying higher rents, but only slightly higher, and for better housing.

Many relocated families—151 of the 886 from Oak Street—have moved into low-income public housing, where they have priority, and where rents are pegged at 21.8 per cent of the family's gross income—usually less than they were paying before. Moreover, many relocated families are on welfare, so that the change, one way or another, in rent has not affected their budget, since the rent is part of their grants.

What about the others? A study just completed of the 100 families most recently relocated into private housing in New Haven shows that they paid an average of 16.8 per cent of their income for rent before relocation and 20.3 per cent afterward. Thus their rents did go up, on the average, but they are still below the 21.8 per cent the public-housing laws regard as standard.

That is the general picture. What about individual cases? Having looked over the case-by-case summary of the 100 families, we found that the extremes have become less extreme. The "worst" case before relocation—in terms of percentage of income paid for rent—was that of a woman with a large family who made $365 a month and paid out $151 a month for rent—40.3 per cent of her income. After being relocated, she is now paying $120 a month—32.9 per cent of her income—and is still the "worst" case.

Most of the increased rent is being paid by those who were paying quite low rents before relocation. The percentages come down from 40 per cent but up from 15 per cent, and more of them now cluster around 20 per cent. These figures do not, of course, tell the whole story about the misery of slum-dwellers, but they do indicate that, on balance, urban renewal has not added to the misery.

Is there a long wait and much scrambling around before these families find new homes? Not if the relocation agency can help it. The New Haven agency's 14 workers go to great lengths to help them find the places they want—even if the family, as has happened, turns down the first five offers, and even to the point of playing Cupid in one celebrated instance so that a couple could meet public-housing standards.

Very well, say some critics, but do the families just move to another slum or Negro ghetto? The answer to this is no. The New Haven family-relocation office has a wall chart showing where all the relocated families have gone from each project.

Negroes cluster only in the public-housing projects. Elsewhere, racial distribution is very mixed throughout the city.

It is clearly apparent that urban renewal does not make *worse* housing for the poor in New Haven, and that holds—despite particular exceptions and soft spots—for the nation as a whole. Nearly 30 per cent of the housing units in New Haven were substandard in the early fifties before the city's urban renewal programs began; today less than 15 per cent are, and by 1970 New Haven may be—in this sense at least—the nation's first slumless city.

The overwhelming majority of the 5,000 families relocated from New Haven's projects—95 per cent from the early Oak Street, Church Street and Wooster Square projects and 99 per cent from the more recent Dixwell and Hill High—have been placed in standard, not slum, housing. In the nation as a whole it is clear from Federal statistics that nine out of 10 families relocated from renewal areas have moved up to standard housing.

All this, however, is part of the defensive answer to the critics of urban renewal. The more positive reply is that it has brought the urban poor to the community's attention and, at its best, provided not only new houses but new neighborhoods and new sets of possibilities.

It is greatly to the credit of recent antipoverty tracts like Michael Harrington's "The Other America," as well as of President Johnson's program and, on a smaller scale, Mayor Richard C. Lee's efforts in New Haven, that the American public has been forced to pay attention to the poor, but urban renewal has been doing the same thing for years. Many liberals uneasy about urban renewal but enthusiastic about the "war on poverty" should remember that experience with family relocation was one of the principal well-springs of the national antipoverty program, uncovering problems of the urban poor that had been kept out of sight for decades and making them a public responsibility.

Urban renewal has a greater potential for eliminating ghettoes and segregated living than any other program yet devised—if a city uses it in the right way. It may be possible, with strong fair-housing efforts, to move a small and select number of Negro families, mostly middle class, out into the lily-white suburbs— but the great mass of Negroes will stay right where they are now, in the center of the cities. (Having middle-class Negroes move out, incidentally, is rather a mixed blessing: these are precisely the leaders who are needed in the center of the city, where problems are concentrated.)

Civil-rights laws alone, therefore, are not going to alter racial patterns in the Harlems of the land. The only way to achieve integrated living in the blighted centers of our great cities is by clearance—by knocking down the worst slums and starting over.

Then comes the question of what is to be built on the cleared land to achieve a balanced mixture of industrial, commercial and residential elements in a city's over-all plan. It has to be said that cities vary widely in their answers to this question, but the Amherst professor and other liberals like him should not condemn *all* urban renewal on the strength of a few failures.

In New Haven, for instance, redevelopment has spread over 1,000 acres, and while it is true that luxury apartments, a telephone building and the Oak Street connector have replaced the old Oak Street fire traps, in other renewal areas throughout the city new low-rent housing projects are a major feature—housing for the elderly in Wooster Square, Newhallville, Dwight and Dixwell, co-op housing in the same neighborhoods. This is new housing, added to New Haven's stock of public housing from the thirties and forties.

One of the cooperative housing ventures now being shown to prospects is directly in the middle of the Dixwell area, New Haven's small version of Harlem. Like all these projects, it will, of course, be integrated. To buy a unit a family has to have $325 to put down, and must be able to pay from $91 to $129 a month, depending on the number of rooms. This does, it is true, put these units out of reach of the very poor, but those who can pay it are not only covering their rent, utilities and property taxes but are building up equity. The other day a young former resident of Dixwell walked wide-eyed and marveling around Florence Virtue Homes and remarked, "I never thought I'd see anything like this built *here*."

Too many people, in New Haven and the nation, equate urban renewal with new business buildings downtown. Important as a healthy downtown is, there is, or can be, much more to it than that. It means the planned rebuilding of the housing and community facilities of deteriorating neighborhoods. Suppose 60 years ago, when Jacob Riis walked Theodore Roosevelt night after night, despairing and angry, through the miserable conditions of Five Points and the Bends, they had had a public agency that could go in, plan, level and rebuild—what could they not have achieved?

Yet there are still people who say: "New Haven's urban renewal is one of the worst in the country. Too few people are involved in the decisions—the inhabitants of the areas to be renewed must be consulted." And then there are those whom Mitchell Sviridoff, director of New Haven's anti-poverty program, calls "slum romantics," represented by a New Haven literary man: "I used to be in favor of urban renewal. But then I talked to artist friends of mine who couldn't any longer find top-floor studios and cheap cold-water flats . . ."

Put these criticisms together and we have a poignant picture of happy slum-dwellers enjoying a varied and interesting life in their cold-water flats until shoved out of their congenial neighborhoods by a few powerful bureaucrats. Their homes are then destroyed and, after a long, messy delay, replaced by badly designed office buildings and luxury apartment. It is a powerful indictment, but it is false.

Although there have been occasions when developers were too quick with the bulldozer, destroying esthetically or historically valuable buildings and viable lower-income communities, since 1954 there has been a growing emphasis on neighborhood conservation and on the rehabilitation of existing structures.

And in the late fifties "planning with the people" became a major theme in urban renewal. In New Haven the Wooster Square project was developed in more than 100 meetings with residents of the area, and the same thing is now going on in Dixwell, Newhallville and the section called "The Hill."

But there are limits. "Planning with the people" cannot always be as dandy and democratic as it sounds. What happens when a neighborhood says it wants no Negroes, no low-income public housing, no site for a public high school? Sometimes that's exactly "what the people in the area themselves want," but it is a little hard to work with on a community-wide basis.

There has been a progression in American efforts to grapple

with the problems of cities and slums. Public housing was the great thing in the late thirties, urban renewal the featured program of the fifties, antipoverty is the rage now. In the beginning the first two were oversold, which led to negative reactions as soon as it was found that neither was a cure-all, and one day the same thing may happen with the "war on poverty." It is important not to look on these programs as panaceas, in the first place, and then not to overdo the criticisms, in the second.

The low-income public-housing projects built in the late thirties and the forties with such hope and promise now are said to have become "legalized slums" or "fireproof slums." At the very least, it is desirable for slums to be fireproof, but in fact far more was accomplished than that. Decent housing was provided for hundreds of thousands of families that simply was not available before and which the "free market" was simply not going to provide.

It is true that public housing did not eliminate slum life and slum behavior, but that merely proved that "decent, safe and sanitary" housing under public control is not, in itself, enough to win the battle against the slum.

Similarly, urban renewal, which grew in part out of the background of public housing, has now reached a stage where it inspires disillusionment among its onetime liberal supporters. But again they should remember that while there have been many failures and deficiencies, it is a complicated program involving a long and difficult journey between cup and lip.

It still represents the expanded role for public planning for public purposes that liberals long have advocated. That conservatives should attack it is understandable. Liberals, however, would surely be better advised to look behind the standard criticisms of urban renewal and work to make it a more effective tool for the social purposes in which they believe.

Battle of Hunger

by Dr. Ancel Keys

WHEN A MAN loses the fight against hunger it is called starvation. There is nothing heroic or romantic about this, one of man's oldest battles, and comparatively little is known about it.

What does starvation do to people? In starving, a person literally begins feeding off his own body, the fat tissues first. His body processes slow down and his body temperature decreases. His heart shrinks and his pulse slows. Progressively he loses much of his strength, most of his endurance and almost all of his will to do physical or mental work. Even in the heat of summer he feels cold. He loses his resistance to disease. His tissues, perhaps a third, waste away and are partly replaced by water (edema). Then, without adequate food, he dehydrates and the battle is lost.

With the help of conscientious objectors and such organizations as the National Dairy Council, the Markle Foundation and the Sugar Research Foundation, the University of Minnesota has found what may be a partial answer to these critical world questions: What is starvation and what is the most effective kind of relief?

The experiment began in 1944. It was an attempt by the Laboratory of Physiological Hygiene to reproduce, under controlled conditions, the starvation which was beginning in Europe at that time; to measure exactly what happens and follow the details of recovery. This could hardly have been done at the scene of dis-

From the *New York Times Magazine,* June 23, 1946, copyright © 1946 by The New York Times Company.

tress, where no relief diets were available and the data would have been confused by the general breakdown of sanitation and medical services.

The "principals" of this reenactment were thirty-six civilian service volunteers. First they were "standardized" by a uniform diet for three months and individual characteristics were analyzed. Then the test began. The "conchies," who later became known to us as "the boys," were housed and fed in a laboratory and subjected to a program of tests, activity, work and study—a regime which normally would require 3,150 calories daily. Instead, during the six months' test, they suffered the stock European famine diet: coarse cereals (mainly wheat), potatoes, cabbage, turnips and minute amounts of meats, fats and dairy products (qualitatively, not a bad diet).

In twelve weeks the average weight of the men fell from 154.5 pounds to 125.5 pounds. At the end of twenty-four weeks it was down to 117 pounds, a gross average loss of 37.5 pounds. During the same period the water content of the body, even in those who did not have puffed faces and swollen ankles, increased about 14 pounds. So the true loss of tissues averaged about 50 pounds, or about one-third of the original living tissues. Of this loss, only about 15 pounds was fat. The rest of the weight loss occurred in the muscles, skin and other tissues.

As the arm and leg muscles atrophied the men became correspondingly weaker. Starvation produced a loss of 25 to 30 per cent in the maximal strength which could be exerted in a single contraction. In endurance tests, where strength had to be used over a period of several minutes, the decline was about 80 per cent.

Edema appeared in some men as early as the end of two months of semi-starvation. All the men suffered from anemia by the end of three months, although it was only slight at that time.

Toward the end of the experiment many men could not even walk up an ordinary flight of stairs without stopping to rest. As their basal metabolism slowed down and bodies began to operate at lower speed, they developed subnormal temperatures. The size of the heart shrank and the heart failed to respond to exercise. In all of the men the pulse rate fell to forty at the highest and in most of them even down to thirty beats per minute.

This deceleration of life processes produced in them the disconcerting sensation of growing old quickly, as indeed, in effect, they were. The body adapts itself to a lack of fuel as an intelligent driver will slow down when his fuel supply is precariously low. The men soon began to complain of feeling cold. In the warm spring air, even in the heat of summer, they could not keep warm. And they became increasingly irritable.

A program of tests was used to measure the loss of mental capacity. Surprisingly, it seemed little affected, although the will to use intellectual power almost entirely disappeared. While the capacity was there, seemingly unimpaired, tests or other special stimuli were required to provoke mental effort. Apathy and list-lessness, both mentally and physically, probably helped to prevent the outright violence that otherwise might have occurred.

It was at this point, six months after the starvation diet began, that they were put on relief diets. They were divided into four matched groups which were fed on varying caloric levels—2,000, 2,400, 2,800 and 3,200 calories daily. The basic diet was the same famine rations, with the addition of soup, more bread and more potatoes. Here again was an attempt to duplicate conditions as they had existed in hunger-stricken areas. In six weeks the men in the lower caloric groups made little, if any, recovery. All diets were then increased by 830 calories daily and later by an additional 200, the caloric differences in the various groups being kept the same. On this diet the men in the lowest caloric group regained only 21 per cent of their lost weight in twelve weeks; the highest caloric group regained 57 per cent. In endurance ("fitness") the lowest calorie volunteers made an 18 per cent recovery, while the men who received more calories recovered 57 per cent.

Special experiments were also conducted to measure the effects of specific dietary deficiencies. Multi-vitamin pills and bread of different protein content were added to the diets of some of the matched groups. The sixteen men receiving extra proteins regained their lost weight slightly faster than other groups. But the provision of extra vitamins slightly retarded the recovery of lost weight.

Recovery from starvation is not as simple as it might seem. Most of the volunteers responded to refeeding by losing the bloat of excess water. Others, who never had it, exhibited edema for the first time. Still others soon lost their edema only to have it recur later in the refeeding.

For some months after the relief diets began, most of the tissues regained were simply fat. Round faces and obvious accumulations of subcutaneous fat gave the men a greatly changed appearance. Clearly, the restitution of muscles which have wasted away in starvation is a slow process.

Although the analyses are still incomplete, a few other important conclusions may be drawn. Starved people cannot be rehabilitated in a few weeks on small hand-outs of vitamin pills and protein concentrates or by a bare subsistence diet. It takes calories —plain cereals in great quantities and all the dried and condensed milk, dried eggs, cheese and meats that we can spare.

No matter what diet is available after starvation, it is months, probably many months, before the full level of vigor and work capacity can be regained. This means long-range planning to help the peoples of Europe and Asia build up their own agricultural production.

The State of the Union's Health

by Howard A. Rusk

AT NO TIME in our history have the American people been so concerned about health. There is evidence of this concern in President Eisenhower's recent move to set up a Council on Youth Fitness, composed of members of the Cabinet, and a Citizens Advisory Committee "to alert America on what can and should be done to reach the much-desired goal of a happier, healthier and more totally fit youth in America."

It is known, too, that the Administration has in the past expressed anxiety over "the increasing number of young men rejected for military service." And there are startling statistics, cited by voluntary organizations and Government agencies in their appeals for private and tax funds, on the extent of heart disease, cancer, mental illness and a host of other conditions. All these circumstances prompt us to ask just what is the physical state—the health—of the union.

In order to consider the question logically, it might be well first to define health. There would seem to be almost as many definitions as there are bacteria. Webster says health is the "state of being sound in body, mind or soul; esp., freedom from physical disease or pain." The definition in a medical dictionary is "a normal condition of the body and mind, i.e., with all the parts functioning normally."

The World Health Organization goes beyond these. It defines health as "a state of complete physical, mental and social well-being and not merely the absence of disease."

But each of these definitions contains words—"sound," "normal," "well-being"—that mean little except within a specific frame of reference. A man who may be judged "sound" and "normal" enough to play ball for the New York Yankees—Mickey Mantle —may still be rejected by the Army. Thus, we cannot ask if we or the next fellow or the nation are "healthy" without asking "healthy for what"?

Physical criteria for evaluating health were drawn up in the first and second decades of this century under the then prevailing "anatomical concept" of medicine. Competency and fitness were measured in terms of anatomical perfection. A man was either fit or unfit depending upon whether or not he was anatomically whole.

But times have changed. We now know physiologically that man can live with one-half of one lung, one-third of a kidney, one-sixty-fourth of a liver, one-half of the normal volume of blood, and without a stomach. Thus, under the current physiological or functional concept of medicine, fitness and health can be determined only in relation to a given task.

To the armed services, being "healthy" means being able to pass their induction tests. There might seem to be cause for alarm in the fact that last November the general rejection rate of potential inductees was approximately 40 per cent and was on an upward trend. This seemed to compare unfavorably with an over-all rejection rate for both enlistees and inductees of approximately 33 per cent for the period from 1940 to 1947. It further seemed to suggest a decline in the health of the nation in general.

But actually these statistics are misleading if they are regarded as an index of the health of the American people. First, these figures include rejections based on mental ability and educational achievement as well as health. Second, standards for draft acceptance are susceptible to broad or tight interpretation depending on the need of the armed forces for manpower.

In 1940-41, before Pearl Harbor, since only a limited number of men were being called up, standards for acceptance could be high and could be rigidly applied. At that time 52.8 per cent of all draftees were rejected. With the national crisis after Pearl Harbor, standards were lowered and the rejection rate dropped to 30 per cent. Today, with the size of our armed forces reduced and the number of volunteers up, standards for induction can again be higher and again rigidly applied.

There are other statistics and criteria one may look into in quest of the state of health of the nation. What of death rates? In 1954, 1,481,000 American men, women and children died; 662,130 or 45 per cent of them were under 65 years. These deaths represent an impressive 19 per cent decline in our mortality rate from 1937 to 1954.

In the ten years between 1944 and 1954 death rates from influenza dropped 91 per cent; from appendicitis, 76 per cent; from acute rheumatic fever and tuberculosis, 73 per cent; from syphilis, 63 per cent; from acute nephritis and other kidney diseases, 60 per cent, and from pneumonia, 43 per cent. Even high blood pressure has begun to decline in the last two years as a cause of death.

Had the same mortality rates prevailed in 1954 as in 1944, there would be 1,244,897 fewer Americans alive today. This is more than the combined population of Maine and Delaware or Rhode Island and Vermont, and almost as many as the total population of North and South Dakota, or of Arizona and New Mexico.

What caused this dramatic drop in our death rate? Better nutrition, better housing, increased personal income and everything that has created a continuing rise in our standards of living, but particularly scientific advances in medicine and the availability of more and better medical care. During the decade 1945-55, domestic consumption of penicillin was nearly 3,000 tons or 3,000 trillion units.

Our national supply of hospital beds has increased from 1,226,245 in 1940 to 1,577,961 in 1954 and the number of hospital admissions has risen by over 50 per cent. Hospital insurance coverage has increased by eight times since 1941 and today more than 100,000,000 Americans have some type of health insurance protection through Blue Cross, Blue Shield, insurance companies and allied efforts.

Thus, our life span is being dramatically extended. However, this seemingly happy fact has an ironic aspect—the greater life expectancy which we all cherish confronts us with new problems of ill health in the late years of life. As the life span is lengthened, our numbers of chronically disabled persons will continue to rise.

But we should not necessarily think of chronically ill persons as sick. It is true that some of them need the same sort of therapeutic services that are required by acutely ill patients. However, most of them require medical services only on occasion, as all of us do. Their problems can be dealt with. And we must recognize their fitness—their "healthiness"—for a great variety of jobs.

What of mental illness? It is recognized as one of the most challenging factors in American life today. Slightly more than half of the hospital beds in our nation are occupied by mental patients; one out of every twelve persons will spend some part of his life in a mental hospital. Yet the current great concern over mental illness indicates a recognition of a problem that has always existed —but was not always treated. Today we can at least speak of encouraging developments in the field.

With modern treatment methods, from 40 to 60 per cent of schizophrenic patients can be helped. As a result of the widespread use of penicillin in the treatment of syphilis, first admission of patients with general paresis to New York State mental hospitals has dropped 50 per cent in five years. With maximum intensive therapy, the Topeka State Hospital in Kansas has been able to discharge 80 per cent of its patients as improved or recovered within the first year.

As a result of new drugs, such as reserpine and thorazine, New York State reports a 19 per cent increase in discharges from its state mental hospitals and expects a net drop in admissions. For the first time since World War II there was a decrease in the number of mental hospital patients in New York State.

Last year, increases in state appropriations for operational budgets of mental hospitals averaged around 10 per cent and ranged up to 45 per cent. Indiana, for example, increased appropriations for its state mental hospitals and schools for the mentally deficient by 40 per cent, and upped its allocation for salaries by 43.9 per cent.

On the whole, the medical prognosis for the nation shows some defects, but by and large we should feel encouraged. Our country is currently at the greatest peak of "health" in its history.

Equal Justice for
the Poor, Too

by Arthur J. Goldberg

IN THEORY, all Americans charged with a crime are, so far as the law is concerned, equal before the bar of justice in every American court. This is guaranteed by the "due process" and the "equal protection" clauses to the Constitution, and the inspiration comes from the Bible: "You shall do no injustice in judgment; you shall not be partial to the poor or defer to the great, but in righteousness shall you judge your neighbor." Justices of the Supreme Court and of many state courts take oaths to "do equal justice to the poor and to the rich."

Unfortunately, despite all these guarantees and safeguards, the poor often meet with less than the same justice as the rich (or reasonably well off) in our courts. As Justice Black has stated, "There can be no equal justice where the kind of trial a man gets depends on the amount of money he has."

It should not be forgotten that problems of equal criminal justice extend to the near-poor and the average wage-earner as well as the indigent, and that such problems begin well before trial and continue after the appeal.

When the police conduct a roundup of "suspects," they generally do so in poor neighborhoods, rarely in middle-class communities. As a result, more poor than rich are arrested for crimes they did not commit. We do not know how many of these people lose or fail to obtain jobs because of an "arrest record" resulting from guiltless involvement in such episodes. Nor do we know how many poor people are even aware of their rights in such situations: for example, their right to consult an attorney, to sue for false arrest, or to have their arrest records expunged (in jurisdictions which have procedures permitting this). Moreover, psychologists and sociologists tell us that young people who are close to choosing criminal identities may have this choice confirmed by their repeated treatment as criminal types.

After arrest, the accused who is poor must often await the disposition of his case in jail because of his inability to raise bail, while the accused who can afford bail is free to return to his family and his job. Equally important, he is free during the critical period between arrest and trial to help his attorney with the investigation and preparation of his defense. In a recent case a defendant was imprisoned well over two years between the time he was arrested and the time he was ultimately acquitted on appeal, solely because he could not raise the small amount of money necessary for bail. This is an example of justice denied, of a man imprisoned for no reason other than his poverty.

In preparing for trial the lawyer appointed to represent an accused who is without funds generally has few, if any, of the investigatory resources available to the prosecution or to an accused with means. He may also be limited in his ability to subpoena necessary witnesses to appear at trial. Under the present Federal rule, for example, a defendant with means may automatically obtain all necessary subpoenas by simply paying a fee and designating the desired witness. A defendant who cannot afford to pay the fee, however, must submit a detailed affidavit stating why he needs the witness and indicating the substance of the expected testimony.

Thus, as a price for obtaining the testimony of a witness, the accused without means must do something not required either of the government or of an accused with means: he must disclose his case in advance. This result might indeed be desirable if disclosure were required of all parties to a criminal case. But fundamental fairness and equality would seem to dictate that this should not be exacted alone from an indigent as the price of exercising his Sixth Amendment right to obtain the testimony of necessary witnesses.

After conviction, the defendant's financial condition may have a significant effect on whether he is placed on probation or sent to the penitentiary, on whether and when he is paroled from the penitentiary and on whether he continues to remain at liberty. Probation and parole frequently depend upon the availability of a job and/or of psychiatric treatment. These conditions can, of course, be met and maintained more easily by one who has means than by one who does not.

The alternative fine/imprisonment penalty still frequently imposed for petty offenses may also be unfair to the defendant without means. The "choice" of paying $100 fine or spending 30 days in jail is really no choice at all to the person who cannot raise $100. The resulting imprisonment is no more or no less than imprisonment for being poor, a doctrine which I trust this nation has long since outgrown. Concern has even been expressed that the most serious penalty of all—death—is imposed with disproportionate frequency on the poor. Warden Lawes, who witnessed the execution of many Sing Sing inmates, remarked:

"If a wealthy man, or the son of a wealthy man kills, he is insane or deranged and usually either goes scot free or to an insane asylum. If a poor and friendless man kills, he is a sane man who committed willful murder for which he must die."

Regrettably, there are still on our statute books some substantive laws which in practice tend to operate unequally against the poor. The vagrancy laws are an example in point. Anatole France would surely have said: "The law in its majestic equality forbids the rich as well as the poor" from being able-bodied persons without visible means of support who do not seek employment and who are unable to account for their lawful presence. These laws, as Justice Douglas has observed, make it a crime to be poor, downtrodden and unemployed. This is reminiscent of Butler's "Erewhon," where it was a felony to be afflicted with pulmonary consumption.

Without intimating any view on whether the "equal protection" clause of the Constitution has any voice on these and similar problems, I will say that the courts and other organs of government, both state and Federal, have not brought their ingenuity sufficiently to bear on these crucial areas of equal justice. In some states, as in the Federal Government, the high courts have power to supervise the administration of criminal justice. This is a source of power from which much good can flow, as demonstrated by some recent decisions of our Court, the Federal Courts of Appeals, and some state courts in the area of equal criminal justice. Certainly the legislative and executive branches have ample powers to remedy these injustices.

In some parts of the world—indeed, in many parts of this country when men of means are involved—arrests are made whenever possible in a dignified manner. The accused is notified that he is being investigated, and he is called to police head-quarters by a summons rather than bodily arrest. I am not sug-gesting that this can be done in every case, but it certainly can and should be done in many.

Recent studies in the area of bail have indicated that if care-fully screened defendants are released pending trial on their own recognizance and treated with dignity, they will appear at trial. Think of the needless waste—to the individual, the family and the community—every time a responsible person presumed by law to be innocent is kept in jail awaiting trial solely because he is unable to raise bail money.

Careful screening and release without bail should be made the rule rather than the exception throughout the country. Again, I am not suggesting that release without bail should be allowed in every case but it should be permitted whenever feasible.

The right to counsel at trial and on appeal may prove hollow if appointed counsel is not armed with the tools of advocacy—investigatory resources, expert witnesses, subpoena, trial tran-script. If the right to counsel is to be given meaningful content, and if our adversary process is to retain its vitality, the appointed attorney, like the retained attorney, must be permitted to perform as an advocate. Courts are not without sources to achieve this end.

In a recent California case, for example, the state supreme court held that if "the attorney is not given a reasonable oppor-tunity to ascertain facts surrounding the charged crime so he can prepare a proper defense, the accused's basic right to effective representation would be denied." Some courts have held that the right to effective representation includes interpreters, accountants and other needed medical and scientific aids. If representation is to be as effective for poor as for rich, it follows that services necessary to make this right effective must be supplied at government expense to those unable to afford them.

The government should also assume a certain degree of responsibility for assuring the poor equal access to probation and parole. It could, for example, provide facilities which would enable the parolee without means to obtain outpatient psychiatric treatment without being institutionalized and losing his job—a privilege heretofore reserved exclusively for the wealthy.

It could also experiment with the idea of the half-way house, a system under which convicted criminals might be released from prison and still remain under the care and responsibility of the government until they have re-established their roots in the community and have found decent jobs.

Our concern, moreover, should not be limited to the very poor alone. The Council of Economic Advisers in its recent report to the President designated the $3,000 annual family income mark as the boundary of poverty. A family of four earning this amount, if it spent a mere $5 per person a week for food and $800 a year for shelter for the family, would have less than $25 a week for clothing, transportation, school supplies, home furnishings, medical care, insurance and everything else. It is clear that if any member of the almost 10,000,000 American families which fit into this category were accused of a serious crime he could not begin to raise the funds necessary for an adequate defense.

But, what about the family earning $4,000 or even $5,000? I would doubt whether half of the families in this affluent country could today afford an adequate defense if one of their members were accused of a serious crime. Perhaps they could raise sufficient money for bail or even for a trial lawyer, but what about an investigator, a psychiatrist or an expert in ballistics or handwriting; and what about a complete transcript to prepare an appeal and the prosecution of the appeal itself?

This is a situation that actually does confront many, many of our families each year. It was recently estimated that "annually more than a million persons stand before our judges for sentencing after conviction." Few of these people fit the misleading stereotype of the wealthy law-breaker well equipped to confront the legal process.

Here, we can learn much from the Scandinavian countries. The services provided there are made available to all accused persons. No test of financial capacity is applied as a condition of receiving them. Far more than the provision of counsel is encompassed within these systems. For example, in preparing the defense, the appointed lawyer may make use of government laboratories and consult with its experts. If the accused is acquitted no effort is made to collect the cost of defense regardless of the defendant's means. If he is convicted some of the countries inquire into his means and if found financially able he is charged with some or all of the costs of his defense. In at least one country no effort is made to establish the means of the defendant or to charge him with costs even if he is convicted.

Even if we choose not to go as far as the Scandinavian countries, we should certainly consider adopting procedures whereby persons erroneously charged with crime could be reimbursed for their expenditures in defending against the charge. Without such procedures, acquittal may often be almost as ruinous to the defendant and his family as conviction.

At the very least, we should extend our provision of free legal services in criminal cases to include many hard-working people who, although not indigent, cannot, without extraordinary sacrifice, raise sufficient funds to defend themselves or members of their families against a criminal charge.

Whenever the government considers extending a needed service to those accused of crime, the question arises: But what about the victim? We should confront the problem of the victim directly; his burden is not alleviated by denying necessary services to the accused. Many countries throughout the world, recognizing that crime is a community problem, have designed systems for government compensation of victims of crime. Serious consideration of this approach is long overdue here. The victim of a robbery or an assault has been denied the "protection" of the laws in a very real sense, and society should assume some responsibility for making him whole.

These are but a few—indeed a very few—of the areas in which

equal justice is lacking. There are many others. It is said that the government cannot be expected to equalize all economic disparities. Of course it cannot, but this does not mean that it should not try to eliminate disparities in certain critical areas like criminal justice. The real question, as put by the Attorney General's Committee on Poverty and the Administration of Federal Criminal Justice, is: "Has government done all that can be reasonably required of it . . . to render the poverty of the litigant an irrelevancy."

In all candor, we must confess that government in this country —both state and Federal—has not done all that can reasonably be required. Equal criminal justice for rich and poor alike is one of the few areas where our country follows rather than leads. If it is true that "the quality of a nation's civilization can be largely measured by the methods it uses in the enforcement of its criminal law," then this situation cannot long be tolerated. We must lead in equality if we are to continue to lead in liberty. But, while we are making efforts to equalize the treatment of rich and poor in the criminal process, we must remember that the criminal process is but one tree in a forest of poverty.

Every criminologist will acknowledge the truth of this linkage between poverty and crime. The great bulk of our prison population comes from the ranks of the economically underprivileged. A root cause of crime is economic distress and its by-products— illiteracy and ignorance. If we are to make inroads on crime and delinquency, therefore, we must as a government and people make inroads on poverty in America.

The recent report of the Attorney General's committee was a milestone which promises to have continued influence. The Justice Department is carrying through many of the suggestions made in that report, and Congress now has under consideration a major item of legislation emanating from it.

The Manhattan Bail Project, conducted in part under the auspices of New York University Law School, also holds great promise. And in the District of Columbia the entire problem of bail is being rethought; just a few weeks ago the first experiment was conducted in releasing an accused on his own recognizance pending trial.

In New Haven, Conn., a "neighborhood social-legal program"

has been put into operation in an effort to confront the basic social, economic, and educational roots of legal problems. A team—consisting of a social worker, a lawyer and an investigator—is assigned to a poor neighborhood in an effort to uncover and deal with the causes of the legal problems at their sources rather than at the litigation stage.

This pioneer program recognizes that problems of poverty cut across the conceptual lines dividing criminal from civil cases, and that the poor person must be made aware of his legal rights and obligations—whether they be in signing a lease, executing a credit agreement, settling a domestic dispute or paying taxes—before he can be expected to participate in the community as a fully responsible citizen. Programs of this sort hold great promise, especially for our urban population centers.

Our substantive criminal law is also undergoing much needed revamping, prompted in part by the American Law Institute's Model Penal Code. More attention is being paid in our law schools as well to this long-neglected area. The practice of criminal law is again becoming as respected as it was at the time of the Constitution and throughout our early history, when it was engaged in by men like John Adams, Daniel Webster and Abraham Lincoln.

It is hoped that many more established lawyers will bring their experience, and that many more young law graduates will bring the most recent academic developments, to bear on the problems of justice. The widespread participation of the bar in the criminal process, which will result from the Supreme Court's recent decisions holding that all criminal defendants, must, upon request, be afforded representation at trial and on appeal, will bring the present inequalities of the criminal process more forcefully to the attention of the bar. This in itself is desirable, for awareness of a problem is the first and most important step toward solution.

Part 5

POVERTY GROUPS, POVERTY AREAS

THE POOR IN America are made up of a variety of groups in terms of age, ethnic background, and geographical location. The aged, for example, are an increasing proportion of the nation's poverty population, despite the old widespread belief that the Social Security system would satisfactorily solve the challenge of security in old age. Fourteen years after the passage of the Social Security Act, it was still possible for Sumner Slichter to write on "The Pressing Problem of Old-Age Security." His article was written partly because of the pending strike over pensions in the steel industry. His criticisms of the private pension plans of that time are relevant even today. The issue of poverty and old age is critical in many ways, not the least being that many of the poor are not born poor: they *become* poor after many years of productive work and comfortable living—once they are removed from the labor force and live "too long."

But age is only one of the many faces of poverty. Another critical dimension is ethnic or racial minority status. The 1947 article on Puerto Ricans in New York portrays the progress and the plight of these Spanish-speaking Americans seeking betterment on the mainland. We must remember conditions in Puerto Rico at that time: the poor were hardly invisible, for 80 per cent of the population had incomes below $500 per year. The island's economic development was not moving ahead rapidly enough to absorb and support a population—even at fixed standards of living—that had grown from 1 million to 2.2 million in less than fifty years, thanks to improved public health measures and no program of birth control.

Oliver LaFarge's "Plea for a Square Deal for the Indian" in 1948 has a tragically eternal character to it. Poverty and frustration, blended with hopelessness and a loss of will, were the inevitable results of the Indian Bureau's policies. Over the years the Bureau combined an inordinate dosage of mistakes, fumbling, inheritance of red tape, inadequate funds, and too few employees.

American Negroes comprise the largest single ethnic minority among the total poverty population (although all poor whites still make up two-thirds of that total population). It may come as a bit of a surprise that the great scholar W. E. B. DuBois, a cultural hero to many black militants today, could write in 1948 about a half-century of Negro progress. While it may be smug to observe that history can be an antidote to exaggeration and hysteria, it is important to recall DuBois' recording of change. For example, the Negro male's life expectancy jumped from thirty-two years in 1900 to fifty-seven years in 1947; and the dramatic exodus from an impoverishing Southern rural farm existence was accompanied by a rise in the proportion of Negroes employed in white-collar occupations, professions, and the arts. DuBois in 1948 was optimistic that fewer and fewer whites believed Negroes to be inherently inferior, and the nation's race problem insoluble.

Six years later, Chester Bowles was writing about not just the progress of the Negro citizen but the challenge he faced. The average income of Negroes tripled from 1940 to 1950 (while whites' average income less than doubled), but it remained only 50 per cent of the white average. We were still creating and perpetuating urban ghettos. Bowles' checklist for alert citizen action on the community level is still a useful one.

C. Eric Lincoln's 1964 article on "The Negro's Middle-Class Dream" was a welcome essay in a time when success and comfort as group and personal goals were being denigrated by blacks and whites. Lincoln's account of the emergence of a relatively nonpoor Negro class credits many of its members with an important contribution to the struggle for first-class citizenship for all Negroes, notwithstanding the indiscriminate labeling of them as "Black Bourgeoisie." If the War Against Poverty is taken at face value, its goal is to move all low-income Americans out of that existence. The further they move from it, the more they will become concerned, black and white, "with being comfortable middle-class—and unhindered in enjoying all that America has to offer."

The last selections are directed at poverty in its geographical dimensions. A. H. Raskin of the *Times* deals with intensive case histories of the long-term unemployed, especially in such poverty pockets as New England, Pennsylvania, and Michigan, and in the classic source of poverty journalism, West Virginia. Raskin's treatment is significant because it recounts the search by John Kennedy for the cures and prevention of such chronic joblessness (for example, through a depressed-areas program) as a first major step toward an organized war against poverty.

The Pressing Problem of Old-Age Security

by Sumner H. Slichter

LESS THAN HALF of the men and less than one out of ten of the women of sixty-five years of age or over in the United States are at work. A man of sixty-five years of age may expect to live on the average about twelve years longer; a woman nearly fourteen years. How are people going to support themselves for twelve or fourteen years without working? An annuity paying $100 a month for life, if purchased at the age of 65, would cost more than $15,000. If it also provided a payment of $75 a month to a wife who survived her husband and who was about the same age as the husband, it would cost several thousand dollars more. Few persons who reach the age of 65 have savings of $15,000 or more. Consequently, the voluntary savings of individuals can meet only a small part of the need. How retired workers shall be supported is plainly one of the biggest economic problems in the United States.

What should be done about the problem of security in old age? Is the problem being made unnecessarily large and difficult by unwise retirement policies on the part of business? How good are the four principal ways through which the country is now attempting to meet the problem—employer-initiated pension plans,

From the *New York Times Magazine,* October 16, 1949, copyright © 1949 by The New York Times Company.

union-negotiated plans, the Federal old-age assistance plan, and the Federal old-age pension plan? Do these plans need to be supplemented or superseded by new arrangements? In particular, how good are the pension plans that have been negotiated by trade unions? The fact-finding board in the steel case said that so long as the Government fails to provide security in "an adequate amount, industry should take up the slack." Is this reasonable? Are union-negotiated plans a good way of meeting the problem of old-age security?

The House of Representatives has just passed a bill extending the Federal old-age pension plan to at least 6 million more persons and raising the monthly benefits by roughly 70 per cent. How far would these changes go in meeting the problem of old-age security?

The seriousness of the problem of old-age security is greatly aggravated by the unwise retirement policies of business. Few people retire voluntarily—most retirements occur against the will of the worker at the decision of the employer. The community obviously would be better off if the older persons who were willing to work had jobs and were producing goods. Furthermore, most persons would be happier at work than they are in retirement. Special reasons for early retirement exist, it is true, in the case of executives, technicians and professional people, who hold jobs that require imagination, originality and resourcefulness. These jobs are best held by relatively young men.

For the great majority of jobs, however, the age of 65 is too early for retirement. Hence, the growing practice of retiring all persons at the age of 65 should be decisively halted. Had the rule of retirement at 65 been generally in effect in August, 1949, 3 million fewer people would have been at work in the United States, and the annual output of the economy would have been nearly $11 billion less—except to the extent that the dropping of older workers might have raised the efficiency of younger workers.

Although a higher age of retirement would diminish the size of the problem of old-age security, it would not eliminate the problem. Even at the age of 70 the average male may expect to live nine years longer. An annuity of $100 a month for life at the age of 70 would cost him in excess of $13,000—certainly more than the average worker of 70 would have. Let us look, therefore, at the four principal ways which are now used to provide retired workers with incomes and let us see whether any of them offers a solution for the problem.

1. Employer-Initiated Plans

These plans have been growing by leaps and bounds—from fewer than 200 in 1915 to more than 400 in 1929 and more than 9,000 today. In the last ten years their growth has been greatly stimulated by the tax laws. More than three-fifths of the employer-initiated plans are non-contributory. Most of the plans were started in order to permit firms to make some overdue retirements. Under the circumstances, managements were hardly able to ask employees to contribute.

Pension plans initiated by private employers have four major deficiencies, and they are clearly not the answer to the problem of old-age security—though they may do much good in the plants where they operate. A primary major deficiency for employer-initiated pension plans is that they will never give adequate coverage. One reason for this is that they do not apply to self-employed persons, of whom there are about 11 million in the United States. They need a source of income after retirement no less than do employes.

Employer-initiated pension plans also fail to give adequate coverage because they are expensive. Hence, only the more prosperous companies will adopt them. Even in the highly prosperous year of 1945, more than one-fourth of all corporations were "in the red." Pensions, depending upon their size, are likely to cost at least 6 to 8 per cent of payrolls. This does not include the special cost of meeting the large accrued liability with which most pension plans start. This special cost is a result of the fact that the plans apply to employes who have worked for the employer for many years and who will soon have reached the age of retirement. No payments have been made before the initiation of the scheme to buy pensions for these employes.

Finally, the employer-initiated plans will not give adequate coverage because they are limited to certain types of employes— usually long-service employes. The present 9,000 employer-initiated plans cover a little more than one-third of the employes of the firms which have the plans.

A second major shortcoming of employer-initiated pension schemes is that they may be abandoned at the will of the employer, leaving the employe without protection. Of 418 plans in existence in 1929, forty-five had been abandoned by 1932.

A third major defect of most employer-initiated pension schemes is that they restrict the movement of workers—a man who leaves one employer to work for another does not ordinarily carry his pension rights with him.

A fourth major defect is the handicap they put on older workers in finding employment. This deficiency is a result of the third one, namely, that employes do not carry their pension rights from one employer to another. Even twenty years' contributions on behalf of a worker will not buy him a very adequate pension unless these contributions are at a high rate. Consequently, a man who is hired at the age of 55 and retired at the age of 65 or 68 would receive a very small pension. Managements do not care to undermine the morale of their workers by giving substandard pensions to employes who are retired, and they avoid this diffi- culty simply by not taking workers of more than about 45 years of age except for temporary jobs.

2. Union-Negotiated Plans

Pension plans negotiated by unions with employers may be less easily abandoned than an employer-initiated plan and they may cover a larger proportion of the employes, but they suffer from the same four major defects as do employer-initiated plans. Consequently, it was a blunder for the fact-finding board in the steel dispute to recommend union-negotiated plans for the various steel companies.

Union-negotiated plans will never give adequate coverage, partly because they do not apply to the self-employed and partly because they can be instituted only in those plants where the employer is making enough money so that he can grant the union demand for pensions, meet the large accrued liability, and hold his own in competition. No matter how strong the union, it can- not impose an adequate pension plan on those employers who are financially weak. The limitation of coverage is especially great when the cost of pensions falls entirely on the employer. Consequently, if union-negotiated plans are established, the workers should contribute part of the cost.

The union-negotiated pension plans which have been established thus far do not, as a rule, permit an employe who leaves an enterprise to carry his pension rights with him to his next job—though some of the stronger unions may be able to correct this defect by negotiating changes in the plans. Union-negotiated pension plans, like employer-initiated plans, discourage employers from hiring older workers and thus handicap older workers in finding jobs.

A special drawback of many union-negotiated pension plans is their financial unsoundness. Many of these plans make no provision for meeting the huge accrued liability with which the plans start. In many cases the cost of the pensions in a decade or so will be so large that the unions will have to consent to a reduction in the pensions in order to gain wage increases. Consequently, the so-called "security" offered by many union-negotiated pension plans is illusory.

The pension fund in the coal industry is a glaring example of an arrangement which provides illusory security because it is financially unsound. No adequate provision has been made to finance the enormous accrued liability with which the scheme started. Nor has the underwriting of the risks been arranged to assure that any part of the payments now being made into the fund will be available to provide pensions ten or twenty years hence for the men who are today counting on getting pensions when they retire. An insurance company which attempted to operate as the miners' welfare fund is being operated would quickly be in trouble with the law.

3. Old-Age Assistance

The old-age assistance program of the Federal Government is the largest single source of income to retired persons. About 2.6 million are drawing old-age assistance, and total old-age assistance payments are roughly twice as large as all of the pension payments made under the Federal old-age pension scheme. More than half of the money now disbursed for old-age assistance comes from the

Federal Government, but administration is in the hands of the states.

The old-age assistance program is open to two major objections. One is that it is demoralizing and the other is that it opens the door to grave political abuses. It is demoralizing for people to have to accept charity after a lifetime of work. And since the money comes from general revenues, recipients of aid do not have the satisfaction of knowing that they have made a specific contribution to help finance the payments which they receive.

The fact that payments are based upon a means test makes the plan difficult to administer. Need is difficult to define, and this creates the danger of political favoritism. The danger is aggravated by the fact that payments are made out of general revenue and that most of the states, which administer the scheme, are paying out more Federal money than state money.

During the last ten years the record of old-age assistance strongly suggests that such a scheme cannot be satisfactorily administered. Although unemployment (which tends to be especially high among older persons) dropped from 9.5 million in 1939 to 2.1 million in 1948, payments for old-age assistance increased 2.7 times. There are wide differences between states in the proportion of persons receiving aid, and there are wide variations in average monthly payments even between adjoining states. In Louisiana no less than four out of five persons of 65 years of age or more are receiving old-age assistance—a sudden doubling of the number since June, 1948.

In Oklahoma and Georgia more than half, and in Texas, Colorado, Alabama and Mississippi nearly half of all persons 65 years of age or over are drawing old-age assistance, but in New York and New Jersey the proportion is only one out of ten.

Wide variation also occurs in the size of payments. In Louisiana the average monthly payment has more than doubled between June, 1948, and June, 1948, rising from $22.87 to $47.05. In the two adjoining states of Arkansas and Mississippi the average monthly payment in June, 1949, was $20.95 and $18.80, respectively. Monthly payments in Massachusetts were nearly twice as large as in Vermont and one-third again as large as in Rhode Island.

4. Old-Age Insurance

The most satisfactory arrangement for providing income for retired persons is the Federal old-age insurance plan. It avoids the principal weaknesses of the other three schemes. In the first place, it is comprehensive, for it covers all jobs in all plants within the covered industries. It is not limited to the generous and prosperous employers or to the plants where unions are strong. In the second place, it gives enduring protection because it cannot be abrogated at the will of an employer, and employes do not lose their pension rights if their employer goes out of business. In the third place, since employes carry their pension rights with them, the plan does not deter employers from hiring older workers.

In the fourth place, the burden on financially weak employers is limited by the fact that the plan applies alike to all competitors in an industry, by the fact that the accrued liability is met very gradually (as is possible only under a compulsory system), and by the fact that half of the cost falls on employes. In the fifth place, the self-respect of the workers is protected because pensions are given as a matter of right without a means test and are financed, not from general revenues, but from a payroll tax to which both employes and employers contribute equally. Finally, the fact that pensions are paid as a matter of right eliminates the chance for political favoritism.

Although the Federal old-age insurance scheme is basically sound, it has three serious defects—its coverage is inadequate, its eligibility requirements are too strict, and the benefit payments are too low. The coverage is inadequate because the plan does not cover certain important types of workers, such as domestic servants, employes of nonprofit institutions, farm employes and the self-employed. All in all, it covers about three out of five jobs. The eligibility requirements are too strict—it takes too long for workers to acquire insured status. As a result, only about one out of five persons of 65 years of age or more is drawing pension benefits or has insured status under the plan. The low benefit payments are indicated by the fact that the average payment for single workers is about $26 a month and for a worker with one dependent, about $40 a month.

The House of Representatives on Oct. 5 passed a bill, H. R.

6,000, which would make substantial improvements in the old-age insurance scheme. The bill would extend the coverage of the act to include nearly one million out of three million domestic service employes, about 200,000 farm laborers, and about 4.5 million urban self-employed. It would extend partial protection, and possibly complete protection, to about 600,000 employes of non-profit institutions.

By voluntary agreement between state governments and the Federal Government, about 3.8 million employes of state and local governments might be covered. The bill would liberalize the eligibility requirements so that newly covered employes would become insured more quickly. Finally, it would raise benefit payments about 70 per cent to an average of between $50 and $60 a month.

The provisions of the bill just passed by the House, though a long step in advance, fall short of the recommendations of the Advisory Council on Social Security appointed two years ago by the Finance Committee of the Senate. This body consisted of seventeen members—six business men, two representatives of organizd labor, four persons from the public service, and five persons from university work and scientific research. The council was unanimous in recommending that coverage of the old-age and survivors' insurance be made virtually universal.

For example, the council would cover farmers and professional workers who would not be covered under the recommendations of the Ways and Means Committee. The council was also unanimous in recommending that eligibility requirements be changed so as to permit workers to qualify more promptly for pensions. The council also recommended increases in benefits which would raise the average benefit of a retired worker without dependents from $26 a month to $55 and of a worker with a wife from $40 to $85 a month.

The Federal old-age pension plan, if its coverage were extended to nearly all of the 25 million uncovered jobs and if the average benefits were substantially raised, would provide the country with an adequate plan of old-age security and would limit the dependence of the country upon unsound employer-initiated or union-negotiated plans which tend to tie the worker to one employer and which handicap older workers in obtaining employment.

A comprehensive and adequate old-age insurance plan is the only way of checking the rapidly snowballing old-age assistance payments. The usefulness of the Federal old-age pension plan in relieving the community of dependence on unsound alternative arrangements will depend upon adequacy of benefit payments. Surely it is not unreasonable that the pension of a man with a wife to support should be at least half of his earnings before retirement. In the case of a man who had been earning $300 a month throughout his working life, the recommendations of the Advisory Council would result in a monthly pension of $106.87— a little more than one-third of his monthly earnings.

Although the Federal old-age pension plan can be easily developed to provide adequate protection to retired workers, some employers and some unions may wish to establish supplementary plans. The Federal Government, however, has an obligation to see that supplementary plans really provide the security which they promise, that they do not tie a worker to a given employer, and that they do not encourage employers to discriminate against older workers.

This can be done by requiring that the plans meet certain standards in order for employer contributions to be a deductible expense under the corporate income tax law. These standards should require that the plan be properly underwritten and that the employes who leave the service of an employer take their pension rights with them. In addition, in order to avoid encouraging noncontributory plans in preference to contributory, the Federal Government should permit the contributions of employes to pension plans to be a deductible expenditure under the personal income tax—at least if the employe's contribution is matched by one from his employer.

Can the country afford an adequate scheme of security for old age? With stiff wage demands constantly being made on industry, with large quantities of goods needed for national defense and to provide help to sixteen countries in Europe, can industry produce enough to give decent pensions to retired workers? And are not all schemes by which the community undertakes to provide security for retired workers wrong in principle? Are not such schemes bound to undermine thrift, initiative, self-reliance, and the spirit of independence?

The cost of an old-age pension plan paying benefits moderately more liberal than those included in the bill recently passed by the House or recommended by the Advisory Council on Social Security may be put roughly at 8 per cent of payrolls. In the past, output per man-hour in the United States has increased about 2 per cent a year. If it continues to grow at the rate of 2 per cent a year, it will increase by over 80 per cent in the next thirty years.

Hence, the total cost of a fairly adequate old-age security program would be about one-tenth the increase in production during the next generation—assuming that output per man-hour grows no faster than in the past. The one thing that must be avoided, in order to keep the cost of old-age security within moderate limits, is a further drop in the usual age of retirement. Universal retirement at 65, depriving the community of nearly $11 billion of product a year, would be ten times as costly as the present old-age pension program is today.

The danger that a system of old-age security will undermine thrift is remote. The usual method by which men have provided for their old age has never been thrift—it has been by having plenty of children and expecting the children to help the parents. Certainly pensions which pay 50 per cent less than average earnings leave much room for thrift. Furthermore, no one need fear that the incentives to practice thrift are about to disappear—there are many good things which the ordinary person can acquire only by practicing thrift quite rigorously. Any wage-earner who buys a house at present prices will have a good opportunity to be thrifty for years to come.

Nor is old-age security likely to undermine initiative, self-reliance and independence—it is likely to strengthen these qualities. The reason is obvious. The worker, small-business man or high executive who has a minimum of protection for his old age is likely to be willing to take some economic chances which he would not otherwise dare take. The extension of old-age security to small-business men may be particularly useful in making them feel better able to take risks. Certainly if the prospect of a pension is likely to undermine initiative or self-reliance, this probability has been overlooked by the many corporations which have provided generous noncontributory pensions for their executives—

the very men who most of all need to have initiative and self-reliance.

One final word of warning. The greatest danger to an adequate old-age security plan is rising prices. A rise of 2 per cent a year in prices would cut the purchasing power of pensions about 45 per cent in thirty years. The greatest danger of rising prices is from wages rising faster than output per man-hour. If unions put up money wages 5 per cent a year and output per man-hour increases 3 per cent a year, prices will have to rise by the difference, or 2 per cent a year. Hence, whether the nation succeeds in providing adequate security for retired workers depends in large measure upon the wage policies of trade unions. If unions push up wages faster than output increases, they undermine the security of all retired workers.

New York Plans Aid for Puerto Ricans

IN FLIGHT from their destitute territory, Puerto Ricans are swelling the city's population by 1,500 new arrivals a week, the Welfare Council of New York City said yesterday.

An estimated 350,000 Americans of Puerto Rican birth now live here, the council reported at a conference of social agencies held in the Hotel Commodore. The figures were averages compiled from several sources.

Absorption by the city, assistance and possible future diversion of the citizens from the impoverished Caribbean sugar-bowl island to other United States areas were suggested as aids in meeting the problem.

Welfare agency officials pictured the Puerto Rico-American as a valuable citizen who would rather work than take relief. His industriousness, they said, is seasoned with artistic ability of commercial use and a laudable moral and religious viewpoint.

G. Howland Shaw, council president and former Assistant Secretary of State, named a thirty-three-member committee on problems of Puerto Rico-Americans to map direct action for social agencies cooperating with the council. Adrian Burke, attorney, president of the Children's Center at 105th Street and Fifth Avenue, is chairman of the committee.

The migration of Puerto Rican natives to New York is a "blood-letting" of the 2,200,000 residents of the overcrowded island, said Dr. A. Fernos-Isern, Resident Commissioner of Puerto Rico in Washington. It may give the island an opportunity to recover economically and build a secure way of life, he told 100 social work executives at the afternoon conference. The Government of Puerto Rico already is establishing agencies to inform its emigrants of other United States areas of opportunity than complex, crowded New York, he said.

"Present conditions in Puerto Rico are simply unbelievable," Dr. Fernos commented. "Eighty per cent of the population are of the underprivileged classes with income not beyond $500 a year. There is terrific economic pressure on the people.

"This resettlement should receive Government aid and should not fall on New York City alone."

He attributed Puerto Rico's plight to its sugar-dependent economy, "half-way" industrialization and population growth from 1,000,000 in 1900 to "about 2,200,000 now." He said it grew through improved public health that cut death rates from twenty-eight for each 1,000 in 1900 to 18.6 in 1941 and 14.1 at the start of 1946.

E. R. Rhatigan, City Welfare Commissioner, said the relief load in Puerto Rican sections of the city was not high and urged that there be no publicity concerning the Puerto Rican situation.

In East Harlem, said Clyde E. Murray, headworker of Union Settlement Association, 237 East 104th Street, twenty-three Puerto Ricans live in four small rooms at one place. At another, fifteen occupy a two-and-one-half room apartment whose owner also runs a day school for ten children on the premises.

"Sleeping bags are at a premium," he said. "It is a marvel that there are not more bad results. We have 400 mothers who would rather work than take relief on our day nursery waiting list."

Other speakers included Msgr. Charles R. Giblin, assistant director of Catholic Charities of the Archdiocese of New York; Ruperto Ruiz, president of the Spanish American Youth Bureau; Manuel Cabranes, executive director of Melrose House, the Bronx; the Rev. James V. Hart, pastor of St. Paul's Roman Catholic Church, 113 East 117th Street, and Robert F. Wagner Jr., City Housing Commissioner.

A Plea for a Square Deal for the Indians

by Oliver La Farge

SANTA FE, N. M.

THE LATEST official figures show that there are more than 420,000 Indians (including a few Eskimos and Aleuts) in the United States and Alaska now under Federal supervision. The figure is surprising. In the early Nineteen Twenties when no one thought Indians important enough to be counted carefully, the official estimates ran around 250,000, and certainly for a long time we have assumed that they were rapidly dying out. Now we learn that they are not; on the contrary, full-bloods as well as mixed-bloods are increasing slightly more rapidly than our general population.

The Indians are going to be with us for quite a while, then. They are a factor in our total citizenry. Some 25,000 of them served in the armed forces in the last war—women as well as men. (A Pueblo Indian woman of my acquaintance recently accepted a Navy offer to return to the Navy as lieutenant, j. g., nurse.) Many thousands served in war industries. The Marines had a special corps of Navajos who were used to communicate by radio from ship to shore in landings—as simply by talking in their own language they used an unbreakable code. One of the men in the famous picture of raising the flag on Mount Surabachi, the one with his arm up, reaching, was a Papago, and shortly after the flag was set up, a Flathead was killed defending it. They sound like a useful and loyal people. We should be glad to have them around.

Yet in one area their situation has become so extreme as to catch public attention. Our greatest tribe, the 60,000 Navajos, is locked by illiteracy and endemic disease into a desert reservation which can hardly support half that number. Their condition has become so shocking that we now have under consideration in Congress a program which typifies what we need throughout. This program contemplates large-scale medical assistance, the building and staffing of schools for some 17,000 children now receiving no schooling, development of resources, encouragement of industries, and general economic rehabilitation which, if carried through, will change the Navajos, perhaps in a generation, from very primitive, half-starved herdsmen into a modern people, engaging in as wide a variety of gainful pursuits as the rest of us, and moving freely in the American world.

It will cost millions, perhaps 150 million before it is done—but then, the present direct relief bill for the Navajos runs to a million dollars a year, and will increase yearly unless their condition is changed.

This is an extreme example, and the remedy required is equally extreme, but in lesser degree this situation is repeated among many of the once famous Plains Indian tribes of the north, and in many other sections.

We took the whole country from the Indians, leaving them tracts of land, often the poorest there was, sometimes purely worthless, on which to try to get by. We shattered the simple and satisfactory life which they had been living, and in return we inflicted upon them a vast variety of diseases, above all tuberculosis, against which they had no immunities. Conquest, despoliation, disease and mistreatment they have repaid with loyalty and patriotism. We owe these people a debt. There is no excuse for us today to follow a course which will prolong and renew the evils of the white man's advent. The Indians deserve a square deal.

They certainly aren't getting it. The predicament of the majority of them is a combination of ignorance and poverty, with ill-health thrown in for good measure. The areas of land, whether reservations or individual holdings, which they have been able to hang on to are too small and too poor to support them as farmers and herders, even if they were taught the most modern agricultural methods. In practice, most of them follow relatively primitive methods, partly because they receive only a fraction of the agricultural extension service extended to every white man living off the land.

In all the years that they have been under our control, the majority of them has still not been brought far enough along in literacy, command of English, and understanding of our complex and often cut-throat civilization, to be able to contemplate leaving their reservation except in desperation, to sink to the lowest slum levels of white communities.

The Indian Bureau, often mistaken, often fumbling, hampered by a magnificent inheritance of red tape, is striving with entirely inadequate funds and far too few employes to bring those hundreds of thousands up across centuries of cultural evolution to a merger with ourselves. So far the result tends to be poverty and a long frustration which ends in hopelessness and the loss of the will to struggle.

One of the reasons why Indians don't get a square deal today is that the American public not only knows almost nothing about them, but is loaded with misinformation. There is the stereotype of the Indian himself, a befeathered, half-human creature of unnatural dignity with a habit of saying "ugh!"

Indians today run from very able lawyers, doctors, business men, trained nurses, to people who speak no English and still retain much of their ancient way of life, although very few now wear Indian costumes except for special occasions. They are notable for their keen sense of humor, ready laughter and fondness for singing. On the whole their greatest desire is to become completely equal to white men in general education and knowledge of the world, and to compete with them on even terms.

All sorts of wild ideas exist as to the status of an Indian and the meaning of the "reservations" on which many of the Indians live. By the exploiting of these misconceptions, millions of acres of Indian land and millions of dollars of Indian money have been stolen from them, and the drive to get the rest still goes on. It is well worth taking a little space to tell what the Indian's status really is.

The average Indian lives on a reservation. This is *not* a sort of large concentration camp. No one is compelled to live on a reservation. The Indians go and come as they please. A reservation is an area of tax-exempt land, owned by the tribe, or originally so owned, and held in trust for the Indians by the United States. It cannot be taxed, levied upon, or alienated. The Indians have received these tracts of land, inadequate though they are, in recognition of their inherent right as the original settlers of this country. Obviously, tax-exempt, inalienable land, even poor land, is a valuable asset.

The Indian is a ward of the United States. Originally, when we were dealing with recently conquered, resentful, warlike tribes, wardships included various restrictions upon personal freedom. Of these restrictions there remains only a law forbidding the sale of liquor to Indians, and this law works about as well as the Volstead Act did with us.

As a person, the Indian is completely free. Wardship consists in the trusteeship over the reservation, and a similar trusteeship over funds which essentially derive from the reservation or from the Indians' status as Indians—that is, such funds as royalties on oil from trust lands, or damages paid to tribes for claims against the Government. It also consists in the right of Indians to receive education, medical care and other such services from the Federal Government. Like reservations, then, wardship is not a restraint, but an asset. In fact, Indians as advanced as the late Vice President Curtis retained wardship status because of the advantages involved.

It is essential to grasp these two points, because the cry of "set the Indians free" by abolishing wardship and reservations is the standard device by which the plunderers lead well-intentioned citizens to acquiesce in new raids upon the Indian estate.

"Setting the Indians free" resulted, between 1880 and 1930, when the process was halted, in the acquisition by various devices —really legalized theft—of more than 100 million acres of Indian land. We have a bill before the Senate today, H. R. 1113, which passed the House without proper debate or hearings, to "emancipate" the Indians out of everything they have.

This bill would, in a short span of years, be booting people who speak no English, know nothing of our world, poverty-stricken primitives, out of all governmental help and protection. It would open the door to the final ruination of all the Indians' hopes. Yet the man who sponsored this bill did so in good faith—and ignorance.

Indians are citizens as well as wards. They enjoy every right of any citizen, except that in the sovereign states of Arizona and New Mexico they are denied the vote and cut off from social security by various trick legal devices. This is the action of the states, not of the Federal Government. Suits are pending in both states now to win Indians the right to vote, and the Department of the Interior has filed briefs *amicus curiae* favorable to the plaintiffs.

It would look, then, as if our Indians enjoyed special advantages. In theory they do. In certain areas, as in parts of Oklahoma, you will find Indians who by means of these aids and their own efforts have advanced themselves to complete equality with the rest of the population. In all too many parts of the United States and Alaska, however, sheer ignorance, widespread disease and wretched economic conditions hold them in a sort of slavery. That is the plight the Navajos enjoy, already described.

In Oklahoma you will find Cherokees in the cities and on good ranches, business men, politicians, professional men—and you will find several thousand Cherokees in the backwoods able to speak very little English and not long ago trying to survive on a per capita income of $34 a year.

We have had these people in our charge for anywhere from seventy-five years to a couple of centuries, and this is what we have to show for it. The usual way of dodging the blame, the shame of such a record is to talk vaguely about the wicked Indian Bureau, as though the citizens were in no way responsible for the failure of a branch of their Government. As a matter of fact, the Indian Bureau of the past twenty years has earnestly tried to help the Indians, although it has made many mistakes. It can do its work only as the people, through Congress, will enable it to do so.

There is a clear goal in our handling of our Indians. That is to give them all the education, medical care and economic assistance which will put them on their feet as healthy, well-informed, self-supporting citizens of the United States. When that is done, there will be no more need for an Indian Bureau. In fact, the Indian Bureau's own brief summary of its policy is that it is trying to work itself out of a job.

When the last Indian is ready to sink or swim in even competition with the rest of us, when we can say that our conquest of what is now the United States has brought full opportunity for a better life than the old one to all the descendants of the conquered, within the limits of their individual abilities, then we can relax. Then it will no longer be necessary to give Indians special status or special advantages.

If we destroy those advantages before the Indians are ready, we simply project them onto the relief rolls, as has been demonstrated over and over again. If we merely keep them in status quo and neglect them, we build up miserable populations who will continue indefinitely to be a drain upon the Federal purse and will increasingly become a liability instead of the very real asset which our Indians potentially are.

The greatest long-range economy we can make in connection with them is to spend enough on them now to give them the opportunity which they themselves so greatly desire. It is worth noting that each white citizen receives an average of $300 per year in services from the Federal, state and local Governments, exclusive of what is spent on the armed forces, while Indians receive an average of $166 per year from the Federal Government and nothing else. This is second-class citizenship.

We need to spend our money as an investment, planning it wisely. It surely should not be necessary to persuade Americans that every American child should go to school. We accept that. But with the Indians we need to go further, into many kinds of training toward true competence, and advice, guidance and assistance in getting themselves established economically.

Wherever the Indians have had a chance they have proved their capacity for advancement. If we will insure them all that chance, we shall get out of it in the end half a million or more (at the rate at which they are increasing now) extremely desirable fellow-citizens whose loyalty to this land goes back even farther, is even deeper, than that of any of us.

If we keep on passing by on the other side, a few of them will pull themselves up by desperate efforts. The spoilers and plunderers who never forget them for a moment will go on "emancipating" them from what few assets they have. The Indians will not solve our problem for us by dying out. They will live on, ever poorer, ever sicker, an infection in our body politic and a disgrace to our nation before the world.

The Negro Since 1900:
A Progress Report

by W. E. B. DuBois

FORTY YEARS AGO Julius Rosenwald, a native and resident of Spring-field, Ill., where Abraham Lincoln lies buried, was shocked by an anti-Negro riot and lynching in the town. That event started him on a long and devoted career of safeguarding rights and gaining wider privileges for all suppressed peoples, in particular Negroes. Along with many other philanthropies in this field he established, in 1917, the Rosenwald Fund with an endowment which was not to be maintained in perpetuity but was to be spent—both interest and principal—within twenty-five years after his death. He said: "We may be certain that * * * the acute social need of tomorrow will be different from that of today and will doubtless call for a new kind of agency to meet it."

This year the last of the Rosenwald Fund was spent; by far the greater part of it had been devoted to the welfare of the Negro. What did the fund, and the many other efforts in this field, accomplish? What progress have Negroes made and what has contributed to that progress?

Between 1900 and 1940 the Negro population of the United States increased from 9,000,000 to 13,000,000; but the increase in the South was but 25 per cent, while in the North and West it was 200 per cent. Since 1940 this increase North and West has been further accentuated. The rural Negro population has remained stationary since 1900, while the city population has increased more than 350 per cent. A million Negroes have left the plantations of the South, where labor is in virtual peonage, to enter domestic and personal service, industry and transport in cities North and South. Large numbers in industry have risen from unskilled to skilled labor. This is shown by the increase of Negro membership in trade unions from about 30,000 in 1900 to 100,000 in 1930, and to an estimated total of 1,000,000 at the height of the war industry.

The Negro is entering business, first as cooperative self-service among his own people, then gradually into general small business, insurance, real estate and banking. A steady increase in white-collar occupations and in the arts and professions has attracted a third of all Negro workers.

Meantime, general conditions have improved. In 1900, a Negro boy baby at birth had a life expectation of thirty-two years; in 1947, this had increased to fifty-seven years. In 1870, nine-tenths of the Negroes were illiterate. The census of 1940 reported the illiterates at 10 per cent, probably an inaccurate figure due to our methods of collecting statistics of reading and writing. Today certainly the Negro illiterates are below 20 per cent. In 1910 there were in school 1,644,000, or 45 per cent, of all Negroes 5 to 20 years of age; in 1940, 64 per cent of such Negro children were in school, or 4,188,000. In 1900, Charles Dudley Warner, speaking for American intellectuals, said that Negroes could not assimilate and use college training. In 1910 not more than 5,000 Negroes were in college. In 1948 more than 88,000 Negroes were enrolled in college.

The year after the Rosenwald Fund went into operation, 324 Negroes received the Bachelor's degree; in 1948 some 5,635 received this degree. There are today more than 1,500 Negro students enrolled in Northern colleges and universities, while from these institutions 279 have received the doctorate in philosophy. In the first edition of "Who's Who in America" there was not, so far as I can ascertain, the name of a single American of Negro descent. The fiftieth edition, in 1948, contains the names of ninety-one Negroes, and in "American Men of Science" seventy-seven

Negroes are listed. There are today on the faculties of the leading universities of the North seventy Negro instructors, ranging from a full professor at the University of Chicago to associate professors and instructors in other institutions.

Advancement has been made in political activity. From 1900 to the first World War the mass of American Negroes, except in Northern cities, had almost stopped voting. In the South, whether voluntarily or because of legal and economic pressure, most Negroes did not try to vote. Today not only do more than 2,500,-000 Negroes in the North and West vote, but in 1947 more than 600,000 Negroes were registered voters in twelve Southern states. Desperate and continued effort in South Carolina, Georgia and Mississippi has not stopped this growth.

In 1947 there were six Negro members of City Councils in the country, and thirty-three members of State Legislatures, including two Senators. More than a dozen Negro judges and magistrates are presiding over courts, and there are two Negro Congressmen. In 1948, for the first time in United States history, all three major parties in their conventions pledged themselves specifically to the upholding of the political and civil rights of American Negroes.

While there is much that is positive in the above record, the continuing struggle requires a full comprehension of all the many negative factors. Even among these negations, however, we can first note some improvement. For one thing, there has been an abatement in mob violence. For another, the fallacy that the Negro is congenitally unable to assimilate American culture has virtually been abandoned.

The most barbarous expression of race hate, lynching, has notably decreased. In 1900 an average of two Negroes each week were lynched by mobs without trial. In 1947 only one lynching was reported for the entire year.

In 1900 and up to World War I it was a common argument that the Negro problem in the United States was insoluble because Negroes were an inferior race and so far below the culture of the nation that they could never expect to live in this land as equal citizens.

Since 1917 this attitude has changed gradually. First, the dogma of "race" has been widely challenged, and the existence of "inferior" races of mankind denied. Many of the old clichés have fallen into disuse: human nature can be changed and most prejudices are neither inborn nor ineradicable. Law can help and hasten human change, and the intermarriage of persons of different races depends on the individuals involved and not on their "racial" characteristics. In science, history, literature and art; in athletics, physique and courage, Negroes have repeatedly proved themselves the equal, and often the superior, of average Americans. There is today scarcely a single field of American culture in which some Negro is not outstanding.

Let no one assume from this record of accomplishment that the American Negro has secured or is about to secure his full rights as an American citizen. Least of all are Negroes themselves satisfied or overoptimistic. The record of progress is impressive not so much because of absolute advance as by comparison with the semi-slavery that marked the condition of Negroes in 1900. If, instead of considering absolute Negro progress, we compare Negro advancement with the condition of the mass of Americans in health, education and political power, it will be clear that the lag is ominous.

Nevertheless, there is a long record of effort on the part of white Americans to help black folk. The successors of the Abolitionists were the teachers and missionaries who went to the South after the Civil War and started the education of the freed men. Large numbers of Northerners and some Southerners supported Negro social uplift and education from 1870 to 1900. In 1902 the General Education Board was endowed by John D. Rockefeller. It succeeded the Capon Springs Conferences and the Southern Education Board, and at first approached the Negro problem from the point of view of the white South.

No schools were helped or projects encouraged which were not approved by the liberal South. Industrial education was emphasized and Hampton and Tuskegee were helped; but higher education for Negroes was discouraged. By 1919, however, a more liberal element of young Southerners became members of the board, and it openly began to help endow Negro colleges, so that at last a broad system of higher education for Negroes was given a large endowment. Andrew Carnegie gave many libraries to Negro colleges and communities.

In 1919 many efforts at interracial cooperation which followed the Atlanta riot of 1906 coalesced into the Commission on Inter-racial Cooperation under the leadership of Will Alexander. This organization did outstanding work against lynching, especially by getting Southern white women from all over the South to deny the excuse of rape as a justifiable cause of mob violence.

The Commission on Race Relations of the Federal Council of Churches of Christ in America was organized in 1921 and insti-tuted "Race Relations Sunday." The Southern Conference on Human Welfare was started in 1939 and took a strong stand for civil and political rights for Negroes. Other organizations like the Carnegie Foundation, the American Civil Liberties Union, the Workers' Defense League and the Congress of Industrial Organi-zations' Committee to Abolish Racial Discrimination helped in the same field. The combined race relations program of the Rosen-wald Fund and the American Missionary Association has done much recently to study and ease racial tensions.

Philanthropy of itself, however, can never free a people. Money and good-will can help; they can at critical times give the indis-pensable push, the encouragement and the confidence. But a care-ful consideration of the facts prove that the chief force behind the progress of the Negro since 1917 came from the Negro himself; his purposive and organized effort, from 1900 until today, and particularly since 1917, has formed the mainspring of Negro progress.

First of all, we must note among American Negroes certain persistent culture patterns: the determination to educate their children; the persistent effort at organization for uplift and prog-ress in church and fraternity; the refusal, despite overwhelming temptation, to adopt entirely white American standards as to the good, the beautiful and the true.

But this individual push upward had to be organized. Organi-zations came early in religion, for social purposes, for specific objects; but the first clear-cut demand for full citizenship rights in the twentieth century came with the meeting of seventeen Negroes in 1906 to form the Niagara Movement. Three years later, in 1909, a small committee of white persons met in New York because of the Springfield riots, and in 1910 these two movements united and formed the National Association for the Advancement of Colored People.

For thirty-eight years this organization has spearheaded the pressure for Negro rights, until it has become a mass movement built deeply into the consciousness of the American Negro. Suggested by white liberals, guided by black radicals, officered increasingly by a black staff, and supported by an overwhelming mass of Negroes with a few whites, it began at the height of the Booker T. Washington appeasement campaign and declared its purpose to make American Negroes "physically free from peonage, politically free from disfranchisement, and socially free from insult." During its existence this organization has raised and spent over $4,000,000, of which 90 per cent came from poor colored workers. It has today a paid membership approximating 300,000 members.

The National Association for the Advancement of Colored People began with a crusade against lynching, starting in 1910 and culminating in 1919, when its address to the nation was signed by a former President of the United States, the Attorney General, seven Governors and heads of chief universities. Its next task was to establish the legal foundation of the Negro's political rights. From 1915 to 1948 the NAACP has brought twenty-seven cases involving the rights of Negroes before the United States Supreme Court and has won twenty-four of them. Included in these was the overthrow of the "Grandfather Clause" in several Southern states, giving certain whites the hereditary right to vote. Next came attacks on the "White Primary," which excluded all Negroes and allowed all whites of any party to vote. Four cases on the white primary had to be brought before the Supreme Court until, in 1944, a clear-cut decision against this form of disfranchisement was obtained. Between 1913 and 1948 six cases legalizing Negro ghettoes, first by law and then by private contract, were fought in the Supreme Court. As late as 1947 ten square miles of Chicago residential districts were by covenant restricted to white people. In 1948 the NAACP obtained a decision denying the legal right to enforce these contracts.

In 1939-40 nine Southern states spent an average of $58 a year on each white elementary school pupil and $18 on each colored pupil; and the South spent public money on colleges and professional schools which Negroes could not enter. The attack of the NAACP on this discrimination began in 1936 and continues. Thirty-two cases were brought to stop discrimination in teachers' salaries on account of race. Of these, 23 were won, 6 by decision and 17 by consent decrees; 4 were lost, 1 dropped and 4 are pending.

Next, the NAACP began to fight for admission of Negroes to professional schools supported by public funds in the South. Cases have been won in Missouri, Oklahoma and Texas ordering the admission of Negroes or the furnishing of equal facilities. In Maryland, Delaware and Arkansas, also by private effort, Negroes have been admitted to state-supported professional schools.

Other decisions have been obtained in three cases outlawing the exclusion of Negroes from jury duty, and a series of cases have been brought and demonstrations staged to stop mob violence and denial of due process of law. In 1923, after the riots at Elaine, Ark., twelve Negroes were sentenced to death and sixty-seven to prison terms. These cases were carried to the Supreme Court, and all seventy-nine Negroes were finally released.

Recently, in Columbia, Tenn., a clerk in a store slapped a colored woman customer for complaining of his service. Her son, a Navy veteran, knocked him through a window. A race riot ensued, and twenty-six Negroes were arrested. The NAACP defended them and obtained the release of all except one. The "third degree" to obtain confessions from Negroes was condemned by the Supreme Court in four cases.

Naturally, the work of the NAACP was not done alone. Not only have white people helped as members of the organization and as advisers in legal cases, but without the help of other Negro organizations the work could not have been done. The Negro churches, with 35,000 congregations, owning $175,000,000 in real estate and spending $28,000,000 a year, helped publicize and support the association. The Negro press, with nearly 150 weekly papers, read by every literate Negro in the nation, has achieved a news coverage which makes Negroes independent of the distortions and suppressions of the white press and lets Negroes know the facts and what is being done about them.

Other Negro organizations, like the National Urban League,

have supplemented the work of the NAACP in areas which it did not reach directly. The league was founded the same year as the NAACP, and they early delimited their fields of operation—the NAACP to fight race discrimination, the Urban League to seek to open opportunities for Negro employment. Its work among employers on the one hand, and among labor leaders on the other, has placed tens of thousands of Negroes in jobs where Negroes had never been hired before. A. Philip Randolph's "March on Washington" led Franklin Roosevelt to initiate the FEPC.

The discouraging note in Negro progress is the continued attitude of the white South. The reaction of the poor and ignorant and their demagogic leaders is understandable. But with notable exceptions, the liberal and educated South has not taken any leading role in Negro progress. It has increased Southern State contributions to Negro education, but the South still gives the Negro child only one-third as much as the white child. Negroes vote in larger numbers, but most Negroes do not vote and are not advised to. Lynching has decreased, but no lyncher has ever been adequately punished.

And in all these cases, it was not so much moral leadership as fear of Federal intervention which was the decisive motive. In general, the liberal white South makes no protest against the fact that in the lower South there is not a single Negro magistrate, no city or county officials and very few Negro members of juries. Meantime the better class of Negro artisans and workers is leaving the South for freer regions.

Why is this? The sudden and dramatic emergence of the Dixiecrats furnishes the explanation: Franklin Roosevelt, with the cooperation of the South, organized a progressive Democratic party. This party, with all other parties, declared for civil rights for all citizens, regardless of race and religion, in accord with the public opinion of the nation and the world. Immediately, a considerable section of the South rebelled, and not only the Talmadges and Rankins, but known liberals of education and character.

The real reason for this revolt was that the progressive white South is not yet ready to attack race discrimination as such in the South. They still stand for Negro disfranchisement, discrimination in education and restriction of Negroes in work and pay. It is not simply because they know that the unlettered crowd opposes this democracy; they themselves, as modern, educated men, oppose such a program. But they are not prepared to proclaim this reactionary belief and prefer to base their opposition to civil rights on the right of states, rather than of the Federal Government, to handle these problems.

Unfortunately for their logic, the nation has decided that most of these matters are already under Federal jurisdiction: the right to vote for Federal officials is a Federal right. A state has no legal right to deny it. If it does and, as in the case of the South, uses the political power of the disfranchised Negro vote to increase the power of the white South in the councils of the nation, this infringes the rights of citizens of New York and Michigan.

Education is a state function; but if the Federal Government helps as it should the schools of poorer states, it has both the right and duty to insist that these funds be distributed without race discrimination. Interstate travel is certainly under Federal control; and the nation's need for intelligent workers makes race discrimination in work and pay of national import (even if it is not under national interdiction). When the nation is pilloried as a nation of lynch law it must have the right to stop jungle law, especially in those states where states' rights have been so surrendered to backward local communities that the state is helpless in its own weal.

The present situation therefore is the direct result of the continued refusal of the liberal South to make a front forward fight on at least the more outrageous aspects of race discrimination. The Dixiecrats, instead of courageously facing a problem that must be faced, sought to disfranchise the South in the Democratic party, in order to retain the right to disfranchise the Negro in the South.

To what future can the Negro look forward? First of all, he faces a changed public opinion. The nation is no longer pessimistic on this problem. Far from believing that black and white cannot live together in peace and progress in one nation, it has awakened to the fact that peoples of all colors and races must live together in one world or perish. This gradual realization of a great revolution following two world wars has made our own problem of races a burning political question.

We begin to see that the Negro is fighting a slow, determined battle and is not going to give up. There is no indication that he will sink into lethargic acceptance of present conditions as inevitable or present progress as satisfactory. He proposes to reach complete equality as an American citizen. And by equality he means abolition of separate schools, the disappearance of "Jim Crow" travel; no segregation in public accommodations; the right to vote, the right to think and the right to speak, the right to work and to live in a decent home, and the right to marry any person who wishes to marry him. The Negro does not expect to reach these goals in a minute or in ten years. He is long-suffering and patient. But whether it takes thirty years or a thousand, equality is his goal and he will never stop until he reaches it.

The Negro, therefore, is not satisfied but encouraged. He firmly believes that if the progress in race relations and Negro advancement which has marked the last thirty years can be maintained for another generation the goal of democracy in America will be in sight, and the transplantation of a nation from Africa to the Western World will have proved a blessing to mankind.

The Negro—
Progress and Challenge

by Chester Bowles

"DO YOU KNOW the Number One obstacle to Asian friendship for America?" a Pakistani business man once asked me. He provided the answer which I had heard over and over again, from Lebanon to Japan. "It's racial discrimination against your own colored citizens. If you want to win our respect and to encourage democracy in our part of the world, you must make dramatic progress in the next few years in establishing full equality for American Negroes. Not only will we Asians admire you for what you accomplish, but your own success will give us new faith that the reforms which are so urgently needed in Asia can be achieved through democratic means."

No American returning from Asia can doubt that the status of the American Negro is a key to our country's relationship with the awakening nations of Asia and Africa. The colored peoples who comprise two-thirds of the world's population simply cannot think about the United States without considering bitterly the limitations under which our 15,000,000 Americans with colored skins are living.

Communist propagandists, of course, exaggerate the picture. They tell Asians that lynch law is the rule with us. They make the fantastic assertion that the atom bomb was dropped on Japan and not on Germany because the Japanese are colored while the Germans are white. But make no mistake about it, the resentment would still be with us if the Communists shut up shop tomorrow. Often it is the most conservative Asian leaders and newspapers who feel most intensely on the subject.

Some thoughtful Americans, fearful that each step may do more harm than good, have cautioned us to move slowly. But the world situation and our responsibilities of leadership enter at this point and tell us that time is running out. The struggle for the very survival of the free way of doing things requires America to show that democratic methods can solve deep-rooted injustice quickly and peacefully.

On Jan. 1, 1963, we will celebrate 100 years of emancipation. How far will we have come by the close of that century toward full freedom for all Americans? Any great change takes time, but 100 years is a long, long time. In these days it seems long enough to accomplish almost anything. A century ago, half the world was dominated by European colonial masters. Communism was a distant spectre advanced in Europe by a few bookish cranks.

In this country, our Pacific West was just being opened to settlement. Free compulsory public education was still a new and questionable proposition; the automobile, airplane and mass production, which have remade our world, were unknown. Looking back, the changes and achievements are breathtaking.

If all this can be done in one century, surely it is not unreasonable to think that 100 years is time enough to see that American Negroes receive the full rights and dignity to which every man is entitled under a democratic government. If 100 years is not long enough, then what will it take?

In the last decade our progress has been rapid. Indeed, it is fair to say that we have done more since the end of the war to eliminate discrimination than in any similar period of our history. The following is only indicative of the many accomplishments which I was happy to be able to report in Asia.

The poll tax has been eliminated in all but five states, and in these remaining states an increasing number of Negroes are paying the tax in order to cast their vote.

Direct attempts to disfranchise Negroes both in general elections and in party primaries have been struck down again and again by the Supreme Court.

In 1948, only 750,000 Negroes were registered to vote in the Southern states. In 1952, this figure increased to 1,300,000, and it is believed that 3,000,000 will be registered by 1956.

The Supreme Court has ruled against segregation in higher education, and now is considering the question of whether any kind of racial separation in public education is constitutional. Only this past week Secretary of Defense Charles E. Wilson ordered an end to the segregation of school children on all U.S. military posts by Sept. 1, 1955.

In the last few years, the courts have also refused to enforce restrictive racial agreements in housing, prohibited segregation in interstate travel and upheld an old law outlawing discrimination in restaurants in the District of Columbia.

The American Negro has made similar progress in improving his economic position. In 1951, our Negro citizens were spending $15 billion annually, which is more than the national income of Canada. Between 1940 and 1950, the average income of Negroes tripled, while that of white citizens increased only one and one-half times.

This adds up to an impressive record. It is doubtful whether any country in the last decade has made as much progress in eliminating such a serious blight on its democracy as has America. Yet no thoughtful person can deny that we have a long way to go before our democracy can be said to belong fully to all of its citizens.

As we approach the 100th anniversary of Lincoln's Emancipation Proclamation, it is essential that we consider objectively and without rancor what remains to be done. The list is substantial.

In practically all of our major cities, there are still segregated ghettoes into which tens of thousands of Negro families are squeezed.

Although the average income of the American Negro has increased tremendously, it is still only half that of the average American white.

Because of inferior medical care, the life expectancy of our Negro population is seven years less than that of whites.

According to the United States census, 9.2 per cent of all

homes occupied by white Americans are dilapidated almost beyond repair, while among Negroes the figure is four times greater. Of the new privately financed dwellings which have been built by private builders in the last twenty years, only 1 per cent has come into possession of the 10 per cent of the population which is Negro.

Although education facilities for Negroes have steadily improved, and some Southern cities such as Atlanta have shown spectacular improvements, the annual expenditures per Negro child in some of our segregated school systems still run far below those for white children.

But perhaps the most deplorable blot on our national record is Washington, D. C., the capital of our nation, which belongs to all the people of America. The Negro one-third of Washington's population still goes to segregated and inferior schools. The Catholic parochial schools alone accept children of all races and on an equal basis. Only one-fourth of Washington's "public" playgrounds are open to both Negro and white children.

When we look at this record of discrimination in terms of our religious and political principles, I am convinced that there are few Americans, North and South, who are not distressed. Most of us believe deeply in the ideals on which this country was based and we know that in the sight of God all men are equal. Most of us also recognize the implication of this faith and know that second-class citizenship in terms of inequality of job opportunities, poll taxes and segregation, whether in public schools, public accommodations or housing, should not and cannot long continue.

Our success in eliminating the remaining road blocks to full freedom for our Negro citizens by the 100th anniversary of the Emancipation Proclamation depends upon the sober and responsible efforts of men of all races. Above all, it requires us in a spirit of good will to abandon some of the fixed positions and weary clichés which have been hampering our progress. The following four points seem to me essential.

(1) *Let us call a halt to racially inspired or politically inspired name-calling.*

It is high time that Republicans and Democrats alike lifted the fight against discrimination out of the political arena and joined hands to get action. Nor do we bring ourselves any closer to a solution when we exchange epithets such as "reactionary Southerners," "Negro extremists" or "Northern radicals."

To call the South of Cordell Hull, Ellis Arnall, Frank Graham, Estes Kefauver, John Sparkman, Lister Hill, Sam Rayburn and William Fulbright "reactionary" is to make a mockery of words. For generations, the South has been in the forefront in the struggle against isolationism and for a responsible world policy. Probably more than any region, the South has supported the United Nations.

Today, the South is America's most dynamic economic and social frontier. On racial matters, a new spirit of good will is coming to the surface, helped on by millions of enlightened citizens and by the hard logic of events.

It is equally inaccurate to call the Negro leadership of today extremist. The present Negro leaders of both the National Association for Advancement of Colored People and the Urban League are moderate and restrained. Although they have been firm in pressing for faster action, they have been both responsible and effective in presenting our racial picture to the world in a fair light.

The loyalty of young Negro fighting men was proved in Korea where Communists exerted their most intense efforts to win over American Negro prisoners. These efforts were a spectacular failure and with very few exceptions the Negro soldiers remained solid in their devotion to democracy.

Nor does it make any sense to charge that "Northern radicals" are the motive behind the pressure for full equality. Some of the most conservative business men have taken the lead. Charles E. Wilson, then the president of General Electric, was chairman of the President's Committee on Civil Rights which produced the now famous report, "To Secure These Rights." In my own Connecticut, as in the state of New York, fair employment practices laws were first enacted under Republican governors.

(2) *We should recognize the fact that racial discrimination is not primarily a sectional problem.*

While some Southern whites too often insist that they know the problem best and that they should be left to solve it in their own good time, too many Northerners, while sanctimoniously criticizing the situation elsewhere, have conveniently disregarded the ugly facts of Negro life in their own urban and rural back yards.

In the midst of the Civil War, Lincoln, in his 1862 message to Congress, wisely stressed that "the people of the South are not more responsible" for slavery than the people of the North. Yankees will do well to remember that there was scarcely an old family in New England which at one time or another did not profit from the slave trade. Most of the slave ships sailed from Northern ports, with Northern captains and Northern crews.

During the Civil War, Lincoln proposed a thirty-seven year program to eliminate racial discrimination, to be completed by 1900, including full compensation to the South. The leaders of his own party turned down his plans as too gradual a compromise and insisted on "total reconstruction" imposed by Federal armies of occupation.

When such compulsion did not succeed, the impatient North all but forgot its concern for the Negro and concentrated its efforts on the economic exploitation of the almost colonial South. Is it any wonder that pride led many embittered Southerners to retreat into the past?

This record is important as a reminder of the need for humility on the part of all Americans in approaching the problem. We need understanding, not only for the Negroes whose full freedom has been so long denied them, but also understanding for the defeated and exploited Southern white, who in years past has suffered so heavily at the hands of Northern politicians and business interests.

Moreover, any fair-minded student of the facts must agree that the inability of the South to solve fully its profoundly difficult problem is no worse than the inability of the rest of the country, under far easier circumstances, to clear up its own shoddy record. Before long, half of the Negro population of the United States will live in the North. In New York State, there are now about as many Negroes as there are in Mississippi. In Pennsylvania, Ohio and Michigan, there are as many as in South Carolina or Louisiana. Any responsible Southerner who examines the Negro slum areas of Chicago, New York and other Northern cities has a right and an obligation to suggest that the North should put its own house in order.

(3) *Laws and court decisions are important but by no means a cure-all.*

Sixteen states have enacted fair employment practices legislation of some kind and in varying degrees they have proved helpful. In Connecticut, our commission on civil rights has investigated hundreds of complaints of discrimination in employment. All but two were settled satisfactorily through conciliation. In these, one against an employer and one against a union, discrimination was clearly established and an order to cease and desist was upheld in the courts. Under this legislation every emphasis is on securing agreement and fostering group education.

The same generally successful record can be told of the enforcement of our laws against discrimination in public accommodations, including housing. These laws in Connecticut and other states have been immensely helpful and have won increasing approval from all concerned.

A national Fair Employment Practices Commission would be an important step forward if it were administered in an understanding, flexible way. But we should not assume that all progress depends on such legislation. If Congress refuses to act, then we must continue to do the best we can.

Among other things, we should recognize the huge cost of eliminating the present system of segregation throughout the South and accept this as a national burden. Indeed, the Northerners who maintain that discrimination in the South is a blot on our entire American democracy should be among the first to agree to some kind of Federal grant-in-aid program to help Southern states achieve an adequate school system for all their citizens. And we should encourage President Eisenhower to use his wide executive power, as he promised, to the fullest extent for a solution of the problem in Washington and elsewhere.

(4) *Vigorous and yet responsible, non-governmental, voluntary efforts in communities throughout America are essential.*

Laws and governmental action, important as they may be, by no means get to the root of the problem in neighborhood and city-wide tensions and attitudes. There should never have been a debate over legal compulsion *versus* education, or Federal *versus* local action. Whatever one may think about Federal laws, local action is indispensable and education is vitally important.

Therefore, despite sharp differences over things like FEPC, we should all get together on a constructive program in the areas where agreement is possible. And we should search for those areas of agreement with diligence and imagination.

I believe that the greatest opportunity for constructive action lies right in our own neighborhoods in our day-to-day relations with our fellow citizens. If our growing concern about discrimination can be channeled into community programs on a national scale, spectacular progress can be achieved in the coming years.

A citizens "check list" for communities both north and south of the Mason-Dixon Line might include the following questions:

How many Negroes are in the Police Force? The Fire Department? City Hall? The School System?

Do Negroes have a full opportunity to get such jobs? And if so are they promoted solely on merit and services?

What kind of housing is available to Negroes—both public and private? What kind of medical and hospital care?

Is there any direct or indirect discrimination in public housing and entertainment facilities?

What about private enterprise jobs? Do Negro workers have jobs which use their skill to the fullest?

Is vocational, professional training freely available to Negroes?

Are the police and the courts as fair to them as to other sections of the population?

Each community might make a list of its strong and weak points and go to work to patch up the latter. A calm, objective study by non-governmental groups in each city, under the leadership of the Mayor and prominent citizens will do much to bring community agreement on the facts, and from those facts can flow constructive, democratic action.

Local civic clubs, universities, labor unions and business organizations should take the lead in what could amount to a massive, nonpartisan, popular campaign of democratic decentralized action in the best American tradition. Montclair, N. J., is one of the pioneers of this kind of community program.

Gunnar Myrdal's monumental study of the problem, "An American Dilemma," provides an important clue to such action. This is the immensely hopeful fact that the very rights which the white people are most ready to grant—equality of opportunity in jobs, equal and adequate social security and housing, and equality before the law—are the very rights which the Negroes are most anxious to secure.

Today, we must look at the problems of race prejudice in America not only in the light of our own moral convictions, but in the added light of the minimum requirements of world leadership. If, as I think likely, the great "uncommitted" world of Asia and Africa is the crucial balance in the cold war, then we must also examine racial discrimination throughout America in terms of our national security and the future of the free world.

If we do not soon end the last vestiges of second-class citizenship in America, I have grave doubts about our ability to achieve understanding with the colored peoples of these powerful, rising continents, who represent two-thirds of all mankind and on whom the future peace of the world may depend.

Just as Lincoln decided upon emancipation of the Negro slaves not only as "an act of justice," but as a "military necessity," so the achievement of racial equality all over America is now demanded on both those grounds. Lincoln was talking about precisely this problem when he said: "The dogmas of the quiet past are inadequate to the stormy present. The occasion is piled high with difficulty and we must rise with the occasion."

The Negro's Middle-Class Dream

by C. Eric Lincoln

A FAMOUS professor at a large university used to begin one of his lectures in social psychology with a description of the characteristics of a typical American family. After he had described the family's income, address, religion, the kind of car they drove, organizations to which they belonged and the occupation of the father, he would then demand to know what social class the family belonged to. But before the students could answer, the professor would add as an apparent afterthought: "Oh, yes, I forgot to mention that this is a *Negro* family!" Inevitably, the students were stymied. What had begun as a simple problem became insolubly complex by the addition of the word "Negro."

Where do Negroes fit into the prevailing American class structure? Most sociologists say they don't. Negroes have a *parallel* social structure, somewhat—but not entirely—analogous to that of whites. This social parallelism, or two-caste society, is created by the color barrier which, with the rarest exceptions, prevents lateral movement from class to class between Negroes and whites. As a prominent Negro matron said in Detroit, "We Negroes and whites visit each other at times, and frequently we belong to the

From the *New York Times Magazine,* October 25, 1964, copyright © 1964 by The New York Times Company same civic organizations and attend the same functions, but the lines are there, and no one has to say where they are."

The Negro class structure had its roots in the institution of American slavery, which, in ignoring the African's cultural presumptions, leveled all classes, and force-fused highly disparate individuals and groups into one conglomerate mass—"the Negro slave," or simply, "the Negro," a word which, in America, became synonymous with "slave" or the "descendant of slaves." Prince and servant, Eboe and Mandingo, Moslem and spirit-worshipper were all the same to the slave master, who saw them only as commodities to be bought and sold, or as a labor supply for his vast plantations.

Whatever the basis of past distinctions, the Negro social structure in America had to evolve out of conditions connected with plantation life, and within a context which recognized the absolute superiority of the white slave owner (although not necessarily that of the small, non-slave-holding white farmers, who supplied the "overseer" class, and who were looked upon by house servants and slave owners alike as "poor white trash").

The Negro's "society," then, had four more or less distinct social classes. In ascending order, they were: (1) field hands (who had least contact with the socializing influences of the white environment); (2) mechanics and artisans (bricklayers, carpenters, iron workers, bakers, etc., who were frequently hired by the month or the year to merchants or builders in the cities); (3) valets, butlers, maids, cooks and other household servants (whose frequent personal contact with whites made them the most "acculturated" class); and (4) free Negroes (who had bought their freedom or had become free by manumission—often because of faithfulness or some heroic exploit).

As slaves, the house-servant class had by far the highest proportion of mulattoes. While this did not by any means exempt them from the normal rigors incident to being slaves, including sale, the light-skinned mistresses of the slave masters were often granted petty privileges and their children were more frequently given their freedom than those of any other class.

At the end of the slave period, the mulattoes sought to establish themselves as a distinct occupational and social class within the Negro subculture. For the most part, they continued as servants and retainers to their erstwhile masters—as dressmakers, barbers, coachmen and the like. For more than a generation they clung tenuously to a certain degree of status derived from catering exclusively to the "quality" folk (as they had done in slavery) under the then current slogan of (serving) "mighty few white folks and no niggers a'tall!"

By the turn of the century, however, as the economy of the South began to revive, the mulatto "retainers" were progressively displaced by European immigrants and poor whites who were suddenly willing to do "Negro work." From that date neither occupation nor color has been a reliable index of social standing among Negroes.

Today, a light skin is not an automatic key to social status. In this day of the Negro's increasing race pride and his subtle impulse to nationalism, a light skin *can* be a handicap, especially if it is associated with "recent" miscegenation. Mass education and the indiscriminate rise to power and money of significant numbers of Negroes irrespective of their grandparents' station in the slave society have all but destroyed the effectiveness of the Negro's private color bar. Leadership in civil rights as well as in the professions has long since passed from the mulatto class. As a matter of fact, the number of mulattoes in the general Negro population seems to be declining steadily, and there is no evidence that legal integration will soon replace clandestine miscegenation in restoring the ratio of light color.

There is no unanimity of opinion as to what proportion of today's Negroes fall into the traditional "lower," middle" and "upper" classes of the Negro social structure. Prof. Tillman Cothran, head of the graduate department of sociology at Atlanta University, estimates that "not more than 25 per cent of the Negro population can be called middle-class by any reasonable standards. And not more than 5 per cent can be called upper class."

Other sociologists have argued that if one applies the full spectrum of criteria by which the white social structure is measured—ranging from income to education, affiliation, residence, etc.—the Negro middle class is reduced to 4 per cent or 5 per cent of the Negro population, and the Negro upper class vanishes altogether.

Such an estimate is, I think, too drastic. If the theory of parallel social structure is valid (and there seems to be no other way to measure "class" in an essentially segregated society), certainly it can be shown that Negroes and whites of similar education and income exhibit many of the same desires, restraints, conformities and general patterns of behavior.

America's self-image is, like that of any essentially equalitarian society, best represented by the middle class. Most Americans concede that there are a few snobs and millionaires at the top, and a few poor people in Appalachia, or somewhere, at the bottom, but America is middle class, and most Americans identify themselves as belonging to the middle class.

Implicit in this identification is a belief in "democracy" and "fair play," and also the expectation of "the good life"—a home, a car, a regular vacation, an education for the children, regular promotions, and maybe even extras like a boat or a summer place. Despite the pessimism of the sociologists, more and more Negroes share this dream, and to an increasing degree they are making it come true for themselves and their children.

The Negro middle class is made up primarily of Negro professionals, with school teachers probably constituting the largest single bloc. Teachers, along with doctors, lawyers, college professors, small businessmen, ministers, and postal workers have traditionally made up the bulk of the Negro middle class.

However, the recent availability of new kinds of jobs not previously held by Negroes has begun to modify the character of this group. Technicians, politicians, clerical and sales personnel, social workers, labor-union officials, minor government bureaucrats, and an increasing managerial class in such agencies as Federal housing and local units of national corporations have helped broaden the occupational range of the Negro middle class.

Under the Kennedy-Johnson Administration a few Negroes have been appointed to the upper echelons of Government officialdom, and within the past two or three years a few Negroes have reached executive status in white corporations. A recent dinner in New York honored seven Negroes who were vice presidents or held managerial positions in major firms. In Washington, Dr. James Nabrit, president of Howard University, and Dr. Frank Jones have been elected to the board of directors of a major bank. And in that city, several Negroes have been elected to the Board of Trade.

It is difficult to set a salary range for a given social class because social status does not depend upon money alone. Some upper-class whites are impoverished, but their families have once held fortunes and they have traditions of culture and attainment. Since the American Negro's family traditions seldom antedate the Civil War, Negro society puts an undue emphasis on money and material acquisitions. It is often said by Negro critics themselves that "anybody with a dollar, no matter where he stole it, can belong to Negro society."

Most Negroes, like most other Americans, earn their living legitimately, of course, but because of job discrimination and lack of skills, the total income of the typical middle-class Negro family will be substantially lower than that of a typical white family of the middle class. An arbitrary figure of $7,500 a year as the average income of a middle-class family would severely limit the number of Negroes who could be called middle-class.

Some Negro families do exceed a $7,500 income, but the vast majority of those who do are families in which both husband and wife work full time. Very frequently among home-buying Negroes, the head of the family works at two jobs, and occasionally at three. Such supplementary work or "moonlighting"—often driving a taxi, waiting on tables, tending bar or bell-hopping—is known as "a hustle," a term quite familiar to the Negro middle class.

In many of the large cities of the North such as New York or Boston where undeveloped land is nonexistent, the middle-class Negro, who has the means and the desire to live elsewhere, is locked in the black ghetto. Only with difficulty can he find a house or apartment outside the ghetto in a white community. As a consequence, many Negroes despair of ever leaving the slums, no matter what their education or income.

Money that would normally go for a new house is spent in the hopeless task of refurbishing antiquated apartments, or in conspicuous consumption which somehow helps them to forget the horror of living in the nation's Harlems. (In the South, the housing problem is not nearly so acute. Space for building can be had in most Southern cities, although it is likely to be in a segregated community.)

The style of living of the Negro middle class does not differ radically from that of its white counterpart. Bridge is a favorite pastime among both men and women. Those who have the leisure belong to innumerable social clubs. An increasing number of Negro men play golf and participate in water sports where facilities are available. In the South, fishing and hunting are favorite pastimes, but only if one has the full regalia of dress, and all the latest equipment shown in the sports magazines.

To a far greater degree than whites, Negroes maintain affiliation in the graduate chapters of their college fraternities and sororities, and these organizations are important indexes of social stratification. Women of a given sorority tend to marry men of its fraternal opposite number. Together, the eight major Negro sororities and fraternities constitute the nucleus of any imaginary "blue book" of Negro society.

The children of the Negro middle class are taught to aspire to middle-class standards. They take lessons in piano and creative dancing on Saturday mornings and attend carefully planned parties on Saturday night. A few are sent East to private schools.

Sometimes the interpretation of middle-class values takes an unusual twist. A Negro matron in a Memphis department store, for example, refused to corral her two children who were busily chasing through the store and littering the aisles with merchandise. She explained: "The white kids do it and the salesclerks think it's cute. I don't want my children inhibited by feeling that they can't do anything any other kids can do."

In Washington, among those aspiring to the middle class, or those who are recently "in," status is measured by the quantity and the cost of whisky served one's guests. The most conspicuous feature in such a home will be the bar appointments, and it is considered equally insulting for a guest to refuse a drink as it is for the host to offer his guests "cheap whisky." One Washingtonian gained prominence in his set by consistently being first to serve rare and expensive imports before they were well known in the Negro community. He learned what was "in" by frequenting an exclusive liquor store patronized by high Government officials.

It used to be said that the difference between a Negro making $50 a week and driving a Cadillac and a white man making $100 a week and driving a Chevrolet was that the Negro, having nowhere to live, needed the bigger car to sleep in! On Atlanta's West Side, where the Cadillac (or Lincoln) frequently comes with a split-level ranch house, it is popular to have the main (or "status") car match the house in color and appointments.

A second car for the Negro professional family is not unusual. Unlike most white middle-class families having two cars, the Negro's second car is likely to be as big and expensive as his first. An expensive automobile to drive to work is often as much a matter of personal prestige for the working Negro woman as for her husband. Hence, it is common to see large numbers of Pontiacs, Oldsmobiles and Mercurys parked near the schools where Negro women are employed as teachers.

A cottage at Oak Bluffs, on Martha's Vineyard, or in Maine or Upper Michigan can be claimed by a few. A very small number of Negroes go to Europe and to the Caribbean or Mexico on vacation. A sort of pilgrimage to Africa has high status value for those seeking to "understand their pre-Western heritage."

Some Negroes are in the middle class because there is nowhere else for them to go. These few might be considered "upper class" but there is a certain incongruity in talking about a Negro "upper class" so long as the color barrier operates to bar Negroes who are otherwise qualified from full participation in American social life. "There may not be an upper class," says Clarence Coleman, southeastern director of the National Urban League, "but there is a 'power élite' which abstracts itself from the rank and file of the middle class and participates to an important extent in the decision-making of the white power structure where Negroes are concerned."

Certainly this power élite does exist. But where it was not created by the white establishment, its power derives from white recognition and respect. Militant civil-rights leaders have discovered this again and again when the white establishment has refused to negotiate with the Negro community except through "recognized channels."

The Negro middle class, like any middle class, is preoccupied with making secure its hard-won social position. This is a characteristic of middle-class aspirations.

Because of this preoccupation the Negro middle class has been criticized frequently for not being more deeply and realistically involved in the struggle for civil rights. The criticism is well placed, for given more manpower, more money and more dedication, it is obvious that more walls could be breached. But this is not the whole story, and the lack of total involvement may not be an accurate index of middle-class feelings and intentions.

Much of the criticism has come from within the ranks of the middle class itself. The Urban League's Clarence Coleman sees the middle class as the buffer between the militants, whose aspirations are frequently unrealistic in terms of present possibilities, and the power élite which seems concerned to protect itself and its privileged positions from too rapid social change.

James A. Tillman Jr., executive director of the Greater Minneapolis Fair Housing Program and a frequent writer on problems of social change, describes the Negro middle class as "that class of Negroes who have bought the inane, invalid and self-defeating notion that the black man can be integrated into a hostile white society without conflict."

Tillman denounces the power élite as "the fixers and go-betweens who cover up rather than expose the violent nature of racism. They are," he declares, "the most dangerous clique in America."

Tillman's sentiments are echoed by Cecil Moore, militant civil-rights attorney and head of the Philadelphia N.A.A.C.P. Moore, who himself came from an accomplished West Virginia family, insists that "the Negro middle class, and all those who consider themselves above the middle class, 'subsist on the blood of the brother down under,' the brother they are supposed to be leading. Who do these Negroes think they're kidding?" he asks, and then answers his own question. "They're kidding nobody but the white folks who are willing to pay 'philanthropy' to keep from having to come to grips with the central problem, which is 'full and complete citizenship for all Americans, *right now!*' "

Despite all such criticism, however, the Negro middle class has borne the brunt of the civil-rights protest. Critics of the so-called "Black Bourgeoisie" have not always given them credit for the maturity and social responsibility upon which the Negro's fight for first-class citizenship has finally depended. The civil-rights fight, at least insofar as it visualizes an integrated society, is a middle-class fight. The N.A.A.C.P., CORE, the Urban League and the followers of Dr. Martin Luther King are all middle-class. (Indeed, the lower-class Negro has yet to be stirred by the promise of integration. He is more concerned with such immediate needs as jobs and housing than with abstract values like integration. He looks neither to Martin Luther King nor to Roy Wilkins; in fact, the leader of the black masses has yet to appear.)

In Atlanta and other Southern cities during the massive sit-ins of 1962-63, housewives baked pies, made sandwiches and provided transportation for the students. Negro businessmen donated food, gasoline and other supplies. Then doctors, nurses, professors and businessmen walked the picket lines. Similar middle-class support has assisted the activities of CORE in New York, Cleveland and other cities in the North. Voter registration is essentially a middle-class project.

Middle-class leadership and support of the civil-rights movement has not been without ambivalence. Desegregated schools frequently mean that Negro teachers will lose their jobs. Negro businessmen often lose their most competent clerical help to recently desegregated industries. Negro restaurants, drug stores, real-estate firms and the like may be adversely affected by desegregation. Some Negro churches have lost members to white churches. In a fully integrated society, the Negro middle class would lose its identity. Indeed, it would cease to exist.

Some Negroes recognize all this, of course, and fight against it. Nor can it be said that the majority of the middle class is active in the rights struggle. What can be said is that the struggle is for the most part led, financed and supported by the Negro middle class and, of course, its white allies.

Certainly, Negro leadership has become a "profession," and

in some cases a lucrative one. Yet most Negroes trying to help improve things are in search of neither fame nor fortune and may be themselves disadvantaged by the race issue. A. Maceo Walker and Jesse Turner of Memphis, for example, both executive officers of a sensitive banking business that has important white as well as Negro depositors, come to mind. These men and others like them have little to gain for themselves personally, yet they have given leadership to the civil-rights movement in their city for years. Other cases could be cited across the country.

In Washington, I talked with the distinguished Negro attorney, Belford Lawson, and his wife, Marjorie McKenzie, who, as associate judge of the Juvenile Court there, is no less distinguished. The Lawsons were undisturbed about the "black backlash" against the Negro middle class, although they felt that the middle class was just beginning to realize its responsibilities to the Negro masses. Nor did they recognize a middle-class backlash against the lower class (which has been roundly criticized by some Negroes for rioting in the streets and undoing the patient and painful accomplishments of middle-class leaders).

"We must press on to the next phase," Lawson said. "And it would be foolish to wait until all of us have reached the place a few of us have reached today. Negroes, like other people, move at different rates of speed. Our circumstances vary. Now we have a handful of civil rights and no money. Our next front is economic. We want to buy stocks in banks and corporations and sit on their boards. Every time a Negro reaches an executive position in a major corporation, he is in a better position to help that Negro in the streets without a job."

Mr. Lawson believes that it is time to stop complaining and to move on into the American mainstream. "Breaking into the white man's economy" he believes to be essential to any further progress on the part of Negroes. "In Washington," he says, "where many social and cultural affairs are integrated, many doors would open if the Negro would only push on them."

Negroes are pushing—for status and respectability and economic security. They are less concerned with integration for integration's sake than they are with being comfortable—middle-class—and unhindered in enjoying all that America has to offer. The riots in the city streets are not the work of sinister Communist agents, except where such agents move in to exploit an already festering social situation. Nor are they the work of hotheads and hoodlums bent on the destruction of the fruits of years of patient interracist effort.

They are the social expressions of pent-up anxiety and frustration which derive from the hopelessness of the conditions under which those people live. *They* cannot hope for "the good life." *They* cannot appropriate the "middle-class image," the American norm for democratic living.

I sat recently in a comfortable middle-class home in northwest Washington talking with Jerry Coward and his wife, both school teachers in the District of Columbia school system. "You know, when we moved into this neighborhood five years ago," Jerry said, "the whites all threatened to move out. A few stayed. And since that time, two brand-new white families have moved in, right down the block. Professional people, too. When white people start moving into, instead of away from, a Negro neighborhood, I guess we've got it made."

I guess they have.

Hard-Core Unemployment a Rising National Problem

by A. H. Raskin

A JOBLESS MINER stood on a sere hillside near Scranton, staring down at the shell of an abandoned Pennsylvania colliery. "I'm one of the lucky ones," he said. "I only have to wait twelve years till I get my Social Security."

In Pittsburgh, a railroad brakeman, out of work for two years, scowled at a stockbroker's ad with the caption, "Buy a Share in America."

"I can't even buy a wheelbarrow," he muttered. "When is America going to buy a share in me?"

The sense of uselessness that afflicts these two long-time foot soldiers in the army of the unemployed points up a problem that has become President Kennedy's most acute domestic worry.

It is the fear that millions of workers will remain on the industrial slag heap after the nation's output of goods and services has shaken off its present slump and moved up to record heights.

Most of the President's economic advisers are convinced that the country will enter 1962 with no significant drop in the present level of 5,500,000 jobless workers. This view is widespread among officials who believe that the recession is near bottom and that business will start perking up in the next few months.

Their pessimism about any quick cut in the idle rate is a compound of concern over the hard core of unemployment that has become ingrained in many major areas and the under-use of productive facilities that has stemmed from the economy's failure to grow fast enough.

How deeply joblessness has settled in is reflected in the rising number on the idle rolls for fifteen weeks or more. The 1,862,000 workers in this category represent one-third of all the unemployed. Eight hundred thousand have been workless for more than a half-year.

The problem of keeping workers like these from becoming frozen into unwantedness is made harder by the pouring into the work force during the Sixties of millions of new workers, the vanguard of a generation born since World War II, eager to help build an expanding America. These youngsters will troop into the overfull labor market at a pace 40 per cent faster than in the Fifties.

They will come at a time when new technology is revolutionizing work methods in offices, factories, farms, mines, transport and distribution. Automation and other far-reaching industrial changes promise a vast expansion in our ability to make more and better goods with fewer and fewer workers.

They hold out the paradoxical vista of a limitless enrichment in our potential for human well-being and of mass misery for men and women whose opportunity to share in the fruits of technological progress may be gobbled up by the same machines that produce the new wealth.

A Congressional subcommittee studying the manpower impact of automation got such an arresting picture recently of the future of electronic brains and mechanical muscles that its chairman, Representative Elmer J. Holland, Democrat of Pennsylvania, told the industrial engineer who presented the testimony:

"These computers scare you. They will do away with Congress."

The engineer discreetly forbore to say whether he felt this should be catalogued under the head of the benefits or of burdens to be derived from automation.

Long-term joblessness has put America's two most famous production centers, Detroit and Pittsburgh, on the chronic distress list alongside the ghost towns left in the wake of the flight of major textile mills from New England to the South many years ago.

Not one of the country's 150 major industrial areas now has an unemployment rate of less than 3 per cent, the dividing line the Labor Department uses to determine when job openings are in balance with job seekers.

Two-thirds of the areas are on the trouble list, with unemployment running above 6 per cent. In thirty big cities one out of every eleven workers is tramping the streets looking for a job he cannot find. In thirteen centers the jobless toll is one out of eight or higher. For the country as a whole, the ratio—adjusted to discount the effect of purely seasonal ups and downs in the job roster—is 6.9 per cent, or roughly one in fifteen without work.

In terms of the Administration's pledge to "put America back to work," the gloomiest thing about these statistics is the memory that each slump since the end of the Korean conflict eight years ago has left the country with a bigger carryover of encrusted joblessness than it had before.

After each downturn in the business cycle, the period of recovery has been shorter and the swing toward re-employment weaker. This has meant more idle workers acting as a drag on the reviving economy and a quicker slip back into recession.

The upward thrust that reached its peak in July, 1953, lasted for forty-five months and brought the unemployment rate down to 2.7 per cent. The slump of 1953-54 was followed by thirty-five months of improvement. This time the prosperity peak in July, 1957, was accompanied by a jobless rate of 4.2 per cent.

The upswing after the 1957-58 recession continued only twenty-five months before it hit its crest last May. The unemployment rate stood at 5.1 per cent and this was the jumping-off point for the present slide to a hard-times level of 6.9 per cent.

What worries the White House is the fear that a sluggish upturn now would not only leave the jobless total close to 7 per cent but would also insure another slump late in 1963 or early in 1964.

This fear is not diminished by the fact that the number of workers with jobs keeps setting new records each month. Shortly before March employment established a high for the month of 65,516,000, the President stressed that record job figures would never satisfy him while the "no-help-wanted" sign stayed up for millions in search of work.

The most optimistic members of the President's inner circle believe that it will be close to the end of next year before the country will approach the 4 per cent jobless rate Mr. Kennedy has fixed as his target for a level of full employment attainable without inflation. Other high officials are doubtful that present programs are adequate to achieve the goal at all.

The most disquieting view of the dimensions of the problem comes from the Cabinet member in closest touch with it, Secretary of Labor Arthur J. Goldberg. He is convinced that the equivalent of 7,000,000 new full-time jobs would have to be created in the next twelve months to bring idleness down to a "true level" in line with the Kennedy yardstick.

This estimate blends the total of those without any work, the "deficit" in employment of those working part time, the hordes of newcomers vying for jobs and the impact of technology. Huge as his figure is, Mr. Goldberg believes it understates the challenge. His own belief is that the Administration should not ease up until it cuts unemployment to 3 per cent. This would bring the job need close to 8,000,000.

The confidential forecasts of Labor Department analysts indicate a strong possibility that total unemployment in the early months of 1962 may top 6,000,000, the highest figure since the Great Depression. This would reflect a losing battle with the growth in the labor force, even if total national production went up by 4 per cent this year. No Administration economists count on a bigger rise in output than that.

The uncertainty over how fast and how far we will move toward re-employment flows from profound changes in the geography, character and composition of the economy, coupled with the thrust of competition from a fast-industrializing world.

These are factors totally distinct from the normal seasonal fluctuations that often create confusion about whether unemployment is getting better or worse. Not the least of the current headaches in Washington is a suspicion that the country will conclude that all is well with the jobless now that their number has started the decline that is a traditional accompaniment of spring.

The hardest thing to understand about unemployment statistics is that the number of work-hunters can vary by as much as 1,900,000 from one part of the year to another with no basic improvement or deterioration in the job situation.

The explanation lies in the extent to which the seasons influence the flow of workers in or out of the labor market, regardless of whether the general business climate is bright or stormy.

Winter brings heavy lay-offs in the building trades and other outdoor jobs. The closing of schools in June means a big influx of youths looking for vacation work. Santa Claus always enrolls a substantial number of helpers in the pre-Christmas season and lets them out before New Year's.

To provide a true index of unemployment in constant terms, the Bureau of Labor Statistics has evolved a complex weighting system for the elimination of the distortions caused by such regular seasonal shifts.

How these work can be seen by studying what would happen if the seasonally adjusted unemployment rate stayed at the March level of 6.9 per cent for a full year. With such a frozen jobless rate, the actual number of unemployed in each month would show these variations:

	1961	
March		5,500,000
April		5,000,000
May		4,800,000
June		5,600,000
July		5,200,000
August		4,600,000
September		4,200,000
October		4,000,000
November		4,600,000
December		4,700,000
	1962	
January		5,700,000
February		5,900,000

A further complication is the extent to which concealed unemployment is built into the statistics in a way that is bound to slow the recall of laid-off employes after output starts climbing.

The present employment total includes 1,745,000 workers on short time who normally work full-time. When business gets better, their employers are likely to lengthen their work week before recalling those dropped from the payroll.

In the hard-hit manufacturing industries, the average work week is running a full hour below the level of a year ago. This is the equivalent of 350,000 jobs that will be filled through more work by people now on the job, rather than by taking back the jobless.

An even more substantial factor in the ability of industrial activity to race ahead of re-employment is the sharp spurt in output per man-hour that invariably attends the first phases of a rising business cycle.

The resurgence of market demand allows businesses, made lean by the enforced austerity of the downturn, to begin cashing in on their squeeze-out of waste and the fuller utilization of their most efficient equipment. Productivity surges forward at double or triple the normal growth rate—and the idle wait to be rehired.

The long-term shrinkage of manpower needs in key sectors of industry is an outgrowth of the same basic trend toward producing more with less human toil. It is a trend that has had much more dramatic expression on the farm than in the factory.

In the last ten years our farms produced 28 per cent more food and fiber with 28 per cent fewer men, women and children at work. This is the climax of a half-century-old move toward machine planting and harvesting that has cut the number of farmers and farm hands from one-third of the national work force to one-tenth and still left us with such vast crops that we pay the farm owners not to grow them.

Newly developed picking machines indicate the probability of even more spectacular gains in farm productivity in the next few years. Many experts believe these machines will eventually end the exploitation of the country's most depressed labor group, the half-million migrant farm workers, whose annual earnings average less than $1,000 and who live in squalor reminiscent of "Tobacco Road."

The question is what will become of these workers when the machines "emancipate" them from their bondage to the crops that pay them so poorly. Uneducated and unused to city life, how will they find jobs in industries that have long waiting lists of experienced workers they are unable to employ?

This is a much starker version of the worry that stalks tens of thousands of workers shaken out of jobs in the railroads, coal mines, steel mills, automobile and aircraft factories and many other branches of industry long before the slump started putting its clamp on work opportunities ten months ago.

Rail employment has gone down from 2,000,000 to 800,000 in the last four decades; the number of soft-coal miners has fallen from 700,000 to 200,000 in the same period. The bright side of these figures is that, without the increased efficiency they reflect, neither industry could have kept alive and there would have been no jobs for anyone.

But these triumphs over rival fuels and transportation systems are more comforting to those still employed than they are to the much larger number whose jobs have evaporated. Even the survivors are made anxious by the argument of rail management that featherbedding remains responsible for $600,000,000 a year in manpower waste. The railroad unions have asked the President and Congress to halt all proposed railroad mergers on the ground that those now contemplated would add 200,000 jobs to the 400,000 abolished in the last five years.

The awareness of such large-scale job dislocations in other industries has heightened apprehension among office and factory workers at the advent of technological marvels that make it possible to do so much more with so much less labor.

No amount of assurances by employers and Federal manpower experts that the end result of new technology will be an expansion of both jobs and living standards have erased this apprehension. It goes beyond the security of present employment to disquiet over whether work doors will be locked against millions of war babies nearing the job market.

Altogether the United States will need 13,500,000 more jobs in the Sixties merely to keep abreast of the expected growth in the labor force. This means an average of 25,000 new jobs each week, on top of those required to drain the reservoir of present unemployment and to replace jobs made superfluous by improved technology.

In the last year, despite the slackness of employment opportunities, 2,500,000 more people came into the job scramble than left it through death, age, sickness or voluntary withdrawal. This was more than double the 835,000 average annual growth in the working population in the last ten years.

By the end of this decade, 3,000,000 youngsters will be starting their quest for jobs each year, as against 2,000,000 now. This almost automatically guarantees trouble in getting the over-all unemployment rate down to 4 per cent because the proportion of idleness among teen-age workers is always far higher than it is among their elders.

Present unemployment among boys between 14 and 19 in the job force is 18 per cent, almost triple the figure for men between 35 and 44. In the 20-to-24 age bracket the rate is over 14 per cent.

The most dismaying aspect of these high figures is that in a period of increased stress on skill and science the Labor Department expects that three out of ten of the 26,000,000 youngsters seeking work in the Sixties will have dropped out of high school without getting their diplomas. The unemployment rate for such dropouts runs close to 30 per cent.

Among workers old enough to vote—and less disposed to hop from job to job when work is available—unemployment has hit hardest at the unskilled and semi-skilled in manufacturing, mining and transportation. One out of every five laborers is jobless, along with one out of every eight semi-skilled mechanics and factory hands.

By contrast, only one out of fifty professional and technical workers is out of a job, one out of forty managers and executives and one out of twenty sales clerks and office workers. Much of this disparity between the plight of manual workers and those in the professional and clerical fields is, of course, attributable to the recession's concentrated impact on autos, steel and other hard-goods industries.

However, many analysts are convinced that a substantial part mirrors the long-term shift in the economy from production to service industries and from blue-collar to white-collar employment. In the last year blue-collar jobs for men dropped by 1,300,000 but white-collar jobs rose by 600,000. Among women the trend was even more startling, with office and service jobs up 700,000 while manual jobs stood almost even.

This highlights one of the most challenging social phases of the hard-core unemployment problem. The freeze-out of heavy jobs for men and the parallel expansion in lighter work openings for women is making the mother the breadwinner in many households while the father stays home with the kids.

In Masontown, Pa., near Pittsburgh, Mrs. Betty Milano tells a story that is a commonplace in many steel and coal towns. She has had to take a job in a shirt factory because her steelworker husband has been out of work for six months. Her third child is due in June.

Two-fifths of all the jobless—a total of 2,400,000—are heads of families, now unable to earn enough to support their dependents. Forty per cent of these have wives or children at work to help pay the family bills.

The trend toward more working women is no recession phenomenon. The Government expects 6,000,000 more women to be in the labor force in 1970 than there were last year. This will bring their number to 30,000,000 in a total force of 87,000,000. More important, it will mean a 25 per cent rise in women workers while the number of men workers goes up only 15 per cent.

Another troublesome social aspect of the squeeze on job opportunities for unskilled and semi-skilled manual workers is the knockout blow it delivers to the employment hopes of many Negro workers. They have tended to find their steadiest and most rewarding jobs in the kind of mine, factory and dock operations that lend themselves most readily to automation.

Despite the anti-discrimination laws that are supposed to immunize them against hiring bias, their current unemployment rate is more than double that of white workers. Handicapped by lack of education and the difficulty of breaking the bias barrier, many see little chance for acquiring the skills that might lead them into new endeavors.

The justification for this despondent view is to be found in the figures on long-term unemployment, which show an even more lopsided proportion of Negroes than the general ranks of the unemployed. Workers over 45 also tend to become glued into chronic joblessness in disproportionate numbers.

An especially disquieting aspect of this condition is the extent to which the list of workers idle fifteen weeks or longer has been climbing in good times as well as bad. In the prosperous period from 1951 through 1953, only about 250,000 workers were listed in this group. In the 1959-1960 period their total had grown to nearly 1,000,000. Now the recession has brought it close to 2,000,000.

For many of these unwanted workers the re-employment problem has been made tougher by the interstate and, increasingly, international battle for industry that has caused a large-scale transfer of work from established production centers in the East and Midwest.

The efficiency gains permitted by automation have stirred new interest by many companies in availing themselves of offers to move into community-built plants and enjoy tax privileges not available in their old locations.

Much of the resistance to the President's plan for aiding distressed areas, which the House passed last week, stemmed from fear in the more industrialized states that the holding out of subsidies by the needy regions would prompt still more employers to move to places where they could get ultramodern plants free, plus lower labor bills and a reprieve from union-enforced curbs on management.

A study by Seymour L. Wolfbein, Deputy Assistant Secretary of Labor, demonstrated recently how the post-war industrial map had changed to create stagnation in some areas while work opportunities multiplied in others.

Florida and the seven Southwest states from California to Texas had an employment growth more than double the national average, while all eighteen Eastern and Midwest states lagged behind the average. New Jersey was one of the few that came close.

Now a global dimension has been added to the industrial tug-of-war. United States companies have been investing nearly $3,000,000,000 a year in foreign properties. Union leaders have complained that much of this investment amounts to an export of American jobs abroad, especially where a significant share of the foreign production is shipped back to this country for sale in the domestic market.

Add to this the jeopardizing of jobs in many sections by the regular flow of low-price imports from low-wage countries, the pooling of facilities through business consolidations and the intensified cost-consciousness induced by the recession and the step-up in competition at home and abroad.

The sum of all these factors has left the White House certain that the gross national product—the yardstick that measures our total output of goods and services—can go up by as much as $20,000,000,000 from its present annual rate of roughly $500,000,000,000 with little or no reduction in the size of the unemployment problem.

White House Seeks Cure for Unemployment Blight

by A. H. Raskin

A DEBATE, muted but intense, is going on inside the White House over next steps in the Administration's fight against unemployment. The question is whether President Kennedy should ask Congress for dramatic new moves to put the jobless back to work or limit himself to pushing the measures he has already proposed for economic revival.

The President, wrestling with urgent international problems, has indicated that he will wait until late this month before making his decision.

It will reflect his promised "second look" at the sufficiency of the anti-recession program he started rushing to Capitol Hill soon after his inauguration Jan. 20. But it will also have to embody the President's evaluation of a contradictory series of political, economic and human considerations.

He must weigh the prospect of new and bitter fights with Congress against the virtually unanimous opinion of his chief economic and labor advisers that the country will go into next year with little or no reduction in the present total of 5,500,000 unemployed.

Few of these advisers see any real likelihood that the present proposals will be adequate any time in 1962 to cut the jobless rate from its March level of nearly 7 per cent to the 4 per cent the President has fixed as his yardstick for full employment.

Nevertheless, the President is under strong counsel from many of his key officials to shun the twin perils of bigger deficits and more inflation that would accompany an intensified back-to-work effort.

A major factor in this caution is the trouble the President is having in getting his current program past the powerful conservative coalition of Republicans and Southern Democrats in Washington.

He was beaten in the House on the minimum wage bill; he squeaked through to a hairline victory in the Senate on the financing of emergency unemployment insurance benefits.

The measures still awaiting action have a cloudy future.

The economy bloc is complaining about the $2,800,000,000 of red ink already contemplated in the Kennedy budget for the fiscal year beginning July 1. Worry over the slow upward creep of prices that has continued through the slump has been aggravated by the nation's unfavorable balance of international payments and by the expectancy of further cheapening of the dollar implicit in the feverish pace of recent trading in Wall Street.

The argument of those who warn against inflaming relations with Congress by asking for anything more is buttressed by the widespread disposition among citizens with jobs to feel that the economy is on the mend and will heal itself without further forced feeding from the Government.

This sentiment is likely to find additional solace in the next two months as the number of workers on the unemployment rolls goes down in response to the regular spring resurgence of construction and other outdoor jobs. The Administration has emphasized that seasonal dips of this kind may often mask a worsening of the basic unemployment situation, but there is scant indication that such reminders have taken hold.

The probability is, too, that each week will bring cheery business news as one economic indicator or another flashes a signal of rising industrial activity. All these factors militate against bold new undertakings directed specifically at hastening the pace of re-employment.

Present indications are that the Administration has shelved

suggestions for giving the economy an extra boost through a temporary tax cut or a large-scale expansion in public services and community improvements. The President's forthcoming tax program is expected to confine its focus on economic stimulation largely to a tax bonus plan to encourage employers to invest in more efficient plants and equipment.

Despite this prospect for limited additional measures to curb joblessness, some members of the White House inner circle are stressing the notion that the Administration will not have fulfilled its pledges to the country if it gets the economy up to record production levels without also restoring the feeling of millions of idle men and women that they have a useful contribution to make in our industrial society.

This is a view the President himself has repeatedly set forth. It is now being expounded with special vigor by Secretary of Labor Arthur J. Goldberg, who is stumping the nation with the message that at least 7,000,000 more jobs will have to be created in the next twelve months if unemployment is to get down to the President's 4 per cent target.

The difficulty with trying to generate so many jobs so fast is that it would require an increase of roughly $70,000,000,000 in the present gross national product of $500,000,000,000. This is more than triple the growth in the economy that anyone in the Administration realistically expects to achieve this year.

In effect, the President will have to cast his own vote on whether he is doing enough to jack up the speed of economic expansion, one of the issues on which he was most critical of the Eisenhower Administration. A favorite Kennedy gibe at the Republicans was that they cared more about balancing the budget than about people.

The decision the President must make is complicated by the multiplicity of factors that have made the unemployment problem so sticky. Even before the recession began last June, the number of jobless workers had shown a persistent tendency to grow in good times as well as bad.

Pockets of ingrained idleness have developed in major manufacturing centers, mining states, textile communities, and other areas left prostrate by the shifting tides of technology and economic geography.

Automation and other radical improvements in ways of doing more with less physical effort have cut manpower needs in many fields of production, distribution and communications. The job problem is made tougher by the necessity for finding work in the next decade for 13,500,000 more workers, by far the largest group entering the labor force in any ten-year period.

This assortment of tribulations necessitates a many-sided attack. On one point, however, there is almost universal agreement. All the approaches will succeed best in a healthy, growing economy. That is the starting point for every attempt to whittle down the jobless rate.

This means that concern for expanding the total output of goods and services must parallel all specialized efforts to retain the hard core of unemployed workers, to pep up distressed communities, to ease the human hardships engendered by technological displacement and to equip youngsters with the skills fast-changing industries may need.

The place where major difference develops is over how much of the task belongs to the Government, how much to management and how much to labor. The difference is equally sharp over how each should fulfill its part of the total responsibility.

The National Association of Manufacturers asserts that the high road to full employment is an end to the "profit squeeze" caused by high corporate taxes and the power of unions to push up wages through industry-wide strikes.

"The profit motive is what gives our economy its dynamic quality, and we can be assured there will be no unused capacity in either manpower or material resources when the possibility exists for employing it at a profit," the association says.

The American Federation of Labor and Congress of Industrial Organizations is convinced that much more Government spending is essential to keep unemployment from growing even bigger. Stanley M. Ruttenberg, its research director, estimates that $20,000,000,000 to $40,000,000,000 will have to be added to the Federal debt in the next few years if the economy is to avoid running downhill.

The one Government remedy the federation likes least is the one the N. A. M. likes best. It is the holding out of tax incentives to spur more investment in new plants and machinery. Labor contends that corporations already enjoy too many tax concessions and that giving them more will simply accelerate another downturn.

A similar division of counsel on what needs doing to restore jobs comes from two former chairmen of the President's Council of Economic Advisers.

Dr. Arthur F. Burns, who headed the Council in President Eisenhower's first term and now serves on President Kennedy's Advisory Committee on Labor-Management Policy, finds no basis for pessimism about the probability of a vigorous upturn without large-scale Government spending.

"We may have a little more of a problem than in the past, but I see no evidence that the nature of the problem is dramatically different," Dr. Burns says. "A jobless rate of nearly 7 per cent can't be cured in six or eight months, though we should make some headway in that period. After that it should start coming down substantially."

Leon H. Keyserling, President Truman's chief economic adviser, feels the present Administration has brought forth a very advanced social program but has failed to give it anything like the economic push it needs.

He recommends that Government outlays be stepped up enough to create a growth rate of 5 per cent, instead of the 3½ per cent now sought. He is fearful that adherence to the present program will limit the actual growth to 2½ per cent, or half the expansion he considers necessary to provide jobs.

While the economists in and out of Government quarrel about how much is not enough, specific attention is being given to two problems that will not automatically solve themselves through the achievement of a high-level general economy.

The first is the restoration of job hopes in areas where unemployment has been heavy for so long that they are classified as chronically depressed. The other is an effort to guarantee that workers will not have to bear the full cost of automation in the form of lost jobs.

Both houses of Congress have passed a bill to provide $394,000,000 in bootstrap aid for distressed communities and their workers. Attracting new industries through loans and grants for new facilities is the bill's main goal. It also makes available

$14,500,000 to retrain workers and supply them with subsistence benefits while they learn.

The big uncertainty is whether the money is sufficient to make any substantial dent in the deeply implanted problems of areas that have upward of 750,000 jobless workers—many out of work so long their capacity for retraining is doubtful. The Republicans opposed the measure on the ground that it would bring only "bitter disillusionment" to the unemployed. Many who voted for it share this fear.

Despite such doubts, Commerce Department officials say they will not let the program degenerate into a show-window operation. They hope the Federal funds will serve as seed corn for intensified industrial development enterprises by state and local bodies.

William L. Batt Jr., Pennsylvania's Secretary of Labor and Industry, is reportedly slated for appointment as administrator of the program. His long identification with efforts to relieve job blight in his home state is cited as an earmark of the department's determination to make the community-rescue venture work.

How to soften the human impact of automation and thus moderate the climate of apprehension that has acted as a brake on the installation of new technological developments in many industries is a matter of top-level attention at the White House.

Unhappily, no one in Government, industry or labor has any precise idea of the dimensions or timetable of the problem that will have to be handled. So explosive has the whole issue become in labor relations that many employers treat information about the manpower effects of future installations of electronically controlled tools or office machines as military secrets.

Representative Elmer J. Holland, Democrat of Pennsylvania, who heads a House Labor subcommittee investigating automation's effects on jobs, has had such a hard time getting industrialists to testify that he threatened to subpoena them.

The Labor Department is moving to overcome the data gap by organizing a special unit to collect and monitor reports on how smoothly or how poorly the process of transition goes in companies that introduce new technological processes.

Some unions have started to press for a shorter work week as their answer to automation. The National Maritime Union wants a thirty-hour week in its contract this June. The United Steelworkers of America is asking Congress for a change in the Wage-Hour Act to cut hours from forty to thirty-two.

President Kennedy has made it plain that he is against any reduction in basic hours. His belief is that the country still has enough uncompleted tasks to keep everybody busy full-time. He regards maximum speed in introducing more efficient machinery as a key to the kind of rapid economic growth that will open the door to such utilization of our manpower. . . .

The President has initiated a search for national answers through the public, labor and industry members of his new Advisory Committee on Labor Management Policy. He assigned the group, under the chairmanship of Secretary Goldberg, the duty of suggesting policies to balance the burdens and blessings of automation.

The group was to have had its second meeting last Monday, but notice that several members could not be present forced a postponement until May 1. The Administration, mindful of the swift collapse of most past efforts to promote top-level labor-management cooperation, is seeking to make sure that everyone shows up the next time.

All this still leaves a substantial question mark over the economy's capacity to bring into being enough new jobs to offset the shrinkage in work opportunities in automated industries and to accommodate the millions flocking into a saturated job market.

The solutions that emerge from collective bargaining are primarily directed at protecting those now in jobs. But the chronic unemployment will not be eased unless equal attention is given to expanded opportunities for those already jobless and those who have not yet had their first jobs.

The pressure for a shorter work week is certain to grow if the only answer for technological displacement is severance pay and retraining for nonexistent jobs. Earlier retirement and longer vacations will also be on labor's list of proposals to spread the work.

More fluidity in seniority, pension and benefit programs, an overhaul of the wage system to put more stress on income guarantees, allowances by the employer or the Government for moving workers from one city to another—all these are in prospect as long-term developments.

All this reflects labor's belief that the cost of helping workers and communities to adjust to changing technology should be considered as essential an investment item as plant or equipment. Industry worries that the piling up of protective charges will be so great as to wipe out the potential gains in efficiency.

The economy's basic vitality is reflected in its ability to keep setting high records in employment at the bottom of a business slump. Even now there are many thousands of unfilled jobs for workers with skills ranging from stenographers to auto mechanics.

An expansion in the size and scope of the Federal-state employment service would help effect a better matching of jobs and job hunters on a national scale. It would also permit a better cataloguing of the growth areas as a guide to useful training.

A permanent overhaul of unemployment insurance standards would help to eliminate the need for stop-gap emergency action in depression periods. Such action usually comes only after many thousands have exhausted their protection and have crossed over into the need for public charity.

The Government's hope is that, once the economy can be spurred to a high rate of growth, much of the anxiety over job security will be erased. It foresees new products and new services as ushering in a new era of abundance marked by high employment.

All that is needed is a bridge over which the millions now idle can walk to jobs. That is the element still missing in the employment picture.

Part 6

SOLUTIONS, STRATEGIES, AND TACTICS

THIS FINAL SECTION leaps from Harry Hopkins' 1935 plea for work instead of mere handouts for the unemployed, to the present. Today the story about income, wealth, and poverty in America is much too variegated and tortuously complex to convey through a few selections a total picture of the efforts to do something about them.

One of the key issues now is that of a minimum income for all persons, regardless of work status or employability. Michael Reagan's article is a strong and straightforward argument for such a guaranteed income, based on Robert Theobald's ideas. In one form or another, and for at least certain segments of our poverty population, some type of guaranteed-income policy may soon become a reality.

Although written only one year after the actual implementation of the anti-poverty program, Nathan Glazer's early 1966 description and analysis of its "grand design" is an excellent document on the patterns and issues that would emerge in later debates over the nation's anti-poverty commitment. Essentially, that blueprint was motivated by the designers' belief that existing welfare and educational institutions needed more than "improvement" and money to break down the obstacles keeping Americans in poverty. The policy-makers may also have entertained a degree of romanticism concerning the idea of giving the poor a voice in their own affairs through new community-action agencies. These agencies would be independent enough to put pressure on other local agencies and practices (such as school authorities, the police, landlords or housing managers, and welfare agencies) to improve conditions for the poor. Glazer's persistent question is whether or not the grand design (especially the community-action component, which received about 40 per cent of anti-poverty funds) can really reduce poverty.

The last two selections are, in a way, continuations of this issue. Patrick Anderson's article about Saul Alinsky, a professional organizer of the poor long before Community Action Agency became a household word, is an in-depth anatomy of Alinsky's ideology and tactics of making the poor into an organization, not merely a movement. The article is pertinent for many reasons today, not the least being its discussion of Alinsky's conviction that the Negro poor must have white allies—perhaps separate and not equal, but nevertheless allies.

Robert Kennedy's support staff of brilliant and idealistic young men included Adam Walinsky, whose 1969 review of Daniel P. Moynihan's *Maximum Feasible Misunderstanding* is the last entry in this book. The book is primarily about the presumed short-comings of social scientists (excluding Moynihan, of course) who allegedly designed and implemented in a naive fashion the community-action component of the War Against Poverty. Despite all the harping and all the justifiable criticisms of the Office of Economic Opportunity, especially its Community Action program, Walinsky reminds us "that for all its terrible failings, it is the only federal agency organized and directed exclusively at improving the life and lot of the American poor." The review of Moynihan's book, which appeared within days after his appointment by President Nixon as a top White House adviser on urban (read: poverty) problems, is a contribution in itself because it gives us the answer to the question not really answered by Moynihan: Why was there a low priority on economic and job-related programs within the Office of Economic Opportunity? Moynihan believes the answer lies in the ignorance and naiveté of community-action romanticists who were apparently more interested in making "maximum feasible participation" an end in itself, rather than one technique among many for reducing poverty.

In contrast, Walinsky lays the failure to emphasize economic development and job programs at the door of the Vietnam War. Such programs would have cost much more than the OEO program as it was originally and subsequently constructed. And the Johnson administration felt it could not effectively fight the Viet Cong and poverty at the same time, its own rhetoric to the contrary. "The great failing of the community action program," in Walinsky's own view, "was that it never had very much to organize about. . . . The organizing should have been around programs to deal with the depression-level unemployment rates that still prevail among the urban poor."

Relief Through Work

by Harry L. Hopkins

THERE ARE NOW around 5,000,000 American families on relief. That is to say that there are 5,000,000 families receiving public assistance because the head of the family has no job. This figure, of course, does not take into account that other extremely important fraction of the American population, the unemployed who have so far staved off going on relief rolls, often by means dangerous to the health of their children.

Our wage-paying habits are such that it frequently takes the pooled earnings of every available member to keep the family going even at a subsistence level. In 1,000,000 of the relief families there is no employable member. But after we have taken into consideration the large numbers who are temporarily on relief because they are victims of the drought, there remain about 3,500,000 relief families containing slightly over 5,000,000 jobless workers, employable in the sense that they are between 16 and 65 years of age, able and willing to work.

The 1,000,000 households which contain no breadwinners present the usual variants of our chronic dependency problem: old age, widowhood, orphanage and physical disability. In these classifications we find our most out-and-out examples of unemployability.

It is important to remember that unemployability is relative and consists of other elements than a man's ability to sustain his

From the *New York Times,* March 10, 1935, copyright © 1935, 1963 by The New York Times Company.

powers at par. Unemployability is measured by private industry. A man is employable if he is sufficiently skilled, quick and strong to be profitable to his employer under highly competitive labor costs. Workers who cannot market their labor in a tightening technological scheme may still have ability and strength to do a full man's work under a less fiercely exclusive economy. We should be very chary of this word "unemployable." It is a word that sticks. It can do a great deal of damage both to our reasoning and to the person to whom it may be applied.

However, let us suppose that for lack of an employable member one-fifth of our relief households are to become quasi-permanent charges upon straight public assistance and that they will have to be given old-age pensions, mothers' aid, straight relief or institutional care. Are we going to make no differentiation between these incapable dependents and the five million workers who are on relief solely because they have no job? Are we going to pursue a course which can have no other end in view than to turn the relief population into a permanent charge upon the public treasury? Can we afford this course financially even if we have no particular interest in the fulfillment of life for as many persons as are physically capable of achieving it?

This last objective is sometimes attributed to the alleged sentimentalism of the social worker, though it has long been the accepted objective of that most realistic of all professions, medicine. Often those economists and financiers who most shy away from the humane objectives of better living for larger numbers and retreat behind what sometimes seem to be irrefutable columns of mounting costs are the very ones who complain that straight relief creates dependency by corroding character. They deplore that once upstanding citizens now accept public money without a murmur and come back for more. It sometimes would appear that the classical economist is a very slipshod social thinker when he faces the human realities of unemployment.

The unemployed worker, watching himself get soft and feeling his skill slip away from him, cannot be so detached. He wants a job and he knows why.

In his desire for a job and in his reasons for wanting it lies the major argument for a work program as over against straight relief. In order to understand this argument we have to analyze the attitudes of the society which still creates the world of the jobless man. Before long we may discover that these are hangover attitudes from times when long hours of labor were prerequisite to the production of whatever wares we used. They are also hangover ideas from the time when any man of energy could make his place in the competitive labor market.

In spite of the fact that we envy those who live on their income, we still, in a time when the push of a button displaces scores of workers, have sufficient regard for the man as producer that we view him with scorn when he is producing nothing. In our more rational moments we conceal this scorn, but deep in their hearts most breadwinners resent the jobless, as the jobless resent their own state. No one, not even the scornful, is so aware of this scorn as the man without a job.

It is easy to understand the worker's hostility to the unemployed as a class. It is historical that the poor support the poorer. Most self-respecting families make a strenuous effort to support their dependents before they turn them over to the public. So, at the beginning, the unemployed man represents a threat to the household budget of his brothers and cousins.

Later, when family resources or patience are exhausted, the unemployed man betakes himself to the relief office. It is then that the worker finds the close relationship between private employment and a glutted labor market.

Neither is the man without a job under illusions as to his popularity with the employer. Although he cheapens labor costs by adding to the labor supply, his chances for re-employment diminish with every week of idleness. Moreover, to the employer as taxpayer, the man without a job has become unpleasantly expensive.

Here of all places he has least choice as to what course to pursue if he would please the business man. If he wants work he is considered too demanding, since work relief costs more than straight relief. But if he accepts straight relief with its deteriorating accompaniments he is accused of wishing to become a permanent dependent of the taxpayer.

Both of these are social and economic problems. There is a third that touches him, if not more importantly, at least more intimately. That is his changing relationship to his family.

If in the past we could have provided the necessaries without working for them, there would never have grown up in us the admiration for work that most of us profess to have. But as it is, we have to deal with the simple truth that the majority of people have associated the chance to earn their living with self-respect. Most of our family habits and customs are constructed around the central fact that the father is the breadwinner. He must be respected. The mother is the domestic guardian. She can be looked to for protection, but she, too—at least this is the traditional notion—should be protected.

Around variations of this theme we have built up many of the fictions of self-advancement, by which individuals have been allowed and even persuaded to believe that any poor boy can rise to the top.

But the unemployed man now has been moved out clean from the world to which he belonged, and from the conventions to which he once subscribed. Not only has he failed to provide for his family what it needs, but the world still believes, except for the fortunate few at the top, that there is something intrinsically good in earning a living. It is a deep-seated conviction. It is, in fact, such a deep-seated conviction that without work men actually go to pieces. They lose the respect of their wives, sons and daughters because they lose respect for themselves; even though they have broken no laws and even though their deportment as fathers and neighbors continues to be above reproach.

It is for this reason that straight relief, direct relief, the dole, or whatever you want to call it, maintains life not at a subsistence level, but at a level of deterioration.

The loss of skill, the loss of work habits, muscle and resolve are only the half of it. The complete loss of any sense of importance to their job, to their families, to society and to themselves is the loss which is being sustained by millions of our workers. By their enforced idleness we are laying by a store of social problems.

Because of these three different enmities which the unemployed have incurred through no fault of their own—that of business, of their recent fellow-workers and in a sense of the forces which sustain and elevate the family as a unit of social life—the unemployed are in danger of being perpetuated as a class. They will have to seek and are already seeking through protest groups social protection as a class.

The most ominous threat which the unemployed can hold over the present structure is that they should as a class be perpetuated, unwillingly unproductive, and held in a straitjacket of idleness.

For a Guaranteed Income

by Michael D. Reagan

THE CONTRAST between America's ability to expand production and her inability to expand employment to keep pace presents a serious problem of public policy, and this is now almost universally conceded. But the solutions enacted and proposed to date— tax cuts, investment incentives, manpower retraining programs, work-study aid for college students, for example—all assume that it still makes sense to work toward the goal of full employment, and that government's major task is to help people prepare themselves for jobs in the private sector of the economy.

One group of publicists, economists and educators (a group which included this writer) has recently presented a more radical analysis, however. This group, calling itself the Ad Hoc Committee on the Triple Revolution,* explicitly challenges the possibility of *ever* reaching full employment in the face of automation's increasing ability to replace human muscle and skills with machines.

Asserting that automation is creating the capacity to produce all the goods and services our society can use without employing all the men and women who will seek places in the labor force, the Ad Hoc Committee (A.H.C.) fears that "the traditional link between jobs and income is being broken." Its prescription is therefore as radical as its analysis: it proposes that "society,

* The revolutions: (1) cybernation, or automated machinery; (2) weaponry—the development of weapons capable of obliterating civilization; (3) civil rights.

through its appropriate legal and governmental institutions, undertake an unqualified commitment to provide every individual and every family with an adequate income as a matter of right." In short, a guaranteed income.

Why is the A.H.C. so pessimistic about full employment? The first reason is the record of over six consecutive years in which the unemployment rate has not fallen below 5 per cent, despite greatly increased production. Worse still, among unskilled laborers the unemployment rate has been above 12 per cent since 1957; among Negroes, above 10 per cent.

This unprecedented nature of the situation we face is revealed in cold statistical terms in the President's 1964 Manpower Report: in the period 1957-63, 4.3 million new jobs were created —but of these only 300,000 full-time jobs were generated by private demand. Even more startling, for the five years prior to 1963 there was an actual net decline in the number of privately generated positions. Most new jobs were the result of increased governmental employment (especially teachers) and procurement (especially military).

The extent to which automation lies behind the present difficulties is a matter of dispute; that it adds considerably to the problem of cyclical unemployment is hardly debatable. Secretary of Labor Wirtz has characterized the automatic machinery that is being introduced widely today as having, on the average, the skills of a high school graduate. The question is, will we ever be able to find jobs for humans whose skills are less developed than those of machines?

How would the guaranteed-income proposal handle the problems? What are the arguments for and against it? Are there any precedents?

The claim that the job-income link is being broken has two levels of meaning, for there are two types of jobs: those arising from production for the market and those—such as teaching, highway construction, public health protection, much of basic research—which are called forth by governmental rather than market demand. As Robert Theobald (in some ways the "father" of the current proposal) says in his book, "Free Men and Free Markets": "Our scarcity is one of market-supported jobs, not of work that needs to be done."

What Theobald and the A.H.C. mean by a guaranteed income

is, in part, that we cannot rely upon privately generated demand to create jobs, but must use government to underwrite income-producing work: to guarantee that public services and public works will take up some of the slack created by the march of automation in the traditional goods-producing industries. This is not too far from the thinking of President Johnson, who said recently that if the tax cut proved to be an insufficient stimulant he would advocate increased public works.

In larger part, and this is the more radical and controversial aspect of the proposal, it is claimed that a guaranteed income—without any work—is needed for the aged, those of low skills and education, those discriminated against by race and those displaced too late in life to learn a new skill and find employment to utilize it—in short, for those whom the A.H.C. expects to be an increasing number.

Suppose that every family were guaranteed $3,000 a year. What would it cost? A detailed answer cannot be given at this point, yet we have one related estimate that is worth considering. The President's Council of Economic Advisers says that "about $11 billion a year would bring all poor families up to the $3,000 income level. . . . The burden—one-fifth of the annual defense budget, less than 2 per cent of Gross National product—would certainly not be intolerable."

The economic hope would be that the giving of income which would be spent by its recipients would, by increasing demand for the goods produced in automated plants, elicit higher profits and market-related incomes from which tax returns would help pay the costs. Whether deficits in the national budget would be involved cannot be foretold at this time. What is known from the experience of recent years is that deficits are definite in the absence of a sufficient stimulus to the full use of resources.

Even if costs were not an obstacle, would anyone be willing to work at all, given the availability of nonwork income? How would the necessary dirty jobs get done?

First of all, loosely following Theobald's suggestions, guaranteed income would be used by the permanently unemployable—the coal miner automated out of the only work he knows at age 45, the clerk replaced by an inventory computer, and others for whom there is no choice because they lack jobs in any case.

Second, there would be some who simply prefer not to work

—perhaps chiefly those already categorized as welfare chiselers. Also, some would use the guaranteed income by preference because they would rather be relatively poor but free to do what they wished than better off financially in jobs alien to their interests. Many creative young people—artists, writers, actors, poets— might make this choice, for our society does little today to provide market or governmental jobs for them.

Third, there would be those workers who earned less than $3,000 a year and whose wages would need to be supplemented to bring their income up to that level.

The unpleasant jobs—the dirty ones that still require human muscle power or dull routine—would, of course, still have to be done. Because one could have an income above the poverty level without doing them, they would have to carry much higher wages than at present to attract workers. In the long run the higher costs would lead toward further automation, further reducing the number of jobs. At the other end of the scale, jobs requiring extremely high skill levels or carrying great burdens of managerial responsibility would continue to attract talent because of their intrinsic interest and increasingly higher incomes.

There would thus be a distribution between the job holders and the workless partly by fate (those who lack the skills called for by any job); partly by economic incentives (most men who can earn $6,000 will not be satisfied with an income of $3,000— witness the extent of moonlighting); and partly by choice (creative activity that society does not otherwise support, or work because of inner drives).

The crux of the proposal is that jobless income would be absolutely guaranteed: an Office of Guaranteed Income would stand ready to provide the agreed minimum income without question to any jobless applicant. Incentives to work would have to be revolutionized: the threats of poverty, starvation or even a means test would no longer be available as goads. Employers would have to make work more attractive; the bargaining position of employes—even as individuals—would be much stronger. The economy would have a vast new "built-in stabilizer" —along with considerable disruption of the labor market.

The average man would face a unique choice when work became voluntary; his largest problem might be to make satisfying use of new-found leisure. Some would doubtless abandon leisure and return to work after a brief fling. Some would find it an agreeable kind of vegetative existence. Yet others might find liberation, independence and an opportunity for self-development through "serious activity without the pressure of necessity," which Paul Goodman reminds us was one meaning of leisure in ancient Greece.

To set forth this description of the plan and its implications is to raise a host of objections—economic, psychological and ethical.

The feeling that a man's character is destroyed if he does not work is deeply ingrained. That man should live by the sweat of his brow is an ancient thought, but one which accords with the experience of many modern men who expire through boredom when retired.

Furthermore, there are strong links between work and self-respect. Ours is a society in which success counts, and it is largely measured by job status and income. The leaf-raking of Depression days was no more popular with those who did it than with those whose taxes paid for it. Is human dignity separable from work? Can leisure be respectable?

It may be that, as Robert Theobald has written, "the discovery of the proper uses of freedom is the fundamental task of the remainder of the twentieth century." But many are doubtful that we can make the discovery. Those who will have the most leisure are those with the least education, the most inadequate backgrounds for making effective use of freedom.

Initially at least, it is hard to dispute the contention that most of us are unfit for leisure. Nor is this view confined to economic conservatives. Norman Thomas said at a recent conference that "money without the pressures most of us need to work will make us a poorer and not a richer nation." (However, he is uncertain that we can provide the work.)

And what of those who would make no pretense of useful activity—those who are just plain lazy? The lazy we will always have with us, we might say, and we do not allow them to starve. But does our sense of social ethics require—or even permit—us to support them with some degree of comfort and as a socially guaranteed *right*?

It takes little imagination to picture the response of the Senate

Finance Committee or of Congress generally to a bill calling for taxes and expenditures to benefit *voluntary* joblessness with no strings attached. And would the proportion of the population opting for a minimal living without work remain constant, or would it jump so drastically that the economy would come to a grinding halt? No one can answer with certainty.

It could also be argued that the A.H.C. is counseling unwarranted defeatism—gloom and doom. Many will fear that such a proposal would become a self-fulfilling prophecy: that if we assume there cannot be enough jobs to go around, then we will bring about that situation by not trying hard enough to create more jobs.

Finally, would not the guaranteed-income plan lead to a government-created class of hereditary wards of the state? Would not children in this class be condemned to fatalistic apathy? And would not the rest of society too easily shrug off the needs of the poor once its conscience had been salved by having provided minimal income? There are, after all, signs that these unwanted outcomes are already present among at least some second-generation welfare families.

Despite the finality that these objections will have for some readers, there are counterarguments and precedents to be considered before the balance sheet is complete.

Jobless pay is not unknown to us—in the form of unemployment compensation, disability insurance, and old age and survivors' benefits under the Social Security program that has been part of our system since 1935. Aid to the blind, to dependent children, to the indigent not covered by insured employment— these, too, are forms of guaranteed income without work.

Nor should we forget two important forms of private separation of income from work: inheritance and property income. If a wealthy relative leaves me $100,000, which I invest in tax-free municipal bonds, I can have a workless income of $4,000 a year. Or if I buy a swamp in Louisiana and the Space Administration then builds a missile base nearby, I can have a very substantial income—even capital gains—from property ownership without lifting a finger to work.

These ways of breaking the income-job link are not universally admired—though perhaps universally envied—yet they are accepted by our society, especially by those likely to be least sympathetic to the A.H.C. proposal.

To the objection that work and self-respect are inseparable, the major reply is that the real necessity is not for a production job, but for meaningful activity. This may or may not be related to income. Voluntary efforts to improve our communities, pursue the arts or participate in public affairs are meaningful—sometimes more so than our regular jobs. Ours might be a richer nation in human and esthetic dimensions if more of us were free to direct our skills and energies toward projects not at present supported by the market.

As for the problem of the lazy, it is difficult to believe that a society noted around the world for the frenetic quality even of its recreation would suddenly turn soporific on any large scale. And of course the man with a family will continue to have both conscience and pressures to keep him seeking the higher incomes available through work—where work is available.

One practical advantage of the guaranteed-income plan is that it would greatly simplify the welfare pattern. A thousand administrative requirements and much overseeing expense could be eliminated if income without work were distributed without needing proof of age, blindness, dependency, length of residence, etc. Also, it would be far more equitable, for existing social-insurance programs—retirement, minimum wage, etc.—leave out many who are most in need simply because they are not in covered types of employment.

Some supplementary action programs would, of course, be required—especially social work and special education to stimulate children of guaranteed-income families and steer them away from apathy, and to aid families in coping with the multiple problems that already beset the unemployed and are not solved simply by the provision of cash. What is necessary is to recognize the need for such programs and their value, and to accord both higher prestige and higher salaries to the enlarged corps of professionals required. One would hope also that the change from grudging welfare to income guaranteed as a right would be accompanied by changes in public attitudes, changes that would lessen the obloquy which underlies the psychological listlessness of some welfare recipients today.

If we learn to educate for life—not just to earn a living—there is no reason, in principle, to assume that we, or at least our children, cannot make productive use of leisure. Let us hope it is possible, because it will have to be. Even without a guaranteed-income plan our working time has on the average been cut to less than half of our waking time. Extended vacations for steelworkers and a 25-hour week for New York electricians are but minimal symbols of the revolution already taking place.

It may be easy to scoff at the A.H.C. proposal, but only if we are unwilling to face up to the problem of automation. How else can we handle it? Long-continued unemployment makes it clear that we do not yet have an adequate alternative.

The particular ways by which we will provide income without jobs in the traditional sense remain to be developed, and the plan discussed here is doubtless not the only possibility. But it is clear now that radical revision of our thoughts, our economic institutions and our style of life are the inescapable accompaniments of man's increasing ability to substitute machines for muscles and computers for clerks.

The Grand Design of the Poverty Program

by Nathan Glazer

THE ANTIPOVERTY program is now a year and a half old. It is running at the rate of about $1.5-billion a year, with about two-fifths going to support the Community Action Programs—the most original and controversial part of the whole antipoverty campaign —and another two-fifths going for the Job Corps, the Neighborhood Youth Corps and the College Work-Study programs. Of the remaining programs, the largest is the work-experience program (primarily for welfare clients)—10 per cent of the total—and the best known is the domestic peace corps or VISTA (Volunteers in Service to America) program, which is budgeted at only 1½ per cent of the total. The entire $1.5-billion for the antipoverty program is about 1½ per cent of the Federal budget, or a quarter of 1 per cent of the Gross National Product.

It is worth keeping these dimensions in mind when we talk about the antipoverty program. Whether the poverty-stricken are 15 per cent or 25 per cent of the American people may be argued. Certainly there are a good number of them. And whatever the causes of poverty—or the definition of poverty—it seems reasonable that a good deal more than the present sums might well be invested in overcoming it. The question the antipoverty program raises most sharply, however, is not the general one—"Shall we do something about poverty?"—but the very specific one: "What shall we do about poverty?" And what we are doing, it seems to me, is by no means the best way of attacking the problem.

Three key decisions underlie the antipoverty program:

First, the framers of the antipoverty program decided that this was not to be a job-creation program, as were the great welfare programs of the New Deal—W.P.A., C.C.C., P.W.A., N.Y.A. Its major efforts are directed toward youth. The aim of these efforts is not so much the *employment* of young people as an end in itself, but rather their *training* for employment, by teaching them the required demeanor for holding any job, as in the Neighborhood Youth Corps, and the specific skills for holding certain jobs, as in the Job Corps. There is little emphasis on conservation of natural resources for its own sake, or on providing additional income to impoverished families through the work of youth, as in the C.C.C. Indeed, one hears remarkably little about conservation work in the publicity of the Job Corps, for it was early decided that saving trees and soil would not teach boys and girls the skills necessary to become productive in an urban society. The income earned is kept by the Job Corps recruit himself—though he can if he wishes have some of it sent back to his family.

The decision to emphasize youth was almost dictated by the nature of the poverty problem. Our poor consist in large measure of old people retired from the labor force on one hand, and young people not yet in it, living in families without adult male providers, on the other. Almost as high a proportion of children as of old people lives in poverty. The best recent study shows that 25 per cent of those under 18, and 30 per cent of those over 65, live in poverty. Among the 35 million poor are 15 million under 18, and 5 million over 65.

The emphasis on youth cannot be argued with. The emphasis on training, however, has been questioned. Does the young man out of school need training, or does he need a job? Is not the training on a real job more effective than the counseling and training attached to a job which is created especially for him, and in which he is under the authority of social workers much of the time?

Most job education in this country occurs on the job. A good deal occurs in public and private vocational schools. Is the special approach of the Job Corps and the Neighborhood Youth Corps necessary to supplement these major forms of job education? Some who argued at the beginning that all that the unemployed, out-of-school youth needed was a job have been convinced by experience that he probably needs a good deal of work counseling, job training, and orientation in what we may call job demeanor as well. But one can still argue that all this might have been better provided by a full-employment economy in which employers would find it worthwhile to train less-skilled and less-motivated workers.

But, of course, the framers of the antipoverty program were not asked to propose policy for the American economy. Asked to handle the problem of poverty, they could, one assumes, have said: "This is a job for high economic policy makers. If we can reduce the unemployment rate to 2 per cent, private industry will undertake the task of job training for youth as it seeks new employes." But we are dealing with problems that are in any case not to be solved by an exclusive reliance on one approach as against another. There is enough evidence that the inability of youth to get jobs, at least in the economy we have, is based to some extent on weak job skills. If we can get some improvement in that, it is certainly worth investing $600 million a year. In addition, we should not forget the fact that this is not only a job-training program, but that the young people are also working. We get some benefit from their work in agencies of city government and in nonprofit institutions, and, in effect, through these programs we subsidize some parts of our affluent society which we know are starved, such as maintenance work in city parks.

The second major decision of the antipoverty program was to set up a new agency, the Office of Economic Opportunity, to direct some of the new programs—in particular, the Community Action Program—and to coordinate other programs that fell under such agencies as the Department of Labor and the Department of Health, Education and Welfare. One can well ask whether this agency was necessary. One could have envisaged a program which expanded existing agencies—the youth counseling and training services of the Department of Labor, the vocational education programs financed by the Office of Education, the programs to overcome dependency that are being undertaken by various welfare departments with the support of the Federal Welfare Administration.

One could even have proposed an antipoverty program that increased grants—though Social Security and old-age assistance and Medicare—to the aged, thus automatically raising five million out of the poverty group, and increased payments to mothers with dependent children, thus doing the same for the majority of those in poverty. Indeed, in the sharp debate between Irving Kristol on the one hand and on the other Michael Harrington and Paul Jacobs (the latter two participated as consultants in the framing of the antipoverty program) in the pages of The New Leader early in 1964, this was just the nub of the argument: Why the fuss about poverty while most poverty could be eliminated by raising payments under *existing* programs above what the Government defined as the poverty level?

The point, once made, is terribly persuasive. It eliminates the need for setting up a new agency with thousands of employes, it eliminates the need for new and complex and inevitably confusing systems of coordination, and it would not have led to the inflation in the salaries of social workers and other poverty fighters which is now becoming an issue in a number of antipoverty programs.

Why then was this course not taken? As to the reasons for the fundamental political decisions, one can only speculate, and one assumes that it would have been something of a dud to implement a new war on poverty with increased Social Security and welfare payments. A war should be more active than that, and welfare payments are not particularly popular with Congress. Furthermore, we were interested in increasing productivity, not in simply raising levels of maintenance.

On the other hand, in view of the great concentration of children and old people in poverty, our only possible hope of improving life for many is simply to increase their level of material comfort. In addition, it may well be that the future productivity of children when they become adult workers can be enhanced by increased money payments permitting better housing, better health, more expenditure for toys and magazines and books, trips to downtown and other broadening experiences.

But there were more than these considerations dictating the decision to set up a new agency: There was a good deal of dissatisfaction with old agencies. This dissatisfaction united right and left together against simply pumping money into old agencies, and when right and left are united, it is irresistibly attractive to propose something new both might unite on. Thus, conservatives do not like welfare agencies because they are expensive and encourage dependency; liberals and radicals dislike them because their requirements restrict freedom and their administration is careful, dull, unimaginative and bureaucratic. Big-city education departments—which to a management expert might seem to be ideal conduits for funds which now flow through the Office of Economic Opportunity under various names, such as Operation Head Start, but which all have education as a major component —are subject to the same criticism. In more muted form, one hears much the same about state employment offices.

The antipoverty program determined on a new agency because it was in revolt against professionalism—the professionalism of welfare agencies, schools, vocational education, employment services, all of which had coexisted too comfortably with poverty. The revolt was signaled by such works as Michael Harrington's "The Other America" and Edgar May's "The Wasted Americans."

In addition to socialists and journalists, many social workers, too, were critical of the public agencies. For some years, progressive social workers had been attacking the public agencies for a number of faults—their inability to cooperate in handling a "multi-problem" family or individual, their emphasis on their specific function as against all the client's needs, their insistence on professional qualifications for workers (making it difficult for them to absorb new views from outsiders), their limited, middle-class orientation in dealing with the problems of lower-class people. The work of the Ford Foundation, which established public-private corporations in a number of cities in the early nineteen-sixties to develop multipronged attacks on social problems, reflected this criticism, as did the work of the President's Committee on Juvenile Delinquency.

Under this attack by liberal and radical critics, the defense of the education and welfare agencies was that they were not given enough money and freedom by legislatures to do a good job. This sounded weak and unconvincing—though there was a good deal of truth in it—and the last thing a progressive critic could bring himself to do was to propose simply giving them more money. And so the Office of Economic Opportunity came into being, with new people and new programs.

But if there already exist—as there do in most communities—departments of education and vocational education, school counseling services and vocational counseling services, welfare departments and public-health departments, and many more public and private agencies, what are these new programs, created in dissatisfaction with the old ones, to do? Here we come to the third major decision of the antipoverty program, and the one that is most controversial. The new programs were to be Community Action Programs. And what is a Community Action Program or Community Action Agency (C.A.A.)? The fact is that no one is as yet very clear what it is, although some 700 are in existence.

Let us begin to approach the Community Action Program the way the blind men approached the elephant, and see if we can make some sense of it.

Historically, it grows out of those joint attacks on social problems financed by the Ford Foundation, the President's Committee on Juvenile Delinquency and the National Institute of Mental Health in the early nineteen-sixties. The best-known example perhaps is still Mobilization for Youth on New York's Lower East Side. The idea was that the problems of low-income people are all interrelated; therefore, an integrated and interrelated program is needed to attack them. Some of these original agencies have now become the C.A.A.'s of their respective communities, or have become the action agencies to which the C.A.A.'s distribute funds.

Administratively, a C.A.A. can be almost anything: It can be public, private or a mixture. It must include representatives of the people in the areas in which it will concentrate, the "target" areas, but these may or may not be poor. The poor people may be a majority of the board of the agency, as in San Francisco, or less than a majority, as in most places, or there may be hardly any of them at all. They may be chosen through elections in the target areas, through appointment by the Mayor—or someone else—or through negotiations among various organizations representing the poor. Administratively, the Community Action Program is the farthest thing possible from Federal uniformity.

Functionally, a C.A.A. may simply support programs proposed by social-work agencies, boards of education and job-counseling and placement agencies. But it can do a lot of other things, too. In particular, it can *organize* communities; indeed, one part of a Community Action Program is generally labeled "community organization."

Politically, the Community Action Program can be a feather in the Mayor's cap, as he demonstrates his vigorous attack on the community's problems—or it can provide political resources, in the form of paid organizers, offices, mimeograph machines and paper supplies, for a variety of groups, and thus frighten political leaders out of their wits. What will all those organizers be up to? Their activities may begin innocuously: They organize the people on a block to discuss their problems, but they may go on to organizing a rent strike against slumlords, or even to throwing garbage on the Mayor's lawn in protest against poor garbage collections. And they may go on to educating the poor to believe that the power structure is against them and will be moved only by militant organization and outrageous actions.

It depends, of course, on who the organizers are. The young men and women who would like to organize in the slums and who are hired as community organizers by these programs are often strongly influenced by the New Left criticism of American society as overstructured, overorganized, restrictive of freedom, hardly democratic and in need of a thorough shaking up. This may not be what the organizers of Community Action Programs have in mind—but it is certainly what many people working in them have in mind.

Financially, the Community Action Program amounts to 1 per cent or 2 per cent of a city's budget, and is hardly enough to make any dent in its needs for schools, welfare, police, parks, public housing and a hundred other city services. And, by law, it cannot be used simply to supplement these budgets—into which it would disappear with hardly any effect. It is, however, supposed to do things which aid the poor—and most of these things bring it into conflict with the older agencies.

Socially, then, the Community Action Program is almost designed to increase conflict. It will organize the poor, and not under the auspices of the schools or the police or the public-housing

authorities. It is not a means to create tame P.-T.A.'s, tame
P.A.L.'s, tame tenants' councils. It will organize the poor to put
pressure on the principals and teachers, the police and the welfare
authorities, the public-housing managers and the housing
inspectors.

Unquestionably, it is giving a new voice to the poor. From the
point of view of city officials, it is a question whether they need
that voice in addition to the vote. From the point of view of the
organizers, it is changing the face of American society by redis-
tributing power, and they fear the powerholders will find out and
stamp out community organization. From the point of view of
the poor themselves, it is a great deal of sound and fury which
has not as yet affected any of the basic circumstances of their
lives—their jobs or lack of them, their housing, their welfare and
Social Security payments—but which promises to do so.

Ideologically, the Community Action Program is based on an
analysis of what ails the poor. The analysis asserts that it is not
their obvious material lack which is the heart of their problem.
It is their lack of power. The vote does not give them power,
because it needs education and money and time and social and
organizational skills to organize the vote, and the poor do not
have these. The imbalance is to be redressed by community organization. The effect, it is hoped, will be to improve education,
welfare service and housing inspection, to make the police more
respectful, to open up new job opportunities and eventually,
through the increase in power, to change the pattern of rewards
and services distributed by the public agencies.

This is, then, the grand design of the Community Action Program. It is only in its initial stages and, by its very nature, one
cannot predict where it is going or what it will do, for it is designed to evoke a distinctive response in each community. Ideally,
it brings into the concert of city government new voices and new
powers which will be able to affect city programs so that they
operate more humanely and more effectively. In doing so, it must
also give opportunities to more radical forces which do not have
such limited meliorative ends in view.

It is a grand spectacle, not simply of democracy at work, but
of democracy trying to stimulate the response that makes it work
better. The danger is that the degree of order that any social

system needs will be undermined. The hope is that a creative disorder will ensue, one that permits welfare agencies to work better, and with a larger participation from their clients.

If we now step back and ask, as Congress will be asking soon, how the antipoverty program is working, I would say as well as permitted by the key decisions that were made when the program was set up—with the concurrence of Congress. But the antipoverty program has by no means as yet proved that those initial decisions were right. It was wrong, I think, to hinge so much of the program on work preparation and work training, and so little on those fundamental programs of social welfare and social insurance that every advanced nation finds it needs to combat deprivation and suffering.

Thus we should have given a much sharper look at our programs of social welfare and social insurance, which are many times larger than the antipoverty program. What revisions are necessary in their levels of support, the nature of Federal contributions to them, their varied requirements and regulations?

At the same time we should have devoted more effort to the creation of jobs, for no economically advanced nation today can tolerate the high unemployment rate with which—even after our five years of prosperity—we continue to live. There have been suggestions as to how we can simultaneously reduce unemployment and increase the level of public services—keeping museums and libraries open at night, doubling mail deliveries, providing attendants in playgrounds and parks. (It is because the Neighborhood Youth Corps provides so much clearly useful work that it may turn out to be one of the most successful and least expensive parts of the poverty program.)

We still have this course open to us, and there is no question that, if we follow it, we will still need at least as much job training and job counseling as is now provided through the poverty program. But training and counseling will become infinitely more effective if we have a tighter employment situation, so that the rewards of training and counseling become immediately evident.

Nor am I sure that the second and third decisions—the creation of a separate agency and the emphasis on Community Action Programs—were correct. The two were closely linked, for while all the other programs in the poverty program could be placed under the Department of Labor or the Department of Health, Education and Welfare, it was not easy to find a home in the established structure of government for Community Action—in part because, as we have seen, one of its main aims was to create conflicts with older, established agencies and programs.

I am convinced conflict can be healthy. I am less convinced that government can successfully support the healthy conflict with its own programs and agencies that produces change. The labor movement had help from the Federal Government in the nineteen-thirties, but it could scarcely have developed its distinctive role in the American economy and society if it had been financed by the Government.

There is a wonderful naiveté about the Community Action Program—as if someone had been convinced by a sociologist that change and reform are spurred by conflict and decided that, since all good things can come from the American Government, it ought to provide conflict, too. But in trying to do so we enter on an incredibly difficult path, one which few administrators, I think, can successfully traverse.

The decisions the administrators of these programs must make are too difficult for almost any mortal. Does one offer jobs in the program to the newly aroused leaders of the poor—and, if so, is one strengthening the program or buying off the leaders of the poor and reducing the pressure? How much pressure does one put on the Mayor to include the representatives of the poor—and is one seeking easy demagogic victories by posing as the leader of the unfortunates against the soulless bureaucracies, or is one really trying to improve the workings of the bureaucracies? And what about the representatives of the poor one is trying to place on C.A.A.'s—is one simply aiding one faction in the Negro community or the civil-rights struggle as against another? Or is one truly changing the fundamental constitution of American local government?

Perhaps the most troublesome aspect of the Community Action Programs is the conflict between the ideology of local control over local programs designed for local problems and the reality of strong Federal control. There is something disingenuous about a program which asserts that we are going to permit each community to design the antipoverty program it needs, and then says:

"But hold on; you don't have enough representatives of the poor; they are not chosen in the right way; your program has too much Community Action and not enough Operation Head Start," and so on. In other words, there is a strain between the theoretical commitment to local independence and the reality of Federal control.

The accents may be those of the poor, but the contents of the programs are too often those proposed by Federal officials influenced by the latest wave of fashion among social critics and social workers. I am not yet convinced the Federal officials will uniformly have a better grasp of the local problems than the local elected officials; they may simply have more power because they control the Federal purse strings.

What were the alternatives to the Community Action Program? Just as I believe we could have gotten—and can still get—more mileage in overcoming poverty through major revisions in Social Security and public welfare, so I believe we should at least consider the possibility of giving united funds directly to city governments. City government today is too often restricted by insufficient tax resources, on the one hand, and by legal commitments and state and Federal requirements which limit how it can spend its money, on the other.

Freeing city government for a more creative role has its dangers, of course, and yet it might produce the kind of ferment the Community Action Program aims at—as city government becomes something worth fighting over, as new Federal funds expand its possibilities of action. And this conflict might be more creative in the end than the present fights over Community Action Program funds, with Federal referees in the background—and often in the foreground.

My reservations about the antipoverty program are much like those of the critic who says the subject of the play should have been a different one. We decided what the subject should be in passing the Economic Opportunity Act, and I think the performance, in view of the difficulties of the script as I have outlined them, is better than we had a right to expect. But I think we still have to take on the jobs which the antipoverty program, as set up under the act, did not address itself to—reducing the unemployment rate, increasing the number of jobs, expanding and revising the Social Security and social-welfare systems, improving the systems of job training, job counseling and job placement, attacking the failures of school systems and police systems. The anti-poverty program will permit us to experiment with a good number of ways of undertaking these tasks. In the end, however, a democratic polity cannot take the position that the major way to improve its institutions of government and welfare is to finance guerrilla warfare against them. It must take up the job of directly improving and transforming them.

Making Trouble Is Alinsky's Business

by Patrick Anderson

SAUL ALINSKY, the middle-aged *deus ex machina* of American slum agitation, is scheduled to descend upon the Negro slums of Buffalo's East Side next month to begin his controversial business of organizing the poor to march against the local powers-that-be. To be more exact, a professional organizer from the 12-man staff of Alinsky's Chicago-based Industrial Areas Foundation will begin organizing in Buffalo; Alinsky, who is currently master-minding several such operations, will stay in the background, giving instructions to his organizer in daily telephone calls and slipping in and out of the city every few months to rally his forces. Alinsky is undertaking his Buffalo project at the invitation of Negro leaders and of white Protestant clergymen; the latter have demonstrated their faith in his talents to the tune of $150,000, which they raised to finance the first two years of his organizing campaign. The money was raised only after a court fight in which Presbyterian lay leaders protested that their church's money should not be used to support Alinsky's slum organizing.

Alinsky's goal in Buffalo, as elsewhere, is to help slum leaders create a disciplined, broad-based power organization capable of wringing concessions—better jobs, better schools, better garbage

From the *New York Times Magazine,* October 9, 1966, copyright © 1966 by The New York Times Company.

collection, better housing—from the local Establishment. He goes after this goal with a fierce belief that the end justifies the means.

"I tell people, 'The hell with charity—the only thing you get is what you're strong enough to get, so you'd better organize,'" Alinsky says. "The only way to upset the power structure is to goad them, confuse them, irritate them, and most of all, make them live by their own rules. If you make them live by their own rules, you'll destroy them."

In a quarter-century as a professional slum organizer, Alinsky, who is 57, has goaded, confused and infuriated the power structures of two score communities. In the process he has perfected what social scientists now call "Alinsky-type protest," an explosive mixture of rigid discipline, brilliant showmanship, and a street fighter's instinct for ruthlessly exploiting his enemy's weakness.

Alinsky has proved that the fastest way for slum tenants to get repairs is to picket their landlords' suburban homes with signs reading: "Your Neighbor Is A Slumlord." He has sent mothers in long black veils to school board meetings to "mourn" their children's segregated schools. When the Federal antipoverty program's VISTA volunteers arrived in Chicago, he spoke of sending Negroes dressed in African tribal costumes to greet them—to underscore his contempt for what he calls the "colonialism" and the "Peace Corps mentality" of the poverty program.

The uses of harassment are endless. Alinsky suggests that a good way to soften up a bank for negotiations would be to send dozens of teen-agers into it at rush hour to open accounts, or simply to get change, thus tying up business. Alinsky is, of course, quite capable of masterminding almost any type of harassment. But as a consummate showman, he also knows that if he can publicize his tactics through newspapers and television, he may so intimidate potential adversaries that he will never have to use them.

He told me recently of another scheme he wants to try out. It would involve buying a number of houses in an all-white neighborhood and sending Negro families to live in them. As Alinsky sees it, there would be one of two results. Either the whites would accept the Negroes, thus providing a measure of integration, or the whites would move out, thus enabling more Negroes to move in and take over the neighborhood's presumably superior schools, parks and other facilities.

Given such tactics, it is no surprise that Alinsky is hated and feared in high places from coast to coast. Nor is it surprising that his services are much in demand in the slums. Besides the forthcoming Buffalo project, he has programs in operation in Rochester and Kansas City, Mo. He recently withdrew from his most famous project, TWO (The Woodlawn Organization, in Chicago's Negro community of Woodlawn), leaving it under 100 per cent local guidance. He is consulting with slum organizing projects in Detroit and elsewhere, and says that only the lack of trained organizers keeps him from accepting invitations to a dozen more cities. He is in constant demand as a lecturer, and he has for several summers conducted training courses in organizing for clergymen.

This success is based on the fact that Alinsky does one job— building effective slum organizations—better than anyone else in sight. And a great many students of today's slum unrest are convinced that militant organization may be an essential first step in a slum's slow ascent from squalor to self-respect. For example, Fortune magazine's Charles Silberman, who approached Alinsky several years ago as a skeptical reporter, ended by writing in his book "Crisis in Black and White" that no other man in America "has proposed a course of action or a philosophy better calculated to rescue Negro or white slum dwellers from their poverty or their degradation."

When considering Alinsky, it is important to understand what he is not, for much of his strength lies in his limitations. He is not a civil-rights leader; he would just as soon organize poor whites or Mexicans or Indians as Negroes. Nor is he, like some youthful members of the New Left, the would-be leader of a national coalition of the poor; he wants to organize slums so they can make their own decisions; he does not want to make the decisions for them. "We're not trying to lead anything," he said recently. "We're just technicians trying to organize people."

What, then, is Alinsky's motivation? Certainly a secondary motive is that he is a born hell-raiser. He is a pudgy, graying man who looks like a suburban dentist and whose joy is unalloyed when he is running the Establishment ragged. But, much more important, Alinsky is a fervent believer in democracy, and to him democracy demands political participation by *all* the people, not just the well-off or the well-educated.

"All I stand for is real democracy and that means popular participation and militant organization," he says. "The have-nots will not just be handed opportunity or freedom on a silver platter; they will have to take it through their own efforts. There is no evolution without revolution, and there are no revolutions without conflict."

Brave talk—but talk is plentiful. How does Alinsky's doctrine translate into deeds in the reality of a slum? What is it likely to mean to Buffalo's East Side slums in the months ahead? There is no better way to answer those questions than to examine the first 18 months of Alinsky's project in Rochester, a militant Negro organization with the appropriately militant name FIGHT, which stands for Freedom, Integration, God, Honor, Today.

FIGHT came about as a direct result of the Negro riots there in July, 1964, riots that ended with hundreds injured, a thousand arrested and property damage estimated at a million dollars.

The effect of these riots on Rochester's community psyche cannot be overestimated. When Alinsky later dubbed it "Smugtown, U.S.A." he was only underscoring an undeniable fact: Rochester is a proud city, proud of its tradition of abundant, locally provided social services, proud of its reputation as a clean, progressive city. (This is what Alinsky calls "welfare colonialism.")

The riots made Rochester face up to the fact of a new, angry, combustible force in its midst. Statistics told the story: the local Negro population had skyrocketed from 8,000 in 1950 to 24,000 in 1960 to 35,000 today. Most of the newcomers are living in a run-down inner-city slum that has no other name than the Third Ward.

In the soul-searching that followed the riots, many white clergymen felt a special obligation to help bind up the city's wounds. Soon after the riots, the Rochester Area Council of Churches invited two of Dr. Martin Luther King's top aides in the Southern Christian Leadership Conference to come and see if they could ease tensions in the Third Ward. But the S.C.L.C. doctrine of nonviolence proved to have little appeal there, and after a few weeks Dr. King's men left, pleading obligations elsewhere. Next the clergymen turned to Alinsky. After initial discussions and fund-raising efforts, they issued a formal invitation to him in January of 1965. Asked why they had called on Alinsky, they explained:

"No one else was available in whom we had faith. . . . There is a missing dynamic in Rochester contributing to anarchy and bitterness—the lack of structural organization among the inner-city people that would give them a voice, cohesion and a sense of identity."

The invitation to Alinsky (with $50,000 a year pledged to his operation for two years) touched off a controversy such as Rochester had never seen. He was denounced as a "hatemonger" and a "rabble-rouser." The city's two Gannett-owned newspapers bitterly opposed him. A local radio station informed the ministers they would have to start paying for the Sunday-morning air time they had been getting free. A settlement house voted to join FIGHT, then was told by the Community Chest that its funds could not be used for that purpose; the settlement house backed down, with some board members resigning in protest. Many ministers put their jobs on the line to support Alinsky's coming. In short, before he ever set foot in Rochester, Alinsky had already forced thousands of its citizens to stop and ask themselves where they stood.

All the controversy, of course, was grist to Alinsky's mill, the kind of advertising he couldn't buy. He observed recently, "When the opposition becomes so intense, as it did in Rochester and Kansas City, the Negroes get to see who our opposition is. Every Uncle Tom is coming out of the woodwork. The Mayor is having hysterics. In Oakland the City Council passed a resolution asking me to stay out. The Negroes have never seen the power structure quake that way. They expect miracles from us; if my men came in walking on the water, it wouldn't surprise anybody."

Much of the opposition in Rochester was based on knowledge of the abrasive tactics Alinsky had used in Chicago. For example, when the president of the Board of Education there had refused to meet with The Woodlawn Organization and had denounced it as a "lunatic fringe," Alinsky replied by sending 18 clergymen to sit-in at the executive offices of Inland Steel, where the school official was a vice president. Other TWO members marched outside with signs denouncing the man as a segregationist. A month later he resigned as school board president, citing "the pressure of company business."

The history of the bitter Chicago conflict led Rochester leaders to expect the worst when Alinsky sent his top organizer, 34-year-old Edward T. Chambers, to begin work in their city in the spring of 1965. Their fears were not eased when Alinsky addressed FIGHT's convention in June and denounced the city as "a Southern plantation transplanted to the North."

But Rochester's leaders were in for a surprise. FIGHT, aside from picketing a few slum landlords, has not gone in much for noisy demonstrations. There are several reasons for this. Ed Chambers says: "They expected conflict so we changed our tactics. Sometimes the threat of a demonstration is worse than the reality; it's like telling your wife you're going to leave her."

Some critics of FIGHT suggest another reason for its go-slow tactics. FIGHT has no conspicuous villain to attack in Rochester, no one like Birmingham's former police commissioner, Bull Connor, to serve as a symbol of oppression. Rochester's Democratic city administration has maintained an open-door policy toward FIGHT. When FIGHT makes a complaint about substandard housing or police brutality, it gets a quick hearing. One local columnist suggested that Rochester is killing FIGHT with kindness. Chambers concedes that the lack of bitter-end resistance makes organizing harder. "This is six years later," he says, comparing FIGHT with Chicago's TWO, "and the enemy is more sophisticated."

There are signs that other communities will try to kill Alinsky with kindness. "I was going into Detroit," he says of a recent experience, "and Cavanagh [Mayor Jerome P. Cavanagh] invited me to meet with him. He said we had a lot in common. Blah, blah, blah. He was making concessions before I got out of the damn airport."

In Rochester much of FIGHT's energies have gone into the quiet, door-to-door, day-in-day-out job of building an organization. It now includes about 100 constituent groups, ranging from churches and block clubs to the patrons of a particular pool hall or barber shop. Just how many people FIGHT speaks for is debatable, but even its critics admit that it represents the Negro community to a degree never before achieved by any organization. In June, 1965, about 1,500 persons attended the convention at which FIGHT adopted its constitution, heard Alinsky's fire-eating speech and elected its first president. He is the Rev. Franklin D. R. Florence, a 32-year-old Church of Christ minister. Minister Florence, as he likes to be known, is very much the New Negro. He is angry and articulate. He wears a "Black Power" button, reveres the memory of Malcolm X and is studiously rude to most whites. Last June, at FIGHT's second annual convention, Minister Florence was opposed for re-election by a younger Negro Episcopal clergyman, who charged that Florence was leading FIGHT down the road of "voluntary black segregation." That may be the road FIGHT prefers, for Minister Florence was re-elected by a 2-to-1 vote. Florence's relationship with Alinsky and Chambers is a delicate one. He very clearly resents the fact that he needs their help. In Rochester, as elsewhere, the days are numbered when white men can lead the black man's revolt.

In its first 18 months, FIGHT's biggest victory came in connection with a $28-million urban-renewal project now beginning in the Third Ward. Negroes feared they would be uprooted from their homes with little provision for their futures. That had happened in a previous project in Rochester in the nineteen-fifties and it has happened all across America for the past 20 years. FIGHT took up the issue and, highlighting its campaign, turned out more than 1,000 people to attend a public hearing on the project early this year.

City Hall was understandably impressed by this turnout and serious negotiations began between FIGHT and the urban-renewal agency.

In the end, FIGHT won specific provision in the urban-renewal plans for new housing on vacant lands before demolition begins, for low-rise public housing on scattered sites, for nonprofit public-housing corporations, and for some 250 units of public housing where only two units had previously been scheduled.

Urban renewal officials say they would eventually have made all these provisions for the poor. "They forced us to be more specific than is customary in plans of this sort," one says, "but there were no significant changes in our plans."

To the Negro-in-the-street, however, the city fathers' largess was by no means to be taken for granted, and the history of urban renewal in America supports his view. The urban-renewal fight is not over. For one example, the school system wants to build an administration building in the renewal area; FIGHT thinks the land should be used for a new school, and FIGHT's members have promised to throw themselves in front of the bulldozers, if necessary, to halt construction of an administration building.

The local "war on poverty" is another area of contention. In its early months FIGHT did not challenge ABC, the city-controlled antipoverty agency, because it was negotiating with City Hall over a program under which FIGHT would recruit and train young Negroes to join the police force. (This program became one of FIGHT's few admitted flops, and Chambers says now, "Negro kids just don't want to be cops.") But once these negotiations were complete, FIGHT began harassing ABC, which it felt did not represent the poor. First, it insisted on the right of its members to attend ABC board meetings. Next, it insisted they should have the right to speak at those meetings. Next, it demanded the right to name six members to ABC's board—and got three. There is a basic Alinsky strategy in this sequence: each time ABC met one FIGHT demand, it was presented with another. Killing FIGHT with kindness is not so easy.

Chambers says with his usual candor:

"We subjected them to constant harassment. Our first issue was that the public business can't be conducted in private. If their board went into private session, we would force our way in. They finally realized FIGHT is here to stay. They said to themselves, 'We'd better give those people something to shut them up.' So they gave us three people on their board and $65,000."

The $65,000 was a Federal antipoverty grant to FIGHT to train about 100 Negroes to pass civil-service examinations. The grant gives FIGHT an added aura of respectability and it also enables its enemies to whisper that it has sold out to City Hall. Minister Florence laughs at this: "We're not looking for money— sure, we'll take their money—we're looking for independence."

In another recent move FIGHT has petitioned New York State Education Commissioner James E. Allen to order greater speed in ending *de facto* segregation in Rochester schools. FIGHT also cooperated in an experimental program in which the Xerox Corporation trained about 15 Negro dropouts for semiskilled jobs in its plant.

FIGHT's next battle may be with the Rochester-based Eastman Kodak Company. FIGHT recently opened negotiations with Kodak over a proposed program in which it would recruit and Kodak would train some 500 Negro youths for semiskilled jobs in Kodak's plants. FIGHT charges Kodak with ignoring Rochester's Negroes while importing white workers from other cities, and argues that Kodak should now give favored treatment to local youths regardless of the extra expense involved. "If Kodak can take pictures of the moon, it can create 500 jobs for our people," says Minister Florence. Ed Chambers says that if FIGHT's demands aren't met, it will resort to direct action—perhaps picketing Kodak's plants, perhaps picketing the homes of its board members.

Another accomplishment has been the organization of some 400 dues-paying liberals—mainly clergymen, teachers, doctors, lawyers—who call themselves Friends of FIGHT. This group has provided FIGHT with money, moral support, legal advice and tutors for its training projects. The alliance between FIGHT and Friends of FIGHT is an uneasy one. There is no social intercourse between them; the whites can attend some FIGHT meetings but they can't speak out; Minister Florence makes it clear that the whites must follow Negro (i.e., his) direction.

"Psychologically, perhaps we're guilt-ridden, but I don't think so," says Louis Martin, president of Friends of FIGHT and assistant librarian at the University of Rochester. "But we accept apartheid because we think it is a way to unity."

Friends of FIGHT is of more than local significance because it reflects Alinsky's increasing belief that the Negro must have white allies. This view flies in the face of the militant, black-good-white-bad mentality now symbolized nationally by Stokeley Carmichael and locally by Minister Florence. So in Rochester a compromise has developed. The Negroes have white allies, but those allies are relegated to a status that might be called separate but not quite equal. Perhaps, given the passions of the day, that is the best arrangement to be reached; that, at least, is what the people involved in Rochester seem to think.

Most FIGHT leaders believe the intangible benefits the organization has provided the people of the Third Ward are more important than the tangible ones. Minister Florence, asked to name FIGHT's biggest achievement, says: "Respect." The Rev. Herbert White, a young clergyman who was instrumental in bringing Alinsky to Rochester, thinks the Alinsky-FIGHT influence has spread through Rochester like ripples on a pond. He cites increased social action by clergymen and new wage demands by local teachers. "I think this is a hell of a lot better town because of Alinsky," Mr. White says. "To do justice to Alinsky and FIGHT you have to look beyond its program to a new spirit that exists in many here."

Charles Silberman reached a similar conclusion when he wrote in "Crisis in Black and White" of Alinsky's work in Chicago: "TWO's greatest contribution, therefore, is its most subtle: it gives Woodlawn residents the sense of dignity that makes it possible for them to accept help. For help now comes (or seems to come, which amounts to the same thing) not as the result of charity, but as the result of their own power . . ."

The irony in Rochester is that for all the cries of "hatemonger" that greeted Alinsky, it is indisputable that FIGHT has been a stabilizing force in the community. FIGHT's tireless efforts deserve at least some of the credit for preventing a repetition of the 1964 riots. FIGHT helped the urban-renewal project gain an acceptance in the Third Ward it had never had before. It has opened the first meaningful dialogue between the Third Ward and City Hall. Alinsky, who loves to be hated, must now live with the irony that in an era of "black power" and irresponsible calls to race violence, he is beginning to look like a pretty solid citizen.

FIGHT would be of no great significance if it were an isolated phenomenon, the chance product of some inspired local leader. But Alinsky, by his work in many cities over a number of years, has come to have a very real impact on today's antipoverty movement: on clergymen who flock to his training courses, on social workers who have studied his techniques and envied his freedom of action, on social work students who have invited him to lecture to them, even on the Federal "war on poverty."

The original antipoverty staff contained several warm admirers of Alinsky and his influence was to some degree reflected in the stress on community organization in the community-action program. However, Alinsky considers the "war on poverty" faulty in conception and cynical in execution. Its misconception, he believes, lies in assuming that the poor can ever make significant gains without fighting for them. In execution, he declares, it has only subsidized existing City Hall welfare programs, while providing absurdly high salaries to social workers and token benefits to the well-behaved poor.

Alinsky's admirers at antipoverty headquarters in Washington do not include the program's chief, Sargent Shriver. Alinsky once declared in an unforgettable outburst that the "war on poverty" was "a prize piece of political pornography . . . a huge political pork barrel, and a feeding trough for the welfare industry, surrounded by sanctimonious, hypocritical, phony, moralistic —." Soon thereafter I was interviewing Shriver and asked him about Alinsky. In one of the few recorded instances of Shriver's losing his cool, he sputtered: "That man—that man—that man called me a *pornographer.*"

Alinsky has won the attention due any man who does a serious job better than anyone else. He says the main reason he went into Woodlawn in 1960 was that Negro leaders told him it was impossible to organize that miserable human jungle. No one with his organizational talent and financial independence had ever before gone into such slums and shown that something could be done; that the poor are not apathetic when given alternatives to apathy; that with the right issues all income levels can be united; that slum organizations can withstand witch hunts; that indigenous slum leadership exists.

An organized slum is, of course, still a slum. Alinsky cannot build schools or raise wages or tear down tenements. Those are the jobs of government. What he can do is teach the disorganized poor how to bring pressure on government, just as every other segment of society is already doing through civic and fraternal clubs, unions, Washington lobbyists, veterans' organizations, political parties and other pressure groups.

Alinsky and his men talk a lot today about the difference between "organization" and "movement." "Organization" is Alinsky's business and it is a slow job; "movement," on the other hand, can be a one-night stand. Alinsky thinks some of the best-known civil-rights leaders are more interested in well-publicized barnstorming than in the dirty work of organizing people. His aide, Ed Chambers, says emotionally: "Look what they did to those poor people in Selma—came and went and left them with nothing. You can't *do* that to those poor bastards!"

"We organize an organization," Alinsky says. "There's a vast difference between that and just organizing a movement which crests into a demonstration and then is gone." In his view such gestures as the recent march to Cicero, Ill., are harmful to the Negro cause because they stiffen white opposition, undercut liberal allies and divert Negro energies to targets from which nothing can be gained—what can you negotiate with a howling mob?

Civil-rights leaders may be coming around to his view. After the recent Atlanta riots Hosea Williams, one of Dr. King's top aides, told reporters that the problem was that the rioters were disorganized—and said Dr. King intended to organize them. If the various civil-rights organizations do step up their heretofore sporadic efforts at slum organizing, they will inevitably be influenced by Alinsky. He has broken a lot of ground for them.

Alinsky was born Jan. 30, 1909, in one of Chicago's worst slums, the son of Russian immigrant parents who were divorced when he was about 14. Chicago is still Alinsky's home, although he and his wife, Jean, keep a summer home near Carmel, Calif.

He entered the University of Chicago in 1926 and from that point forward his whole career seems, in retrospect, to have been pointed at the break he made in 1939 when he began his career as a slum organizer. His college sociology courses only impressed on him the gap between academic theories and the slum realities he knew. His first taste of social action—and his first arrest— came when he and other students took food to Southern Illinois coal miners who were rebelling against the United Mine Workers.

After graduate study in criminology, he took a job with the Illinois State Division of Criminology, which led him into work with Italian youth gangs. This was followed by a couple of years as a criminologist at the state prison at Joliet. In addition, Alinsky lectured at various colleges, but as his career boomed, his interest waned. ("I've never encountered such a mass of morons as in the field of criminology," he says.)

He kept his prison job but in his free time he became active in various social causes of the nineteen-thirties: raising money for the International Brigade in the Spanish Civil War, for the newly formed Newspaper Guild, for Southern sharecroppers; fighting the eviction of slum dwellers who couldn't pay rent; fighting for public housing. He often worked closely with the C.I.O.

He reached a turning point in 1938 when he was offered a high-paying job as head of probation and parole in Philadelphia. "It was very tempting," he recalled years later. "I could see myself with a house in the beautiful Philadelphia suburbs and money in the bank." But his instincts pulled elsewhere, he rejected the offer and decided to make a career of helping the poor. However, there still remained the question of how he could do the most good.

Using his training in sociology and criminology, he might have comforted and counseled the poor in society's traditional manner. But Alinsky was unimpressed with the traditional ways; they were too little, too late, too condescending. Instead, he turned for a model to the techniques he had learned from the labor movement of the thirties—from John L. Lewis, from the C.I.O.'s organizing campaigns, from the Auto Workers' sit-down strikes in Flint, Mich. If labor's organizing techniques could be applied to entire slum communities, he believed, organized poor people might wrest a higher standard of living as a matter of right instead of waiting passively for the crumbs of charity. Alinsky saw American society as did Jefferson and Madison, as an endless political struggle between conflicting interest groups; the trouble was that the group he cared about was outside the struggle and would be until it was organized for political power. So he set out to do that job.

He started in Chicago's Back of the Yards slum district, which he remembers now as having been "a hellhole of hate—the Poles, Mexicans, Negroes, Lithuanians, Hungarians and Germans all hating each other, and all of them hating the Irish because the Irish were the power structure."

In Back of the Yards, Alinsky worked with Catholic priests, left-wing labor leaders and stockyards workers to form a mass movement directed against the meat packers, slumlords, bankers who exploited small businessmen and small homeowners, and the local political machine. Picketing, boycotts, rent strikes and sit-downs helped win concessions for the slum dwellers.

Alinsky's work led Chicago's Marshall Field to put up funds to allow Alinsky to organize elsewhere, no strings attached. In 1940 the non-profit Industrial Areas Foundation was created. Other money came in time from the Catholic Church, other church organizations, and other foundations and philanthropists. Today, the I.A.F.'s governing board includes business, labor and religious leaders. Alinsky draws a $25,000-a-year salary; his staff organizers are paid from $10,000 to $15,000.

Throughout the nineteen-forties and fifties, he organized some 30 Mexican-American slums—*barrios*—in California, and others in Chicago, Detroit, the Chelsea section in New York and elsewhere. In those years he built an underground following among social workers, but he did not become a national figure until he entered Woodlawn—his first Negro slum—in 1960. His success there, coupled with mounting racial tensions across the nation, focused increasing attention on his methods.

He has, of course, many critics. At various times he has been denounced as a Communist and a Fascist, a segregationist and an integrationist, a pawn of the Catholic Church (because it has financed him) and an anti-Catholic (because he once called Los Angeles' conservative Cardinal McIntyre "an un-Christian prehistoric muttonhead").

Members of the New Left generally dismiss him as a "mercenary who manipulates the poor." Some academics complain he has been much overrated by a friendly press. It is true that Alinsky's candor tends to win him friends among reporters (he is the only public figure in modern times who has stated categorically that "Brotherhood Week is a lot of ——!") but it is also true that he has encountered overwhelming editorial opposition in the cities he has worked in.

Dr. Harold Fey, editor of The Christian Century, has charged Alinsky with encouraging "a political movement whose object is to establish control over urban society by raising up from its ruins a 'power structure' dictatorship based on slum dwellers." A spokesman for the University of Chicago, Alinsky's bitter enemy in the organization of TWO, accused him of copying the tactics of "lynch mobs."

Philip M. Hauser, head of the University of Chicago's department of sociology (which Alinsky describes as "a tribe of head counters") has warned that any Negro who follows Alinsky down the path of social conflict ". . . may be the victim of a cruel, even if unintended, hoax . . . The methods by which (Alinsky) organized TWO may actually have impeded the achievement of consensus and thus delayed the attaining of Woodlawn's objectives."

Alinsky has a ready response: "One thing we instill in all our organizations is that old Spanish Civil War slogan: 'Better to die on your feet than to live on your knees.' Social scientists don't like to think in these terms. They would rather talk about politics being a matter of accommodation, consensus—and not this conflict business. This is typical academic drivel. How do you have consensus before you have conflict? There has to be a rearrangement of power and then you get consensus."

Critics in Rochester sometimes charge that all Alinsky is doing is making the Third Ward a "better ghetto," that is, he is an inadvertent segregationist. In truth, Alinsky is not concerned with integration or segregation but with self-determination. He wants to help people win the power to choose their own paths; he is not much concerned about what paths they choose—not because he is callous, but because he has faith in people to make the right choices.

As an organizer, he has found that integration, as a far-off ideal, makes a poor rallying cry. Negro parents, he says, will support the idea of desegregation, "but the issue that will bring them out to meetings and into vigorous action is to have something done about the schools which their children go to right now." Of the "black power" controversy, he says: "I agree with the concept. We've always called it community power, and if the community is black, it's black power."

Alinsky has no illusions about the nobility of poverty. He said in an interview with Harper's Magazine last year: "Too often I've seen the have-nots turn into haves and become just as crummy as the haves they used to envy. Some of the fruit ranchers in California steam around in Cadillacs and treat the Mexican-American field hands like vermin. Know who those bastards are? They're the characters who rode west in Steinbeck's trucks, in 'The Grapes of Wrath.' "

Reformers are supposed to have a vision of the future. Alinsky's is a deceptively simple one: "Regardless of what the situation is, people will not be able to do anything constructive, anything in the true democratic spirit for themselves, unless they have the power to cope with the situation, whatever it may be and whenever it occurs. So I'm just holding at that point—build the organization and cross each bridge as we come to it."

Alinsky says the scope of his operations is limited only by the scarcity of trained organizers. It takes about three years to train an organizer, the working conditions are bad and the turnover is high. Some of his ex-organizers have made names for themselves: one is Cesar Chavez who led the recent grapepickers' strike in California; another is Nicholas von Hoffman, now a brilliant reporter on the civil-rights movement for The Washington Post.

Alinsky says that if the money can be found he hopes to start a permanent training institute for organizers. He says the institute would be in either New York City or the San Francisco area; if the former, he would begin an organizing project in either Jersey City or Spanish Harlem; if the latter, in either Oakland or San Francisco's Mission District. Probably the money will be found; Alinsky is nearing that level of respectability at which foundation funds can be had.

Indeed, one of his toughest fights these days is to keep from being crowned the Grand Old Man of Radicalism. His words and deeds have made him the darling of the liberals—and a liberal in Alinsky's book is somebody who disappears when a fight starts. But Alinsky has no intention of becoming the Harry Golden of social work: "I called my staff together the other day and told them. 'Don't worry, men, we're going to pull through this storm of approval just as hated as we ever were.'"

Maximum Feasible Misunderstanding

by Adam Walinsky

MAXIMUM FEASIBLE MISUNDERSTANDING: Community Action in the War on Poverty. By Daniel P. Moynihan. 218 pp. An Arkville Press Book. New York: Macmillan-The Free Press.

THERE IS A real and serious study to be made of the war on poverty, and especially of its heart, the community action program. Such a study would trace the roots of the community-action concept against the demonstrated inadequacies of New Deal-style social welfare legislation to the political and economic crises of the 1960's. It would view the current effort as part of the continuing tension between representative and participatory forms of democratic government which Hannah Arendt treats brilliantly in "On Revolution."

Such a book would view community action in the politics of the Johnson years: its place in the Great Society; in the struggles with Robert Kennedy for the allegiance of the American poor, which both men, in vastly different ways, took for their special constituency; in the developing group consciousness of blacks, Mexican-Americans and others; and in relation to the politics of the Vietnam war, which crippled the program even as its first appropriation was coming up for renewal.

Lastly, such a book would examine, however cursorily, the history of community action—what it did and did not accomplish, and why, in some of the thousands of cities and counties across the nation where these programs, in less than five years, have become a fixture of government. It would, in short, be a thoughtful study of one of the few real innovations in the structure of American government since the formation of the T.V.A.

This is not that book. What Daniel Patrick Moynihan has given us instead is a slight, selective tour through such parts of community action theory, most of them out of date, as can be blamed upon the "maximum feasible misunderstanding" of "activist social scientists" in general, and "the literary reviews, the salons, the intellectual élite" of New York in particular. It is his contention, broadly, that the social-work intellectuals, having conceived the community action program on inexact guesses about the roots of human behavior, imposed these theories on a too-willing Government, which in an effort to "effect such outcomes as who *thinks* what, who *acts* when, who *lives* where, who *feels* how," intensified social conflict among Americans, especially between the poor and nearly everyone else, and thus were largely responsible for the pro-Wallace reaction of 1967-68.

There is the germ of an idea here. But one comes away from the book much as one might from a desultory after-dinner conversation, in which all sharpness and bite of analysis have dissolved in self-contradiction, vague ellipses and archly flattering references to the really important people at the next table; afterwards there is the sense that he was not really talking to us, but for them. (Republican politicians, in this book, get the following adjectives: "flexible and alert," "active and informed," "redoubtable," and "young, gifted.") From his new position as poverty adviser to President Nixon, we may assume that they have overheard.

This is *not* the slashing, all-out attack on the community-action program that the press and some excerpts have led us to expect. Indeed, Moynihan calls community action "the most notable effort to date to mount a systematic social response" to the problem of national integration of ethnic minorities which do not participate satisfactorily in the process of government: "it must stand," he says, "as a perceptive and timely initiative." The book proposes neither to scrap the program, nor to amend it substantially. His most clear and forceful call is for a better system of social accounting—to be accomplished through an office of legislative evaluation in the General Accounting Office.

I myself would not defend the administration of the community action program, which has been, over-all, abominable. But what I and other critics of the O.E.O. must not ignore is that for all its terrible failings, it is the only Federal agency organized and directed exclusively at improving the life and lot of the American poor. To attack it now, unless we also offer serious alternative programs and commitments, is to say that we do not care, that we will let O.E.O. die, and the hopes of the poor with it.

That is why what is distressing is the tone of the book: basically anti-intellectual, anti-participatory, quietist, above all flattering of that very political passivity which we may now, I suppose, expect to be the domestic keynote of Mr. Moynihan's new Administration. What he is telling us, most clearly, is that we should study more and do less. Against this tone, against the complacency it encourages, his defenses of community action are small beer indeed; and basically ineffectual, since like so much else in the book, they are pure assertion. (Though Mr. Moynihan speaks ex cathedra, he seems to combine Rome and Avignon in one. Thus, speaking of the civil-rights movement as of the summer of 1963, he assures us on page 24 that "there was almost no economic content to the protest." By page 63, he has remembered that the March on Washington was for "Jobs and Freedom," and we are told that "Negro protest . . . at this time . . . frequently focused on unemployment as an issue.")

Moynihan comes closest to an alternative approach in a suggestion that he would have preferred to build the antipoverty strategy around employment. To this we should give hearty assent. The great failing of the community action program, in my own judgment, was that it never had very much to organize about; and there is no question that the organizing should have been around programs to deal with the depression-level unemployment rates that still prevail among the urban poor. "Unemployment," in the words of Robert Kennedy, "is having nothing to do; which means nothing to do with the rest of us." It was and remains the "master problem."

The real question is why the major effort on jobs was never made. In Moynihan's view, "an immense opportunity to institute more or less permanent social changes—a fixed full-employment program, a measure of income maintenance—was lost while energies were expended in ways that very probably hastened the end of the brief period when such options were open, that is to say the three years from the assassination of [John F.] Kennedy to the election of the Ninety-first Congress." Moynihan's assertion—it comes close to being the prime conclusion of his book—is that the faulty priority of community action, far overshadowing the minor efforts made on employment and income, was the work of social scientists and Government officials who should have known better; that it was their free choice, largely influenced by highly speculative theories of human behavior, that led them to choose the tiger.

The fact is otherwise. The overwhelming priority placed on community action was due only in small part to social theorizing. The real reason was that job programs cost money, and a great deal of it. To undertake the massive public-works programs urged by Gunnar Myrdal and Philip Randolph—which alone could have quickly created the jobs that were lacking—would have required at least an additional $2 billion to start, and perhaps $10 billion a year within a short time. But as early as February, 1964, President Johnson had vetoed a $1.25-billion unemployment plan, to be financed by a special 5-cent tax on cigarettes. "He was," as Moynihan says, "seeking that year to cut taxes, not to raise them."

Nor would there be money thereafter. By July of 1965, when O.E.O.'s funding came up for its first renewal, the war in Vietnam had begun to exact its remorseless toll of American resources and energy, and the annual rate of O.E.O. spending was cut back. A number of the participants in the early poverty-planning sessions had pushed hard for an employment strategy. Now the poverty warriors sought to build up enough political strength to force a major program through—to fulfill Johnson's constant pledges that we could fight the Viet Cong and poverty all at the same time. They knew—at least the best and brightest knew—that the poor were without the political weight to command large shifts in the allocations of Federal resources; the 1964 tax cut, with its benefits directed overwhelmingly to the middle and business classes, was evidence enough. But perhaps, in a year of organization, with $340 million in community action funds, they could seize the nation's swelling current for social justice, bring the message of need fully home to an awakened public, and then capture the major share of the new Federal resources being generated by a booming economy.

But by January of 1966, the battle was already lost. First, the development of manpower and job programs was largely delegated to Mr. Moynihan's Labor Department (Mr. Moynihan was Assistant Secretary of Labor for Policy Planning and Research under Presidents Kennedy and Johnson), which never came up with more than a few palliatives—new acronyms for the same old programs and bureaucracies. Second was the rivalry that had sprung up between Labor and O.E.O.; a weakening of Government efforts further aggravated by Sargent Shriver's complete inattention to employment problems, while he pursued high-visibility national programs like Legal Services and Head Start.

Third and greatest of all was the spreading war in Vietnam— which would dictate that the total poverty budget could not go significantly above $2 billion a year, a sum grossly insufficient for any major job-creation efforts. Those the war would not allow; and Shriver, who had confidently told the Senate in 1966 that American poverty could be eliminated in a decade, would say in 1967 that "the war on poverty is not fought on any single, simple battlefield and it will not be won in a generation."

Where does all this leave Moynihan's argument that the war on poverty was lost by social-science theorists, whose "maximum feasible misunderstanding" threw away this once-in-a generation opportunity? Without much to stand on, I think.

At all times, the major decisions that crippled community action—the low initial budgets spread thin for maximum publicity, without adequate planning or targeting of goals—these, and above all the Vietnam war, were political—made less by theorists than by politicians, and on wholly political grounds. (Administrative confusion and incompetence, another major handicap, was itself largely a product of these political decisions.) The great virtue of community action was that it could be done—they thought—on the cheap.

About the war, and its effects on the poverty program, Moynihan has very little to say. Of course he is opposed to it and recognizes its malign effect, as do all men of intelligence and decent intent. But so intent is he on sticking the social scientists with the responsibility for community action's failures, that he does not anywhere discuss what difference might have been made if funds had been available to couple it with a major employment program.

This is of great relevance today, when the Vietnam war seems at last ready to exhaust itself, and thus to offer us another bite at the apple of 1964. For to turn now to an employment strategy, without the element of community action, would be as great an error as we committed before. It took the community action programs to bring public attention to the needs of the poor in the first place; and there is little likelihood that great sums will be spent on unemployment, much less spent well, without effective political organs for the poor. But more important is the question of whether employment—and on its fundamental importance I have no disagreement with Mr. Moynihan—is or can ever be enough.

For a moment, elsewhere in the book, Moynihan seems to agree. He begins with a chapter on "The Quest for Community," quoting Robert Nisbet, whom he praises lavishly. (Nisbet has reciprocated with a jacket blurb, as has James Q. Wilson, also the object of textual bouquets.) Says Nisbet, of the necessary response to "the profound dislocations," the "growing sense of isolation in society":

"To create the conditions within which autonomous *individuals* could prosper, could be emancipated from the binding ties of kinship, class, community, was the objective of the older laissez faire. To create conditions within which *autonomous* groups may prosper must be . . . the prime object of the new *laissez faire*."

Though there were, as Moynihan correctly points out, lamentable failures of examination and articulation at every stage of the process, still *the community action programs were pointed directly at this profound need.* And Moynihan later follows with approving citation of the radical community organizer Saul Alinsky, who has always maintained that conflict between organized groups is the only way to serious social change.

In between these sensible and perceptive observations, however, Moynihan spends much of the book decrying militancy in the community action programs. The drive for community control, he says, "took the form of denying the legitimacy of those institutions of electoral representation that had developed over the years—indeed the centuries—and which nominally did provide community control." "The institutions of representative government," he continues, "have the singular virtue of defining who speaks for the community." But "the assumption that established symptoms were somehow not meeting the needs of the people, was certainly much encouraged by the community action era."

But this is the most blatant kind of question-begging. Who is "the community" that "nominally" exercises "control" through the representative process? In the Bedford-Stuyvesant ghetto of New York there are 450,000 people—as many as in the entire city of Cincinnati, more than in the entire state of Vermont. Yet the area has only one high school, and 80 per cent of its teenagers are dropouts; the infant mortality rate is twice the national average; there are over 800 buildings abandoned by everyone but the rats, yet the area received not one dollar of urban renewal funds during the entire first 15 years of that program's operation; the unemployment rate is known only to God.

Clearly, Bedford-Stuyvesant has some special needs; yet it has always been lost in the midst of the city's eight million. In fact, it took a lawsuit to win for this vast area, in the year 1968, its first Congressman. In what sense can the representative system be said to have "spoken for" this community, during the long years of neglect and decay? Yet Moynihan rejects efforts to develop community control as leading inevitably to community conflict.

Of course this is no new argument. Political thinkers from Jefferson to Hannah Arendt, urban critics like Lewis Mumford and Jane Jacobs, and many others have given sustained and reasoned consideration—and support—to schemes for decentralization and "community control." It was a major element—one which struck deeply responsive chords all over the country—in the Presidential campaign of Robert Kennedy. From Moynihan we have the right to expect that he will at least engage the argument, in the same serious terms that it has been put forward by others. But this we do not get.

Do not get, I am afraid, for not very good reasons. Moynihan seems to believe in the exercise of the critical faculties only when those doing the exercise are people like himself. Thus he criticizes the O.E.O., among other things, for giving its principal benefits to middle-class professionals, and observes that Shriver's interest in community action "declined" in February, 1964, "when he learned that the time it would take to produce a comprehensive community-action program would preclude any dramatic results for the war on poverty in time, for example, to influence the 1964 election, or even the selection of the President's running mate." Serious criticisms, yet fair comment.

But when representatives of the poor make similar statements, Moynihan is scornful. Describing a 1966 meeting between Shriver and the Citizens' Crusade Against Poverty, he writes of how a militant minority raged at the director of O.E.O. " 'He hasn't done anything for us,' cried one delegate, 'Where do the poor have an opportunity? It's just a big publicity deal,' shouted another. . . . 'The poverty program is a laugh,' declared a mother of six from Watts. 'When all the money is spent, the rich will get richer and I will still be receiving a welfare check.' " These statements Moynihan characterizes as "the kind of bad manners and arrogance that are more the mark of the rich than the poor, or perhaps more accurately, the too-common attributes of the radical right and left."

It might seem that this "militant minority" is only saying somewhat more directly what Moynihan is writing a book about; but for this—for them—he has no tolerance. When attacking the sensitivity of the social scientists he is criticizing, Moynihan says, "Those who with Hobbes would seek a 'quiet corner' from which to observe it all, must deny themselves some of the excitements of the fray, or else not complain when bashed." Unless, apparently, it is poor folk who are doing the bashing.

Which brings us back to the central question of tone. I hope I am wrong, but what this book seems to be is a long exercise in condescension: to Government officials, to social thinkers, above all to the poor themselves. If this should become the domestic hallmark of the Nixon Administration, then we are in for very difficult times, indeed. Moynihan sums up his case by saying that "men of whom the nation had a right to expect better did inexcusably sloppy work," and that "enough snake oil has been sold in this Republic to warrant the expectation that public officials will begin reading labels." True enough. But judging by this book, of which we had a right to expect better, Mr. Moynihan's appointment is evidence that in some high places, snake oil still passes for medicine.

Suggested Reading

Alan Batchelder, *The Economics of Poverty*, New York, Wiley, 1966.

Warner Bloomberg and Henry J. Schmandt, eds. *Power, Poverty, and Urban Policy*, Beverly Hills, Calif., Sage Publications, 1968.

Harry M. Caudill, *Night Comes to the Cumberlands*, Boston, Atlantic-Little, Brown, 1962 (Little, Brown paperback).

Richard Elman, *The Poorhouse State: The American Way of Life on Public Assistance*, New York, Pantheon, 1966 (Delta paperback).

Louis Ferman with Joyce L. Kornbluh and Alan Haber, eds., *Poverty in America: A Book of Readings*, revised edition, Ann Arbor, University of Michigan Press, 1968.

Thomas Gladwin, *Poverty: USA*, Boston, Little, Brown, 1967.

Michael Harrington, *The Other America*, New York, Macmillan, 1962 (Penguin paperback).

Robert Hunter, *Poverty: Social Conscience in the Progressive Era*, New York, Harper and Row paperback, 1965 (original 1904).

Gerald Leinwald, ed., *Poverty and the Poor*, New York, Washington Square Press paperback, 1968.

Sar A. Levitan, *The Great Society's Poor Law*, Baltimore, Johns Hopkins Press, 1969.

Peter Marris and Martin Rein, *Dilemmas of Social Reform: Poverty and Community Action in the United States*, New York, Atherton Press, 1967.

Herman P. Miller, *Rich Man, Poor Man*, New York, Crowell, 1964 (Signet paperback).

Frank Riessman with Jerome Cohen and Arthur Pearl, eds., *Mental Health of the Poor*, New York, Free Press, 1964.

Ben B. Seligman, *Permanent Poverty: An American Syndrome*, Chicago, Quadrangle Books, 1968.

Ben B. Seligman, ed., *Poverty as a Public Issue*, New York, Free Press, 1965 (Free Press paperback).

Charles A. Valentine, *Culture and Poverty: Critique and Counterproposals*, Chicago, University of Chicago Press, 1968.

Index

Ad Hoc Committee on the Triple Revolution, 227–229, 232–234
Adams, John, 145
Advisory Committee on Labor-Management Policy, 214, 217
Advisory Council on Social Security, 51, 157
Affluent Society (Galbraith), 32–33
AFL-CIO, 213
Aged, 49, 52–53, 72–73, 147; and pension plans, 150–160
Alexander, Will, 174
Alinsky, Saul, 220, 247–262, 268–269
Allen, James E., 254
American Civil Liberties Union, 174
American Dilemma (Myrdal), 187
American Law Institute, 145
American Medical Assn., 85
American Missionary Assn., 174
Anderson, Patrick, 220, 247–262
Anti-inflation efforts: "classical," 109; and unemployment, 5–6
Anti-poverty program, 235–246; Alinsky's criticisms of, 257; and Community Action Programs, 240–245; vs. existing agencies, 237–240; harassment of, 248–254; and Vietnam War, 221, 264, 266–268; and youth, 236–237. *See also* Community action; War Against Poverty.
Appleby, Thomas, 115–116, 121–128
Area Redevelopment Administration, 12
Arendt, Hannah, 263, 269
Armour & Co., 216–217
Arnall, Ellis, 184
Astor, John Jacob, 83
Automation, 201, 208, 209, 213–218, 227–228, 230, 234

Bail, 139, 141, 144
Batt, William L., Jr., 215
Bedford-Stuyvesant area, 269
Beecher, Henry Ward, 88
Bendiner, Robert, 36–37, 76–88
Bilbo, Theodore, 97–98
Black, Hugo L., 138
Blind, aid to, 51
Bowles, Chester, 148, 180–188
Brady, Dorothy S., 71
Brannan Plan, 54
Bridges, Harry, 216
Broken families, 35–36, 49, 51–52, 72–73
Brown, Claude, 80–81
Bureau of Home Economics, 39–40
Burke, Adrian, 161
Burns, Arthur F., 36, 56, 214
Butler, Samuel, 140

Cabranes, Manuel, 162
Capon Springs Conferences, 173
Carmichael, Stokely, 255
Carnegie, Andrew, 173, 174
Carpenter, Rowena Schmidt, 39
Cavanagh, Jerome P., 79, 252
Chambers, Edward T., 252–255, 258
Chavez, Cesar, 262
Chicago, slum organization in, 249, 251–252, 256, 257, 259–261
Children, dependent: in families of disabled workers, 50–51; in families headed by women, 52; increase of, 15
Chrysler Corp., 94
Citizens' Crusade Against Poverty, 270
Civil rights movement, 175–176, 197–198, 258, 265
Civilian Conservation Corps, 236
Civilian Production Administration, 99

Clark, Kenneth, 10
Coleman, Clarence, 195, 196
College Work-Study program, 235
Commission on Interracial Cooperation, 174
Commission on Race Relations, 174
Committee to Abolish Racial Discrimination, 174
Community action, 10, 13, 85, 186–187, 220–221, 235, 237, 240–245, 257, 263–271; criticism of, 265–271
Connor, Bull, 252
CORE, 197
Cothran, Tillman, 191
Council of Economic Advisers, 4, 5, 33–34, 69, 73, 113, 142, 214, 229
Council on Youth Fitness, 133
Coward, Jerry, 199
Crider, John R., 38–40
Crime, 144–145. *See also* Justice, criminal.
Crisis in Black and White (Silberman), 249, 256
Culture of poverty, 33
Curtis, Charles, 166

Danzig, Louis, 120
Death penalty, 135
Death rates, 135
Depressed-areas bill, 11–12, 70, 149, 209, 214–215
Depression vs. 1960's: anti-poverty efforts of, 236; poverty in, 76–88; and race, 79–81
Disability insurance, 51
Disabled persons, 48–51
Distribution: and economic growth, 110; vs. technology, 93
Dixiecrats, 177–178
Douglas, Paul, 11–12
Douglas, William O., 140
DuBois, W. E. B., 148, 170–179

Eastman Kodak Co., 255
Economic Development Administration, 12

Economic growth, 105–114; and distribution, 110; and federal spending, 105–106, 112; and inflation, 109–110; objections to, 109–111; and private enterprise, 109, 112–113; proposals for, 111–114; and tax policy, 112; in USSR, 106, 111. *See also* Reconversion, post–World War II.
Economic Opportunity Act, 6, 13, 245
Eisenhower, Dwight D., 11, 36, 105, 133, 186
Ellison, Ralph, 79
Employment Act of 1946, 111
Equal pay for equal work, 97–98
Erewhon (Butler), 140

Fair Employment Practices Commission, 177, 186, 187
Family income. *See* Income, family.
Farm families, in Depression, 38–40
Farm price supports, 54
Federal Housing Authority, 100, 101
Fernos-Isern, A., 162
Fey, Harold, 260
Field, Marshall, 260
FIGHT, 250–256; and anti-poverty program, 254; and urban renewal, 253–254, 256
Fisher, Irving, 17, 20–21
Florence, Franklin D. R., 253–256
Ford Foundation, 239, 240
Ford Motor Co., 94
France, Anatole, 140
Free Men and Free Markets (Theobald), 228
Friedman, Milton, 87
Fulbright, J. William, 184

Galbraith, John Kenneth, 32–33, 85
General Education Board, 173
General Motors Corp., 94, 97
Giblin, Charles R., 162
Glazer, Nathan, 219–220, 235–246

Goldberg, Arthur J., 117, 138–145, 203, 212, 217
Goldwater, Barry, 87
Goodman, Paul, 231
Graham, Frank, 184
Grapes of Wrath (Steinbeck), 261
Grutzner, Charles, 115, 118–120
Guaranteed annual wage, 97–98
Guaranteed income, 219, 227–234; advantages of, 229–230, 233–234; cost of, 229; and leisure, 231, 234; objections to, 231–233

Harlan County, Ky., 69–70
Harrington, Michael, 18, 32–34, 78–79, 125, 238, 239
Hart, James V., 162
Hauser, Philip M., 261
Head Start program, 6, 13, 239
Health, 117, 133–137; and Army rejection rates, 134–135; criteria of, 134; and death rates, 135; and medical care, 117, 135–137; and mental illness, 136–137
Health insurance, 135–136
Hereditary poverty, 84
Hill, Lister, 184
Hobbes, Thomas, 270
Holland, Elmer J., 201, 215
Home ownership, 115, 118–120
Hoover, Herbert, 23
Hopkins, Harry, 219, 222–226
Housing: post–World War II shortage of, 99–101, 103–104; proposed program for, 93–95. *See also* Home ownership; Urban renewal.
Housing Acts of 1949 and 1954, 122
Hull, Cordell, 184

Income, family: distribution of, 1959 and 1967, 7–8; median, annual growth rates in, for whites and nonwhites, 1947–1967, 5–6; of poor, 1926, 20

Income, guaranteed. *See* Guaranteed income.
Income distribution: on basis of need, 55; changes in, 1947–1967, 4–6; range of, 1959–1967, 7–8
Income gap, 7–9, 25, 36, 56–63; chart, 58; in Depression, rural Negro vs. urban white poor, 40; within Negro population, 9, 14, 81; among occupational groups, 60–62; white-nonwhite, 5–6, 36, 59–60
Income tax: of millionaires, 67–68; negative, 87
Indian Bureau, 148, 165, 167–168
Indians, 148, 163–169; as citizens, 167–168; and reservations, 164–166; and wardship, 166. *See also* Minority groups; Nonwhites.
Industrial Areas Foundation, 247, 260
Industrial Revolution, 20
Inflation, 5–6, 109–110
International Longshoremen's and Warehousemen's Union, 216

Jacobs, Jane, 269
Jacobs, Paul, 238
Jefferson, Thomas, 269
Job Corps, 6, 235–237
Jobs vs. training, 236–237, 243
Johnson, Lee F., 120
Johnson, Lyndon B., 13, 36, 76, 79; and anti-poverty program, 221, 229, 266; and urban renewal, 122, 125
Joint Congressional Economic Committee, 63, 113
Jones, Frank, 193
Justice, criminal, 117, 138–145; and alternative sentences, 140; and arrest procedure, 141; and bail, 139, 141, 144; and court-appointed counsel, 141–142; and criminal lawyers, 145; and death penalty, 140; and defense costs,

Justice, criminal (*cont.*)
142–143; and probation and parole, 140, 142; and social problems, 144–145; and subpoenas, 139–140; and victim compensation, 144

Kefauver, Estes, 184
Keller, K. T., 94
Kennedy, John F., 18, 36, 56, 78, 79; and unemployment, 11–12, 62, 149, 200, 202–203, 209, 210–212, 214–217
Kennedy, Robert F., 220, 263, 265–266, 269
Keys, Ancel, 116, 129–132
Keyserling, Leon, 69, 70, 74, 86, 90, 105–114, 214
Kimball, Dexter S., 17, 19–25
King, Martin Luther, 197, 250, 258
Kristol, Irving, 238
Krug, J. A., 91

LaFarge, Oliver, 148, 163–169
Lawes, Lewis E., 140
Lawson, Belford, 198
Lawyers: court-appointed, 141–142; and criminal practice, 145
Lee, Richard C., 125
Legal counsel. *See* Lawyers.
Legal defense costs, 142–143
Legal system. *See* Justice, criminal.
Lewis, John L., 259
Lincoln, Abraham, 145, 185, 188
Lincoln, C. Eric, 148–149, 189–199
Living costs: post–World War II, 41–47, 102; urban vs. rural, 40
Long, Huey, 77
Low, Fred, 22
Lynching, 172, 174, 177

Manchild in the Promised Land (Brown), 80–81
Manhattan Bail Project, 144
Manpower Development and Training Act, 12
Mantle, Mickey, 134

Markle Foundation, 129
Martin, Louis, 255
Marx, Karl, 9
Maximum Feasible Misunderstanding (Moynihan), 220, 263–271
May, Edgar, 239
McKenzie, Marjorie, 198
Medical care, 117, 135–137
Mental illness, 136–137
Milano, Betty, 207–208
Miller, Herman P., 36, 37, 56–63, 69–75
Miller, William Lee, 115–116, 121–128
Millionaires, 64–68; ages of, 67; geographical distribution of, 65–66; nontaxpaying, 67; and sources of income, 66; tax deductions of, 67; tax rate of, 67–68
Minority groups, growth rates in median family income of, during Democratic and Republican administrations, 5. *See also* Indians; Negroes; Nonwhites; Puerto Ricans.
Mobilization for Youth, 240
Moore, Cecil, 196
Moynihan, Daniel P., 220, 263–271
Mumford, Lewis, 269
Murray, Clyde E., 162
Muscle Shoals, 24
Myrdal, Gunnar, 187, 266

NAACP, 175–177, 184, 196, 197
Nabrit, James, 193
National Assn. of Manufacturers, 213
National Dairy Council, 129
National Housing Conference, 115, 118–120
National Institute of Mental Health, 240
National Maritime Union, 215
National Resources Committee, 38–40
National Urban League, 176–177, 184, 196, 197

National War Labor Board, 97
National Youth Administration, 236
Negative income tax, 87
Negro colleges, 173
Negroes: and civil rights movement, 175–176, 197–198; class structure of, 189–192; and discrimination, 73–74, 177–188; educational attainment of, rise in, 59, 171–172, 176; income gap among, 9, 14, 81; income growth of, vs. whites, 5–6, 36, 59–60, 148; and legal activity, 175–176; middle-class, 81, 148–149, 191–199; occupational status of, change in, 59, 171–172, 177, 192–193; and philanthropy, 170, 173–174; and political activity, 172, 175; and poverty of 1960's vs. 1930's, 79–81; power elite among, 195–196; and progress against discrimination, 172–177, 181–182, 186; rural poor, Depression income and costs of, vs. poor urban whites, 40; and slum organization, 247–262; as soldiers, 184; and unemployment, 208, 216, 228; urban poor, and sex, 80; and urban renewal, 121, 123–127; and urban riots, 198–199; and white allies, 220, 255. *See also* Minority groups; Nonwhites.
Neighborhood Youth Corps, 6, 235–237, 243
Neuberger, Richard, 35, 41–47, 89, 99–104
New Deal, 76, 79, 83, 87, 116, 236
New Haven, Conn.: neighborhood social-legal program in, 144–145; urban renewal in, 121–127
New Left, 85–86, 88, 241, 260
New York City, urban renewal in, 122
Newark Housing Authority, 120
Niagara Movement, 174
Nisbet, Robert, 268
Nixon, Richard M., 36, 220, 264

Nonfarm families, low-income, 48–55; and expenditures for food, 49; property owned by, 50; proposed measures to benefit, 51–54
Nonwhites: as percentage of poor families, 1951 and 1960, 72; and whites, income gap between, 5–6, 36, 59–60. *See also* Indians; Minority groups; Negroes; Puerto Ricans.
Nutrition and motivation, 117

Occupations: income gap among, 60–62; of Negroes, changes in, 59, 171–172, 177, 192–193; unskilled, decline of, 54, 62–63, 207–208, 216–217, 228
Office of Economic Opportunity, 77, 85, 220–221, 237, 239, 240, 265–267, 270
Office of Price Administration, 97, 102
Old-age assistance, 51–53, 154–155; and work clause, 52–53
Old-age and survivors' insurance. *See* Social security.
Other America (Harrington), 18, 32–34, 78–79, 125, 239

Participatory democracy, 10. *See also* Community action.
Pensions: employer-initiated, 147, 152–153; federal old-age, 151, 156–160; union-negotiated, 153–154. *See also* Old-age assistance; Social security.
Post–World War II period: difficulties of veterans in, 99–104; housing shortage in, 99–101; industrial reconversion in, 91–98; living costs in, 41–47, 102
Poverty: as culturally defined, 36, 57, 69–71, 75; culture of, 33; decline in, 4; in Depression vs. 1960's, 76–88; hereditary, 84; structural vs. cyclical, 84

Poverty program. *See* Anti-poverty program; War Against Poverty.
President's Committee on Juvenile Delinquency, 239, 240
Private enterprise and economic growth, 109, 112–113
Probation and parole, 140, 142
"Psychological poor," 81. *See also* Poverty, as culturally defined.
Public Housing Administration, 120
Public Works Administration, 236
Puerto Ricans, 147–148. *See also* Minority groups.

Racial discrimination, social costs of, 73–74
Randolph, A. Philip, 86, 177, 266
Raskin, A. H., 32–34, 149, 200–218
Rayburn, Sam, 184
Reagan, Michael D., 219, 227–234
Recession, inflation during, 109–110
Reconversion, post–World War II, 91–98
Relief vs. work programs, 222–226
Retirement, 52, 151, 159, 218. *See also* Pensions.
Reuther, Walter, 89, 91–98
Rhatigan, E. R., 162
Riis, Jacob, 127
Riots, urban, 198–199
Rochester, N.Y., slum organization in, 249–256, 261
Rockefeller, John D., 173
Rogers, Will, 83
Roosevelt, Franklin D., 17, 38, 75, 76–77, 82–83, 103, 177; 1937 Inaugural Address of, 26–31
Roosevelt, Theodore, 127
Rosenwald, Julius, 170, 174
Ruiz, Ruperto, 162
Rusk, Howard, 117, 133–137
Ruttenberg, Stanley M., 213

Samuelson, Paul, 36, 56
Shaw, G. Howland, 161

Shriver, Sargent, 36, 257, 267, 270
Shuster, Alvin, 64–68
Silberman, Charles, 249, 256
Simpson, H. V., 100
Slavery: ancient defense of, 19; and Negro class structure, 190
Slichter, Sumner H., 35–36, 48–55, 147, 150–160
Slum organizations, 247–262
Social security, 51–52, 112, 147, 156–160; inadequacies of, 156
South, racial discrimination in, 175–178, 184–186
Southern Christian Leadership Conference, 250
Southern Conference on Human Welfare, 174
Southern Education Board, 173
Sparkman, John, 119, 184
Starvation, 116–117, 129–132
Steinbeck, John, 261
Stiebeling, Hazel K., 39
Structural vs. cyclical poverty, 84
Sviridoff, Mitchell, 127

Taft-Hartley Act, 53–54
Tax policy, 112. *See also* Income tax.
Teamsters' Union, 216
Tennessee Valley Authority, 93. *See also* Muscle Shoals.
Theobald, Robert, 219, 228, 229, 231
Thomas, Norman, 231
Tillman, James A., Jr., 196
Titmuss, Richard, 15
Townsend, Francis E., 77
Truman, Harry S., 91
Turner, Jesse, 198
TWO. *See* Woodlawn Organization.

Unemployment, 24, 63; and anti-inflation efforts, 5–6; chronic, 11–12, 149, 200–218; geographical aspects of, 209; and guaranteed-income proposal, 227–234; Ken-

nedy's efforts against, 11–12, 62, 149, 200, 202–203, 209, 210–212, 214–217; management-union differences on, 213–214; among Negroes, 208, 216, 228; in 1957–1958 recession, 11; vs. unemployables, 87, 222–223; vs. work programs, 223–226. See also Unskilled.
Unions: initiation fees of, 53–54; vs. management, on unemployment remedies, 213–214; pension plans negotiated by, 153–154
United Automobile Workers, 93, 98
United Steelworkers, 215–216
Unskilled, decline in employment for, 54, 62–63, 207–208, 216–217, 228
Urban areas: income gap in, 7–9; increase of dependent children in, 15; and Negro poor, 79–81
Urban families. See Nonfarm families.
Urban League. See National Urban League.
Urban renewal, 115–116, 120, 121–128, 253–254, 256

Vandenberg, Arthur, 98
Veblen, Thorstein, 92–93
Vietnam War, effect of, on antipoverty program, 221, 264, 266–268
VISTA, 235
Von Hoffman, Nicholas, 262

Wage-price spiral, 102; and retired workers, 160
Wage-price structure, 96–98
Wagner, Robert F., 98

Wagner, Robert F., Jr., 162
Walinsky, Adam, 220–221, 263–271
Walker, A. Maceo, 198
Wallace, George, 264
War Against Poverty, 6, 18, 36, 116, 128, 149, 220, 235–246; vs. New Deal philosophy, 76–79. See also Anti-poverty program; Community action.
War Production Board, 97
Warner, Charles Dudley, 171
Washington, Booker T., 175
Washington, D.C., racial discrimination in, 183
Wasted Americans (May), 239
Wealth: per capita, 1850 vs. 1928, 20; vs. income, 65
Webster, Daniel, 145
White, Herbert, 256
Wilkins, Roy, 197
Williams, Hosea, 258
Wilson, Charles E., 182, 184
Wilson, James Q., 268
Wirtz, Willard, 228
Wolfbein, Seymour L., 209
Women: families headed by, 35–36, 49, 51–52, 72–73; in labor force, 207–208
Woodlawn Organization, 249, 251–252, 256, 257, 260, 261
Work programs vs. relief, 222–226
Workers' Defense League, 174
Works Progress Administration, 236
World Health Organization, 134
World War II, industrial conversion during, 94

Xerox Corp., 255

Youth and anti-poverty program, 236–237

A Note on the Editor

Harold L. Sheppard is a staff social scientist at the Upjohn Institute for Employment Research in Washington, D.C. Born in Baltimore, he studied at the University of Chicago and the University of Wisconsin, and has been a Fulbright Research Professor. Mr. Sheppard has served on the staff on the Senate Subcommittee on Manpower, Employment, and Poverty, has been assistant administrator of the Area Redevelopment Administration and staff director of the Special Senate Committee on Aging, and is co-author of *When Labor Votes; Economic Failure, Alienation and Extremism;* and *The Job Hunt.* He is now a consultant to the National Urban Coalition.